PATTERNS OF NATIONALITY

AMERICAN CULTURAL HERITAGE SERIES 7
Jack Salzman, *General Editor*

PATTERNS OF NATIONALITY

**Twentieth-Century
Literary Versions of America**

BENJAMIN T. SPENCER

Burt Franklin & Company

Published by Burt Franklin & Co.
235 East Forty-fourth Street
New York, New York 10017

© 1981 by Burt Franklin & Co., Inc.
All rights reserved

Library of Congress Cataloging in Publication Data

Spencer, Benjamin Townley.
Patterns of nationality.

(American cultural heritage series ; 7)
Includes bibliographical references and index.
1. American literature—20th century—History
and criticism. 2. National characteristics in
literature. 3. United States in literature.
I. Title. II. Series: American cultural
heritage ; 7.
PS228.N38S65   810′.9′3273   80-36833
ISBN 0-89102-199-X

Designed by Bernard Schleifer

Manufactured in the United States of America

For Helen

CONTENTS

FOREWORD

THIS VOLUME IS a sequel and supplement to *The Quest for Nationality*, which traced the evolving concepts of an American literature from colonial times to the end of the nineteenth century. The structure and aims of *Patterns of Nationality*, however, are somewhat different from those of the earlier study. On the assumption that the ultimate shape and development of twentieth-century American literature are still in the making, I have chosen eight major authors to represent the diverse trends of nationality during the two most recent literary generations. The implication of *Patterns*, therefore, is pluralistic: There are a number of valid modes and levels in which the imagination may flow to embody or adumbrate "America." Through both the critical statements and the literary works of these eight authors, I believe, one can discern the most cogent views of an American literature that have emerged during the first three quarters of this century. The first three essays provide a general background for the eight authors by examining the nature of nationality from the point of view of both literary history and literary criticism.

The completion of the essays in *Patterns* would not have been possible by my efforts alone. My wife, Virginia, has spent countless hours in proofreading and otherwise substantiating the authenticity of the text. For over three decades Edwin Cady has provided invaluable counsel and encouragement in my quest to understand "literary nationalism," and he must be credited with much of whatever scholarly contribution to American studies this volume makes. My colleagues Richard Bauerle and Randall Waldron have given generously of their time in making constructive suggestions that appreciably improved the structure and style of several of the essays. With his insights into Whitman and modern American poets, Edwin Folsom has prompted further explorations that have led to a substantial enrichment of the essays that involve American poetry. And I do not forget the competence and patience of my typist, Peggy Maxwell.

Acknowledgments are also due those persons and publishers who granted permission for the use of copyrighted material: Professor Robert Falk, editor of *Literature and Ideas in America* (Ohio University Press) for "Gertrude Stein: Non-Expatriate"; Jack Salzman, editor, and Burt Franklin & Co., publishers of *Prospects 2* (1976) for "Mr. Mailer's American Dreams"; *American Literature* for "Nationality During the Interregnum (1892–1912)" and "Sherwood Anderson: American Mythopoeist"; *The South Atlantic Quarterly* for "Fitzgerald and the American Ambivalence"; *The Sewanee Review* for "An American Literature Again"; *PMLA* (Publications of the Modern Language Association of America) for "Pound: The American Strain"; *Tennessee Studies in Literature* for "Doctor Williams's American Grain"; *Twentieth Century Literature* for "American Literature as Black Mass: Edward Dahlberg." Thanks are also due to Brom Weber for permission to use brief quotations from *The Letters of Hart Crane, 1916–1932* (Heritage House, 1952) and from *The Complete Poems and Selected Letters and Prose of Hart Crane* (Doubleday and Company, 1966), and to the Columbia University Press for brief quotations from *Letters of Hart Crane and His Family*, ed. Thomas S. W. Lewis.

PART ONE

The Nature of Nationality

TWENTIETH-CENTURY NATIONALITY: CONTINUITY AND CHANGE

ALTHOUGH THE UNITED STATES has been a nation for two centuries, the conviction that her literature still bears the stamp of transatlantic culture persists in varying degrees among many of her major writers. In the colonial era authors as dissimilar as Cotton Mather and St. Jean de Crèvecoeur were aware that existence in the New World had nurtured a cisatlantic "plain" style, but not until the political birth of the nation did this awareness coalesce into a conscious movement for an "American" literature. Educators, editors, and men and women of letters then began to issue various prescriptions whereby, in Noah Webster's words, the United States could "be as independent in *literature* as she is in politics."[1] Before the War of 1812, Webster in his *Grammatical Institute* initiated the movement toward an American language, magazines suggested native themes and settings worthy of imaginative treatment, and a number of poets aspired to write an American epic.[2]

The arrival of a convincingly national literature, however, lagged decade by decade, and hence Emerson in 1836 felt impelled to devote his Phi Beta Kappa address at Harvard ("The American Scholar," termed by Oliver Wendell Holmes "our Declaration of Literary Independence") to a transcendental view of man out of which a New World literature might most substantially arise (*Quest*, pp. 158–60). Whitman's 1855 preface to *Leaves of Grass* and the poems in that volume afforded additional stimulus for a literature "transcendent and new" (*Quest*, Chap. 7). This cumulative attempt to define and achieve a distinctive American literature has persisted among twentieth-century au-

3

thors. To the varied nature of their concerns and expectations
and to the relationship of their views to those of earlier decades
this introductory chapter will be devoted. So far as the scope
of a single essay permits, the issue of nationality during the first
two literary generations of this century will be presented as some
one hundred of the prominent authors of the period perceived
it. Emerging most prominently among the topics that concerned
them are the following: the lingering of colonial attitudes, ob-
structions in the American milieu, indigenous potentialities, the
example of Whitman, the claims of regionalism and localism,
and the nature of an American style.

I

During World War I Theodore Dreiser with his German
heritage understandably could deplore the "accursed English
domination"; but in the 1920s Waldo Frank, novelist and mystic,
from a more indigenous point of view castigated those American
cultural leaders who cast an obsequious eye on London, indifferent to the fact that America could not "grow up through a
dump-heap of discarded customs and ideas." A decade later
Edgar Lee Masters implicitly concurred with Frank in lamenting
that Whitman's attempt to emancipate us from English literary
tradition had been in vain: The "virus . . . we inherited from
England and Europe is still alive."[3]

Even in the 1920s, however, a more radical and persuasive
voice—that of William Carlos Williams—had begun to sound its
lifelong admonition to "ex-British colonials" in the United States
that culturally speaking, Europe is our "Enemy" and is "unrelated to us in any way."[4] Somewhat more temperately Wallace
Stevens in his "Adagia," collected and edited by S. F. Morse
in the poet's *Opus Posthumous* (New York, 1957), declared,
"Nothing could be more inappropriate to American literature
than its English source since the Americans are not British in
sensibility" (p. 176).

Although Williams and Stevens disagreed about certain aspects of poetics, the latter ventures close to Williams's American

"ground" through his comic hero Crispin, who, in "The Comedian as the Letter C," is a "searcher for the fecund minimum." Accordingly, in his sustained dialectic on the relative authority and proper fusion of sensory phenomena and the imagination, Stevens steers Crispin from Europe, where presumably "man is the intelligence of his soil" to a "colony" in Carolina in an America that "was always north to him, / . . . polar-purple, chilled / And lank." Reversing in Carolina his earlier "Nota" that "man is the intelligence of his soil" to "his soil is man's intelligence," Crispin would seem to be making an implicit subscription to Williams's view that "colonies" in the new American world must develop an autochthonous intelligence and culture through "things" and the "ground." Or, as Crispin concludes, "Exit the mental moonlight . . . / . . . exit the whole shebang. . . . Here was prose / More exquisite than any tumbling verse: / A still new continent in which to dwell." Was not the purpose of his voyage, Crispin asks, to be released from the "stale intelligence" of "his fellows in the skies" and "to make a new intelligence prevail?"[5] With whatever element of parody, is not Crispin the voice of Williams?

A generation later a more substantial reliance on American objects as the prime means of exorcising the European mentality and of enhancing the cisatlantic consciousness was advocated by Charles Olson. As Robert Creeley notes in his Introduction to Olson's *Selected Writings* (New York, 1966), Olson began his *Call Me Ishmael* (1947) with the stated assumption that the "central fact to man born in America" is "space" (pp. 1–2). Like Williams, Olson liked to derive ideas from things and hence approvingly remarked of Melville that "as an American" he was "down to his hips in things" and that he equated "visible truth" with the "apprehension of the absolute condition of present things" (pp. 46–47). Convinced that the "objectivism" Williams and Pound had espoused had become outmoded, Olson in "Projective Verse" proposed a "more valid formulation" in "objectism," whereby there would be an elimination of the "lyrical interference" of the individual as "ego" or "soul," which had been interposed by "western man" between "what he is as a creature of nature . . . and those other creations of nature which we may . . . call objects" (p. 24). All comparison and *symbology* he deemed dangerous because they impinged on the "self-existence" of things (p. 56). Such respect for objects had, of course, been enunciated a century earlier in Whitman's principle of "identity" and embodied in his poetry. Whitman, however, supposed no absolute renunciation of the past and the Logos either possible or desirable, and his supposition no doubt reflected not only the national mind of his own day but also the preternaturalism of its aboriginal beginnings. As he implied in his *Democratic Vistas*, a national literature must embody a larger psychic range than that based predominantly on Olson's "little brains" of the "skin" (p. 60).

If in his anticolonialism Williams assumed that in tapping their aboriginal heritage to discover the American grain his countrymen would recapitulate aboriginal experience, he was mistaken. Few of them, so to speak, were ready to reinvent the cisatlantic cultural wheel. What they generally did (if they responded at all) was to accept the aesthetic or ecological or mythical results that had accrued from aboriginal experience. With the growth of the Southwest, the granting of statehood to Arizona and New Mexico in 1912, and the presence of a large Indian population in the area, renewed attention was drawn to the aboriginal culture and history, as is suggested by the large number of Indian names given Arizona counties. Yet this heritage, achieved though it had been over many centuries from cisatlantic "things," had evolved into a rich complex of arts and rituals; and it was to this high cultural level that American writers and artists were generally attracted, although some, such as Sherwood Anderson and Edward Dahlberg, briefly envisioned a reversion to the Indian life close to the mythically endowed American earth. Hart Crane, however, in *The Bridge*, realized that in an urban, corporate, and technological society only his few nomadic hoboes would risk an Indian existence; and indeed the Indian was very slowly absorbed and honored as an integral part of the American literature or culture.

In "Amerindian Verse," an essay in W.S. Braithwaite's *Anthology of Magazine Verse for 1926* (Boston, 1926), Mary Austin, a California author of many works dealing with the desert and the Indians, berated American scholars and critics for their lack of a "sufficiently informed and genuine feeling for Americanness" and also for persisting in their mistaken dream that "an adequate American culture should spring all cap-a-pie from the fountain head of Europe" (p. 104). It was an unspecialized audience, she said, that discovered that those poets "credited with being most American" (Amy Lowell, Carl Sandburg, and Anderson) were writing in patterns "genetically related" to those of the first Americans; indeed, there were striking "alikenesses" in the thought processes of "early and late United Statesers" (pp. 105, 108). Contemporaneously in Paris the expatriate editor of *transition* (No. 9, December 1927) found a potent counteragent to the "mechanistic psychology" of America in a cultivation of such aboriginal qualities as simplicity and naiveté (p. 192). Toward this end he urged the American poet to "absorb the rhythms of the indigenous Afro-American and Indian traditions," to "find the skyscrapers of the fourth dimension he dreams of," and thus in effect to follow Williams's proposal for a return to the origins of American mythology in the Mound-Builders, Mayas, Aztecs, and Negroes as a means of returning to the serenity and stability of the earth (pp. 195–96).

The absorption and imaginative projection of aboriginal attitudes and values can be seen in Anderson's *Mid-American Chants* (1918) and in Hart Crane's *Bridge* (1929), and during subsequent decades this process accrued into the pervasive counterculture of the 1960s, which had its own espression in the West Coast poet Gary Snyder. In his "Passage to More than India," in *Earth House Hold* (New York, 1968), he declares, "The American Indian is the vengeful ghost lurking in the back of the troubled American mind. . . . That ghost will claim the next generation as its own. When this has happened, citizens of the U.S.A. will at last begin to be Americans . . . in love with their land" (p. 112). Whether or not Snyder's prophecy is valid, the impact of Williams's attack on the colonial tradition is clear.

Coincident with the aboriginal role in cisatlantic cultural liberation from Europe, the Indian inevitably achieved a new esteem among many of his countrymen and thereby completely reversed his seventeenth-century image as a diabolic threat to national well-being. During the intervening generations (1650–1950) he had been rarely portrayed as a noble savage; more often he became—especially in Hollywood films—the hap-

less and expendable animal in a continental conquest viewed as
manifest destiny. In this conquest, as Richard Slotkin persuasively argues in *Regeneration Through Violence* (1973), he
nurtured a covert frontier myth in which the white man as a
hunter found in violence his vital mode of being. By the mid-
1900s, however, in an ecologically troubled America, the Indian's rapport with, and veneration of, his natural environment
conferred on him a redemptive role and an elevation in the
national literature heretofore denied him.

II

In addition to being overwhelmed by the massive literary
heritage of Europe, American writers have been continuously
aware of obstacles inherent in their own native milieu. In the
early nineteenth century, to be sure, the national pride of many
literary patriots did not allow them to discriminate sufficiently
between the achievement of nationalism and nationality—between, on the one hand, the political will that could
found a new nation in a decade and a half and, on the other, the
accumulation of affective attachments to the cisatlantic experience that issue in a homogeneous culture and, in turn, a national
literature.

Impatient with the gulf between the growth of national
power and the relatively mediocre literary achievement (internationally considered), men and women of letters since the
beginning of the nineteenth century have sought to explain their
failure by pointing to the aesthetic limitations and liabilities of
the American scene. Some of these putative liabilities have remained essentially constant; a few have disappeared or reappeared in new formulations. In the early nineteenth century the
chief factors in the anemia of the national literature were adjudged to be the dominantly mercenary spirit of the country,
the philistinism of the well-to-do classes, the lowly status of and
condescension toward native authors, political factions, and the
absence of a "polite society" (*Quest*, pp. 63–70). By midcentury,
authors were also troubled by the virtual lack of remuneration

for literary works, the absence of a national past and a landscape with rich associations, the paucity of legends and myths, the anesthetic effect of utilitarian "progress" and well-being, and America's youthful stage in the normal cycle of national cultures (pp. 97, 199–209, 310–11). In the preface to *The Blithedale Romance* (1852) Hawthorne stressed the difficulties for the American "romancer" who had no enchanted "Faery Land" approximating the "real world"; and later Henry James in his *Hawthorne* (New York, 1879) made an inventory of America's impoverishment in history, manners, customs, and institutions requisite "for a fund of suggestion for a novelist" (p. 42).

In the early decades of the twentieth century, despite the achievements of the "American Renaissance" comprising the internationally known works of Emerson, Thoreau, Hawthorne, Melville, Poe, Whitman, and somewhat later Dickinson and Twain, the native milieu was suprisingly still often adjudged unpropitious for, and even hostile to, the literary imagination. One of the intractable enigmas was space, the vast raw territory unhallowed by memorable deeds and associations. In *The Grandmothers* (New York, 1927) Glenway Wescott uses his protagonist, Alwyn Tower, to relate the pioneer saga of his ancestors in the Midwest (pp. 17 ff.) and to conclude that this saga was essentially that of a rapacious conquest that exterminated all culture as a form of weakness (pp. 30–31). Hence "Neither Chicago nor Wisconsin had justified its existence. . . . Maturity, responsibility, immorality, virtue are offspring of memory; try not to remember. America had as yet nothing worth remembering—no palaces, no enchanting antiquity, even the plunder of Tenochtitlan . . . had been taken away. The past was by nature tragic [but] tragedy was treason" (pp. 372, 378). In a similar vein Edgar Lee Masters's Archibald Higbie, feeling "weighted down with Western soil," escaped to Europe because he wanted the West of Spoon River "rooted out" of his soul.[6]

Yet it was not the Midwest alone that was disenchanting for the imagination, as Dos Passos lamented during World War I. Echoing Hawthorne and James, he found the whole country colorless, with monotonously similar cities, no "jewelled accretions" of the ages, no folklore, no "earth-feeling," and no "ghosts." American literature, like American life, was bodiless,

abstract, and rootless—a "cutting from England's sturdy . . . oak";
or, in another metaphor, America was the "Sicily of the modern
world," producing nothing but "steel and oil and grain."[7]

Through the 1920s, however, the dominant concern seems
to have been the unalterably slow accrual of a homogeneous
national consciousness. Thus, although Zona Gale, the Wisconsin novelist and dramatist, found a resource in the many wise
and simple people in the towns across America, she also sensed
a "lack in the national life of that indefinable control by the
ordered, the accustomed, the mellow, the dreaming, the old."
Admitting that we are without "our memories and our echoes,"
she nevertheless urged American writers to sustain "that nas-
cency" that Whitman began in his provocative expression of
American life. The "novel of tomorrow," she concluded, might
well focus on uncovering "the beauty of our . . . commonplace
living as the novel today has triumphantly uncovered its ugliness." After all, she said, "There are only an Old World and a
New. You make your choice."[8]

For the less provincial Archibald MacLeish, who was contemporaneously struggling with the problem of the allegiance
of the imagination to the Old World or the New, the commitment to the latter did not come so readily. Nostalgic in his own
dry land for the transatlantic delights of "red roofs and the ol-
ives," he asked himself how a wise man could have two countries.
"It is a strange thing—to be an American," he wrote in his well-
known "American Letter," for America is not a place or a "blood
name" but is "West and the wind blowing"; it is a "great word,"
a "white bird, the rain falling / A shining thing in the mind and
the gull's call"; it is "neither a land nor a people, / A word's
shape it is, a wind's sweep— / America is alone: many together,
/ . . . and none brothers among them." Yet sick at heart as he
was for the "south water," he concluded that this "raw earth"
is our "ancient ground," and "here we must live or live only as
shadows." This sense of the impoverished resonance of the
American scene lingered through mid-century, as Howard Nemerov's poem "Deep Woods" attests. Even the brilliance of October foliage in New England, the poet realizes, cannot in this
"unlegended" land have the same rich overtones as the "Black

Forest where the wizard lived" or as a Chinese forest on a mountainside. In this land "unmitigated by myth / . . . common splendors are comparable only to / themselves."[9]

Although the writers of a romantic predilection realized that only time could resolve their longing for a fund of associations, the realists and naturalists could inaugurate a campagn to lessen their frustrations. Hence, no doubt encouraged by Whitman's example, they increasingly attacked the inhibiting Puritan heritage. Avowing in 1912 that the spirit of America had eaten into his heart, and impressed by "the technique of Poe and the social conscience of Whitman," the immigrant George Sylvester Vierick attacked the Puritanism which "crucified Whitman and slandered Poe; its breath is deadly to art."[10] A few years later in *Salvos* Waldo Frank, attacking the narrow canons of art in America, asserted that native writers need a freer imagery than Puritan taboos allow (pp. 109–10). Not suprisingly H. L. Mencken added his anti-Puritanical voice by praising E. W. Howe's *Ventures in Common Sense* for its "rare quality of honesty . . . so seldom encountered in American writing" and for its "austere intellectual passion which exalts a bald fact"—a passion absent from American writing because of the "crushing heritage of Puritanical poshposh."[11]

A third major impediment to a mature national literature, so numerous authors believed, was the stolidity, callousness, or naiveté of the public. Such was the implication of E. A. Robinson's view in the early 1920s that there is "no such animal" as the "democratization of art" and that a brain "100% American" cannot have "many percent left over." Contemporaneously Robert Frost blamed popular attitudes, charging that "as a nation we are being kept out of our greatness in literature by . . . the columnar attitude of mind. . . . Our habit is to be smart and guarded."[12] More sardonically in *The Seven Arts* Dreiser concluded that America is inhabited mainly by Bottom the Weavers who are devoted to machines and trades and are indifferent to the mind and spirit as expressed in the arts; and a decade later Thomas Wolfe wrote his mother that "for the most part we are a nation of overgrown and illbred children . . . insolent to everything but money, servile, boastful, and cowardly."[13] A generation later William Faulkner concurred: "We seem to have neither taste nor courtesy, and know and believe in nothing but money and it doesn't matter much how you get it."[14]

Somewhat more discriminatingly, however, Van Wyck Brooks in *America's Coming of Age* (New York, 1914) had observed that the American populace was split into a highbrow minority and a lowbrow majority—a bifurcation that had a dessicating effect on American letters: The popular culture was untouched by the "pure" literary modes imported from abroad and, conversely, the range and vitality of the national life received little mature expression (pp. 7–15). That indeed the highbrows of the late nineteenth century felt little respect for native literature and authors is clearly indicated by Edith Wharton's observation in *A Backward Glance* (New York, 1934) that her parents' generation regarded "authorship . . . as something between a black art and a form of manual labor" (pp. 68–69). In view of the author's lowly status as well as of the oft noted "rawness" of the American scene, the massive resort to expatriation among native writers in the 1920s is not difficult to understand.

III

Despite lingering colonialism and cisatlantic liabilities, however, there was an increasing tide of literary affirmation as the century progressed. Such had been the pattern a century earlier when, with the dynamic expansion of the country, the national imagination shifted from retrospect to the present and to prospect. Hence in literature some of the initial emphases receded. The early nineteenth-century assumption that the grandeur of American scenery would issue in a sublime literature or that the rich variety of American flora and fauna would usher in a new Arcadia had proved to be illusory (*Quest*, pp. 12–18, 22–24, 39–53). The post-Revolutionary aspiration for an American epic evolved after the Civil War into the long debate over the Great American Novel (*Quest*, pp. 328–31), which in turn yielded to the vogues of local color and regionalism. The intensive antebellum concern for a national literature, given a positive metaphysical context by the New England Transcendentalists, issued variously in a search for both the romantic and the unique in American life and history, in a renewed attention to the Indian, in a projection of the democratic ideal of independence and self-reliance, and in an increasing reliance on the American idiom. The major authors of the resultant "renaissance" of the mid-nineteenth century helped to nourish, as this essay will subsequently indicate, a second mid-century renaissance in the mid-1900s (*Quest*, pp. 90–95, 102–27, 156–61).

The twentieth-century exemplars and proponents of an American strain were generally less explicit in their national stance than their predecessors of a century earlier. Wallace Stevens, for instance, often regarded as only tangentially or ambivalently American in his poetry (as noted previously in comments on his "Comedian as the Letter C"), emerges in his *Letters* as persistently devoted to both his country and its indigenous image. Writing to his young Cuban friend José Feo in 1945, he urged him to express "the genius of your country, disengaging it from the mere mass of things"; and he was giving this advice, he added, "for my own sake." Soon thereafter he spoke of his contemporary John Crowe Ransom as "very American and, therefore, very valuable." Writing to Feo a decade later, Stevens disclosed that his emphasis on nationality extended into music and painting. If in listening to a piece of music for the first time he wanted to identify it, he said, he did so "by trying to fix the nationality of the musician." American music he characterized as "slow, thin, and often a bit affected." Most American paintings, moreover, seemed imitative and "nothing but unpleasant color which does not seem . . . in the least American."[15]

Stevens's interest in a national literature was, indeed, rooted in a deep devotion to his country past and present. After reading an account of America by a French visitor at the end of the Revolution, he remarked that going back to Washington's America was a "pleasant thing" and that it is a "curious thing that virtue should show itself in the love of one's country. . . . The only profoundly displaced persons are those who have cut that attachment or those who may never have had it." Hence his admiration for a friend who, for all his cosmopolitan habits, had "clung to his American origin faithfully and affectionately." He could even go so far as to say, "I like natives: people in civilized countries whose only civilization is that of their own land."[16] However much his own reading of transatlantic and especially French authors may have extended his technical proficiency, his imagination, affections, and style remained strongly indigenous.

Though Stevens's strong national piety was generally expressed obliquely in his poetry, some twentieth-century authors saw a need of focused exhortation. Such were those committed to Dos Passos's view (noted in the previous section) that since America had no "ghosts," the country's writers should follow Whitman's example and look toward the future. This visionary mode in varying degrees left its imprint on Crane, Wolfe, and MacLeish; but its major spokesman was Waldo Frank, who foresaw the possibility of a new cultural-religious unity in which artists and writers as messengers of the redemptive Word would supplant the former priesthood (*Salvos*, pp. 24 ff.). For the younger generation, Frank said in *Our America* (New York, 1919), America is a promise and a dream—"the first generation of Americans engaged in spiritual pioneering" (pp. 9–10).

A decade later, however, the "promise" and the "dream" of Frank's vision were blighted by the stringencies of the economic depression; and hence the socio-ethical strain that had long been an aspect of the national literature reappeared. As a century earlier such religious humanitarians as Orestes Brownson, Theodore Parker, and Harriet Beecher Stowe had proclaimed the ideal of "Brotherhood" to be the nation's *raison d'être* (*Quest*, pp. 124–27), so Michael Gold in the 1935 leftist American Writers Congress expressed the hope that the assembly would be the "beginning of a great new literature which will reflect . . . the soul of the basic American human being."[17] In the second Congress in 1937 there was an even stronger insistence by Joseph Freeman that the Congress was espousing a literature "American in theme and language" though differing from customary motifs in its focus on the American workers in their factories and homes and city slums. Likewise Newton Arvin construed the emphasis of the Congress as a "culmination of a long native development" through Thomas Hooker, John Wise, Roger Williams, and Whitman. The national past, he declared, should be explored not as sentimental provincialism or "romantic nationalism," for one of the "truest things" to be said about American literature is its "gradual maturing, rationalization, and deepening of the democratic idea."[18]

In the 1940s most American writers were drawn by the tension of international events away from both the visionary and proletarian commitments. Although Archibald MacLeish was committed to neither, on the eve of America's entrance into World War II his own new insistence on a politicocultural involvement by the writer appeared in *A Time to Speak* (Boston, 1941)—a collection of recent essays that having been written over several years, presented the writer with mutually incompatible literary principles. In an essay on Marx from the mid-1930s he could proclaim that there is "no substitute for art," and that to criticize a writer "for not writing of political issues of his day is to risk being ridiculous" (p. 43). An author who serves a Cause becomes a special pleader, he added, and loses "artistic disinterestedness" (p. 49). By 1939, however, he censured Eliot and Pound for writing poetry which evaded the "human political necessities of our own world" (p. 92). In 1940 in "The Irresponsibles" he deplored the failure of most American writers to oppose fascism on the ground that "There are things in the world—ideas, conceptions, ways of thinking—which the writer should defend from attack" (p. 119). The war had indeed brought MacLeish a long way from his "Ars Poetica," which by its concluding declaration that a poem "should not mean but be" ironically nullified the validity of either the stated conclusion or the poem. Those writers who agreed with MacLeish's earlier views inclined to see "The Irresponsibles" as a betrayal; the adherents of his later principle of involvement probably needed no new incentive.

As MacLeish, Frank, and the Writers Congress have implied, most American writers were lukewarm to causes, whether visionary, proletarian, or international, and were content to allow the national literature to take its generic course. Thus Frost, with a predilection for distinctiveness in nations as in persons, concluded that the national must precede the international in our arts—a view reflected in his poem "Build Soil." Similarly in commenting on his "Mending Wall" as being a "New Englandish" poem about boundaries, Frost added that "nationality" was something that he"couldn't live without."[19] Amy Lowell, also concerned with America's identity and convinced that a truly national literature is contingent on a new "race" with a homogeneous mind and spirit, was heartened in 1916 by evidence that "slowly before our eyes the American race is being born."[20] Sinclair Lewis, on the other hand, found the chief hope for a vital American literature in an eclipse of the "genteel tradition." In his Nobel Prize address on "The American Fear of Literature" in December 1930, he cited such varied writers as Dreiser, O'Neill, James Branch Cabell, Cather, Mencken, Anderson, and Hemingway as having inaugurated a new era by their renunciation of the "bucolic and Puritanic simplicity of Uncle Sam" and their expression of the "sweep and strength and beauty-in-ugliness of the American empire."[21]

In the early twentieth-century search for the indigenous, native folklore and folkways were given a new emphasis. To be sure, in the previous century Washington Irving had made imaginative use of Dutch legends, Joel Chandler Harris through his Uncle Remus had reflected the fables of the slaves, and the Western humorists had made tall tales of frontier life a staple part of their journalistic anecdotes. In an attempt to link folk and high art, however, and in the belief that national art grows upward from the simple to the complex, the editors of *The Seven Arts* in their first volume (November and December 1916) cited the role of community spirit and artisanship in the building of the great cathedrals of Western Europe (pp. 153, 154–56). Coincidentally in the Midwest Vachel Lindsay had begun to preach his "gospel of beauty" with the conviction (inspired in part by Whitman) that the humblest citizens as gardeners or dancers or craftsmen could effect a transformation in the national life. Lindsay's passion for such "completely democratic art" was essentially a pastoral dream of "old-fashioned Americanism" in which he envisaged city laborers escaping from skyscrapers and slums to a rural existence rooted in nature.[22]

Scarcely less enthusiastic about communal and folk resources was the more learned poet and playwright Percy MacKaye, who during World War I declared in *Community Drama* (Boston, 1917) that international harmony "does not imply less nationality in our culture, but more civilized culture in our nationalism" (pp. 5–6). Such culture he found in community drama, which he interpreted as essentially the "ritual of [a] democratic religion" of neighborliness. Modern cultures, he reminded his readers near the end of the war, were the "remnants and ruins of these communal folk arts" left standing by "the armored tanks of Machine Industrialism," and rather than remodel the ruins America should build new "temples of the communal imagination" (pp. 13–14). A few years later in the preface to *This Fine Pretty World* (New York, 1924) he praised as literary resources for the communal imagination the rich imagery, the flexibility of the mountain vocabulary, and the tradition of a spoken language that he found during his sojourn in the Kentucky mountains (p. xvi). In such diversity of lore and language he discerned a "natively American" counteragent to offset the nation's increasing standardization and "ultimate sterility of creative power" (pp. xix–xx). It is not surprising that Frost, whose poetry so often derived from New England rural life, should have praised MacKaye in *Percy MacKaye: A Symposium* (Hanover, N.H., 1925) for his "campaign . . . to hasten the day when our national life, the raw material of our poetry, shall at last cease to be raw at all" (p. 21).

Among the folk sources of American arts the blacks of the Deep South were, except for their music, only tardily recognized. In the 1935 *American Writers Congress* Eugene Jordan called attention to the Black Belt as a "suppressed nation" whose frustrations were expressed in folk tales, hymns of futility, spirituals, and work songs (p. 143). This subculture constituted, indeed, a renunciation of not only the antebellum image of the blacks in such fiction as that of Thomas Nelson Page but also the upper-class Negro authors such as W. E. B. DuBois and James Weldon Johnson as being out of touch with the indigenous "folk" art of the Black Belt (pp. 144 ff.). In the urban Northeast a generation later Ralph Ellison, who had impressively projected the covert plight of the underprivileged city black in *Invisible Man*, was similarly repudiated by militant blacks, who felt Ellison's art tainted by a disciplined proficiency acquired from such writers as Hemingway. The Black Belt "nation" was essentially a cultural unity, a "nationality" whose expression developed through generations of shared exigencies; its later urban counterpart was essentially ideological, conscious, and willed, a "nationalism" whose pattern ironically was, unlike that of the Black Belt, largely derived from sophisticated white models.

Though the Black Belt "folk" expression has become a durable part of the national culture, the indigenous folklore of the whites has proved to be less substantially rooted. "We have more myths and legends than the Greeks," wrote Norman Rosten in *Return Again, Traveler* in 1940; and as evidence he cited Johnny Appleseed, Shays, pioneer and Indian legends, "the big men, with money," and the immigrant builders of railroads. Yet how superficial and stereotyped such folk elements have tended to become has been cogently stated by Randall Jarrell in his assessment of Conrad Aiken's treatment of the legendary Southwestern desperado W. H. Bonney, or Billy the Kid. *The Kid*, Jarrell declared, is "one of those manufactured, sponsored, 'American epics': a . . . crude hodgepodge of store-bought homespun, of Madison Square Garden patriotism, of Johnny Appleseed and Moby Dick and Paul Revere and the Grand Canyon."[23] Indeed folk tales and culture can all too easily become the packaged picturesque for an urbanized America. There is, of course, nothing antithetical to the literary imagination in the motifs and themes mentioned by Rosten and Jarrell, although the Western desperado is more effectively projected in Aaron Copland's music and by Hollywood films than by Aiken's "epic." Indeed, Moby-Dick is Melville's rich creation, the "big men, with money" are assessed by Dreiser, Paul Revere is appropriately memorialized by Longfellow, and frontier violence is treated in a rich Jeffersonian context in Robert Penn Warren's *Brother to Dragons*. These works are surely not merely "manufactured"—to use Jarrell's key word. They derive from, but require more than, the stock responses of stereotypes.

The most inclusive portrayal and affirmation of the richness and variety of the American land and people in the first half of the century undoubtedly came from Thomas Wolfe, who sought to emulate Whitman in expressing both the spirit and body of the nation. How comprehensively he depicted the effects of space and the character of various sections of the country is reflected in *The Face of the Nation* (New York, 1953), a selection of passages from his fiction made by John Hall Wheelock. In *Of*

Time and the River, remembering his own return home at his father's death in October, Wolfe traced the advent of autumn across the country with reiterated allusion to leaves and the wind, and he recalled the harvests of shocked corn in the October light—an "immeasurable richness . . . a cry, a space, an ecstasy!—American earth in old October" (pp. 156–68). In his evocation of the nation Wolfe included all levels of society, and he also embraced the activities and moods of cities (especially of New York) as they impinged crucially on the lives of their inhabitants and in their heartlessness contrasted with the atmosphere of moonlit landscapes.

Within the vast beauty of its countryside and the anonymity of the cities, however, Wolfe's America bred loneliness—the absence of "brothers" and the isolation from the old cultures, which MacLeish earlier had lamented in "American Letter." In *Look Homeward, Angel* Eugene Gant, Wolfe's autobiographical persona, reflecting disconsolately on "this broad terrific earth that had no ghosts to haunt it," concluded that he must walk alone (pp. 48–50). Again in *Of Time and the River*, Eugene "plundered" the library shelves of a rich man's home and heard the "voices" of the great poets and chroniclers of Greece and England; and he could but feel himself, culturally speaking, a "poor, nameless child" hounded by an all but impossible dream of portraying the "huge historical mass of the dark wilderness of America" (pp. 211–18).

Similar moods pervade *You Can't Go Home Again* (New York, 1942), the novel in which Wolfe projected his final attitudes toward his country. Like Whitman, he realized that America had its collective guilt and corruption, which the protagonist, George Webber, is determined to disclose (p. 328). Yet America with its rich diversity also has its promises for those who would defy time and intensely seek for fame (pp. 503–8). Indeed, for "every man" there remains the "promise of America"—his "shining, golden opportunity," his "right to live . . . and become whatever thing his manhood and his vision can combine to make him" (p. 508). Those expatriates who supposed that their aspirations could be satisfied in the slower-paced life of England or France, Webber discovered, lacked passion and hence remained "pallid half-men of the arts" (pp. 610–11).

America's enemy, he concluded, is selfishness and greed; but if the nation is now "lost," it will be "found": "The true discovery of America is before us" (pp. 741–43). Thus in the mingled and troubled realistic-visionary vein of Whitman, Wolfe provided both a lyric and an epic version of the nation to complement the sterner realism or naturalism of Lewis and Dreiser. The generation of readers after his death inclined to disparage his intensity and rhetorical extravagance; but Faulkner may be justified in placing him, because of his grand design, in the highest rank of novelists in the first half of the century.

IV

In the early twentieth century for the first time in the long effort to define and create a national literature, American writers moved toward a basic unity in their discovery of a literary avatar: Walt Whitman. Although both Emerson and Poe had been and continued to be valued for the indigenous distinctiveness of their pronouncements or their art, neither quite reflected as did Whitman the American "psychosis," to use Hart Crane's term in his description of Whitman's harmonizing of the diverse aspirations and impulses in the national life and literature. (Crane's "ode" to Whitman as "our Meistersinger" in *The Bridge* and his debt to the elder poet are discussed later in this book.) As early as 1909 Pound began grudgingly to concede that Whitman was essentially the "America" of his time, that he had broken "the new wood . . . for carving" a new literary image, and that as he wrote in "A Pact," because "We have one sap and one root— / Let there be commerce between us." Yet, Pound did not realize how profound that "commerce" had been until his imprisonment in Italy at the end of the war evoked many reassessments of his life in the *Pisan Cantos*.

Pound was but one of many spokesmen who, in the surprising surge of recognition two decades or so after Whitman's death, attested to his provocative example. In the Midwest before World War I, Vachel Lindsay, in *Adventures While Preaching the Gospel of Beauty*, espousing a local and "democratic beauty" that would transform American neighborhoods, supposed himself affined to the Whitman who had heard all "America singing" (pp. 16–17). In the East, Van Wyck Brooks in *America's Coming of Age* (New York, 1914) declared that Whitman for the first time had fused the extremes of the American temperament and "precipitated the American character"; he had provided a focal center, "a national point of rest" (pp. 112, 118, 120). A few years later in *The New Era in American Poetry* (New York, 1919) Louis Untermeyer praised Whitman as the great liberator and model from the preceding century (pp. 10–12).

Meanwhile in England Henry James for several years before his death in 1916 had made clear his awareness of the richness of Whitman's poetic art. In his *Notes of a Son and Brother* (1914), recalling the Civil War years, he remarked the "tender elegiac tone in which Walt Whitman was later on so admirably to commemorate" the Civil War soldier; and remembering his own ministrations to a few soldiers, he inevitably thought of "dear old Walt" and "good Walt." A year earlier in *A Small Boy and Others* in commenting on the "indigenous vogues" of the 1850s, he asserted that only "*The Scarlet Letter* and *The Seven Gables*" had the "deep tone" until "Walt Whitman broke out in the later fifties—and I was to know nothing of that happy genius till long after."[24] It was this "deep tone," one may suppose, which Edith Wharton felt in James's evocative reading of Whitman's poems one evening when they agreed that he was "the greatest of American poets." That evening, she recalled, James's voices ranged from an "organ adagio" in "When Lilacs Last" to a "subdued ecstasy" as he conveyed "the mysterious music of 'Out of the Cradle.' "[25]

The acclaim and acceptance of Whitman as the liberator of American literature have persisted more than half a century since James's death. Wallace Stevens, despite reservations about Whitman's prosody and frequent crudity, gave him a quasi-mythic image in "Like Decorations in a Nigger Cemetery" by picturing him as "walking along a ruddy shore" and "singing and chanting the things that are a part of him / . . . . Nothing is final, he chants, No man shall see the end. / His beard is of fire and his staff is a leaping flame." Yet most of Whitman's "eleves," as he addressed his auditors in "Song of Myself," were drawn to him on less mythic grounds: In 1940 Norman Rosten in *Return Again, Traveler* valued him because he "gave us a Western belief" (p. 40); contemporaneously Kenneth Fearing acknowledged indebtedness to his flexible and organic prosody;[26] and a few years later in *Essay on Rime* (New York, 1945) Karl Shapiro credited him with fathering a "new form" and freeing us "from the traditional" as well as making "his leap / Into the personal infinite" (pp. 16, 30). How pervasive Whitman's influence has been is convincingly assessed in Roy Harvey Pearce's "Whitman and Our Hope for Poetry," wherein he notes the widely acknowledged indebtedness of mid-century poets, including Robert Duncan, Charles Olson, Louis Simpson, Robert Bly, Robert Lowell, Allen Ginsburg, and Denise Levertov.[27]

V

Among the persistent modes of nationality that enjoyed a resurgence in the twentieth century was that of regionalism. In the antebellum decades three dominant and diverse "styles" were generally recognized: those of New England, of New York and the Middle Atlantic states, and of Virginia and the Carolinas. Although New England writers through the 1850s frequently assumed that their works essentially constituted American literature, most of them (Hawthorne, Emerson, Thoreau, Margaret Fuller, James Russell Lowell, Whittier) in temper and point of view were distinctly and consciously regional. In contrast, the Dutch heritage of New York and the religious diversity and scientific interests of Pennsylvania nurtured a wider range of theme and attitude. In South Carolina William Gilmore Simms, though a vocal proponent of a "national literature," reflected the plantation South, as did John Pendleton Kennedy in Virginia (*Quest*, pp. 262–64). After the Civil War the Midwest heartland, conscious of its distance from coastal and transatlantic influences, felt its writers such as Twain and Edward Eggleston to be more indigenously and representatively American; the Deep South had its distinctive materials, whether the Lost Cause or Uncle Remus or the Creoles; and by the 1870s the uniqueness of the Far West had its popular interpretation in Bret Harte. For the literary imagination, America had indeed increasingly become a nation of nations (*Quest*, pp. 264–89).

That in the early twentieth century a regional or local focus had been adjudged the most viable mode for an authentic national literature is indicated by the widespread dismissal of the possibility or desirability of the "Great American Novel"—a literary shibboleth that had been influential in the post–Civil War decades (*Quest*, pp. 328–31). Although in 1916 Dreiser could recall his earlier excitement on reading Frank Norris's *McTeague*, "the first real American book I had ever read," in 1920, scoffing at the discussion of the Great American Novel as "silly palaver," he prophesied that there would never be such "a sole and glistening luminary blazing unrivaled in the literary heavens" (*Letters*, I, 211, 310–11). A few years earlier in an interview with Joyce Kilmer, who spoke of the Great American Novel as "that venerable mirage," Booth Tarkington added, "The only safe thing to say . . . is that the author will never know he wrote it."[28] The same year James Gibbons Huneker, devoting a chapter to the subject in *Unicorns* (New York, 1917), maintained that "The idea of a great American novel is an 'absolute,' and nature abhors an absolute"; moreover, since "America is a chord of many nations," such a novel "will be in the plural; thousands perhaps" (pp. 82–83). Similarly Stanley Braithwaite in the introduction to his *Anthology of Magazine Verse for 1925* (Boston, 1925), noting that America is as various as her forty-eight states, hailed the "passing of that so long dominant illusion of achieving 'The Great American Novel' " (pp. x–xi). Soon thereafter in a poem, "Critical Observations," MacLeish reminded his countrymen that, since the American population was a bastard mixture talking "those English Spich," they should lower their expectations from "Let us await the great American novel" to "Let us await (can we wait?) the American novel."[29]

In the 1930s this literary trend away from a nationally inclusive perspective was enhanced by the disruption of the urban economy and the corporate system. Moreover, as Van Wyck Brooks observed in *Opinions of Oliver Allston* (New York, 1941), the regional movement was in part a protest against New York's failure as a literary capital to express either the primary or the universal in the life of the country; and furthermore, "Except in the case of the strongest talents, the attempt to embrace the whole country tends to make one's emotional life sketchy, thin and vague" (pp. 262–64, 265). Such essentially was also the conviction of the Nashville group of Southern agrarians who had previously in *I'll Take My Stand* (New York, 1930) decried the cultural consequences of corporate, urban, and technological dominance. Indeed, in that manifesto Donald Davidson charged the industrial civilization with an indifference to the arts. Asserting that cities merchandise art but don't produce it, he maintained that in agrarian societies the folk arts especially were a part of routine living (pp. 47, 52, 57).

For more than a decade John Crowe Ransom, Robert Penn Warren, Cleanth Brooks, and Allen Tate in sustaining Davidson's general thesis wrote, in effect, the nation's most impressive apology for regionalism as the essentially organic mode for achieving an autochthonous and distinctive American literature. Viewing man as motivated by both economic and aesthetic needs, Ransom in 1934 declared that art grows out of a whole life that must differ from place to place, and hence cities must always draw on the regional hinterlands, where "objects and activities have their real or pious meaning." Regional culture is an importation "lived with and adapted for so long that finally it fits, and looks 'native.' " The next year in the Spring issue of the *Virginia Quarterly Review* (1935) both Ransom and Cleanth Brooks disparaged the unrepresentative character of such local-color versions of the South as those of DuBose Heyward and Julia Peterkin. A year later Warren in "Some Don'ts for Literary Regionalists" added further strictures on local color as well as on "touristic" regionalism and cultivated simplemindedness. Recognizing the current vogue of regionalism as in part a reaction to the economic depression, he nevertheless perceived its durability as a permanent "centrifugal force" in American life—a belated reminder that a circle must have a circumference as well as a center. A decade later Allen Tate continued to strengthen and refine the regional principle by attacking literary nationalism and its by-product, local color, as nurturing a superficial and uninformed literature. Indeed, he asserted, "no literature can be mature without the regional consciousness"—that is, without a "local continuity in tradition and belief." Regionalism, he concluded, is "limited" in space but not in time; its antithesis is provincialism, which is limited in time but not in space. The ideal regional literature would be one that avoided being provincial by keeping in touch with suprapolitical verities.[30]

Other sections of the country were not so assured or articulate as the South in presenting either regional principles or their own distinctive resources. To be sure, the Southwest had its Indian heritage and deserts admirably espoused by Mary Austin, as heretofore noted, and impressively embodied in such works as Scott Momaday's *House Made of Dawn* (1968) and Cather's earlier *Death Comes for the Archbishop* (1927). The New England local color of eccentric Yankees, pointed firs, and the coastal picturesque had in part yielded priority to the agonized hereditary probings and confessions of Robert Lowell's poetry. The Rocky Mountain regional consciousness, lacking as it did the "continuity in tradition and belief" specified by Tate, was still in the 1940s apparently unsure of its literary bearings. In *The Rocky Mountain Reader* (New York, 1946) W. O. Clough, convinced that the "truly regional writer is not a transplanted adult . . . but one to the country born," conceded that the character of the landscape and the inhabitants had not yet been fused integrally into an imaginative whole. Thus far the literary reflection of the area had been (in Tate's terms) "provincial" local color (pp. 415–16). By the end of the 1950s, in fact, Wallace Stegner could persuasively argue in the *Saturday Review* (May 2, 1959) that the Rocky Mountain area, like California, had little interest in an idiosyncratic culture or spirit such as that which characterized the Nashville Fugitive group. The West, indeed, felt itself to be "the national culture at its most energetic end" (pp. 15, 17, 41).

As Allen Tate has implied, "place" and region often fuse; a locale though in part idiosyncratic, may also typify a region or, more rarely, the nation, or, as William Carlos Williams would have it, the universal. Faulkner is a case in point. In *The Private World of William Faulkner* (New York, 1954) Robert Coughlan reports the novelist as saying that "to be a writer, one has first to get to be what he is, what he was born; . . . to be an American and a writer, one does not necessarily have to pay lip-service to any conventional American image. . . . 'You have to have somewhere to start from . . . ,' he told me. . . . 'one place . . . is just as important as any other. You're a country boy; all you know is that little patch up there in Mississippi where you started from. But that's all right too'" (pp. 62–63). For Faulkner, of course, this "little patch" expanded into Yoknapatawpha County, which in turn expanded into a reflection of much of the Deep South, and finally into what Faulkner in his Nobel Prize speech called the "the truths of the heart." Yet often his fiction was, though at times a tragic view of the South, an apology for the region. In *Intruder in the Dust* (New York, 1948) the county attorney, in his attempt to obtain justice for the alleged Negro murderer, Lucas Beauchamp, echoes Ransom and Tate in his defense of the regional as a cultural homogeneity out of which everything of durable value—the arts and literature and even liberty for the Negro—can emerge. As the only homogeneous section remaining in America, the attorney argues, the South itself must set the blacks free and resist extraregional imposition (pp. 150–55).

"There are those to whom place is unimportant, / But this place, where sea and fresh water meet, is important—" wrote Theodore Roethke as the first lines of "The Rose"; and then he proceeded to elaborate the rich symbol of the "rose in the sea wind" into a mystical experience in which he became "A something wholly other." At times Roethke proceeds on a "national" level when he ponders "American sounds in this silence," as he also does again in "The Journey to the Interior" (another poem in the "North American Sequence") where the verisimilitude of his "drive in gravel" is essentially a rich metaphor for the "long journey out of the self." As his earlier experiences in his father's greenhouse in Michigan had ultimately been, for all their precise botanical detail, an exaltation of the thrust of organic life toward the light, so "place" was "important" to Roethke for its metaphorical and, at times, its mystical overtones. In an almost diametric contrast, "place" was for the novelist William Maxwell, as he said in *Time Will Darken It* (New York, 1948), an index to cultural change. Hence his focus on "a certain street in a Middle Western small town" from whose residents' manners and houses and tastes he supposed he could bring to life the culture of the area just before World War I. Perceiving the current residents of Elm Street as belonging "to a different civilization," he felt obliged to focus on neither the continuity stressed by the Southern regionalists nor the mystical ultimates of Roethke but on American life as sociological flux (pp. 7–8).

For Wallace Stevens "place" could be his native Pennsylvania in the Reading area, or the Hartford region in Connecticut, or parts of the South (Florida or the Carolinas). In "all these Southern places and among the people there," as he wrote Harriet Monroe in 1922, he felt "something integrally American." Yet a generation later he more specifically fixed his regional heritage: "Whatever I am comes from Pennsylvania and Connecticut and from nowhere else."[31] Whatever the settings, Stevens inclined to use them as points of departure for his perennial reflection on the interrelationship between the imagination and the world of phenomena. In "The Idea of Order at Key West" the girl's singing voice is the "maker" of the "world / In which she sang"; and in "An Ordinary Evening in New Haven" the poet speaks, in Stevens's words, "By sight and insight" (Section v); but in general the poem moves toward "the exterior made interior" (Section vii). In "Dutch Graves in Bucks County" the Dutch pioneers "whose ecstasy / Was the glory of heaven" are the occasion for a consideration of cultural change—of modern war and the death of the religious imagination. Especially in his later poems Stevens continues to stress "the exterior made interior."

Thus in "A Mythology Reflects Its Region" he surmises that if there were a mythology of Connecticut, it would reflect "the nature of its creator": It would be "he in the substance of his region / Wood of his forests and stone out of his fields." In "Local Objects" he concluded that in a "world without a foyer, / Without a remembered past, a present past, / Or a present future" a "few things, the objects of insight, the integrations / Of feeling" could yield "moments of the classic, the beautiful," which moved "As toward an absolute foyer beyond romance."[32] Indeed, Stevens like Twain or Dickinson or Faulkner could well substantiate the dictum of T. S. Eliot that great literature combines a strong localism and unconscious universality.[33]

VI

From colonial times to the twentieth century, American writers have often been self-conscious about the relationship between the national environment or character and their literary style. As colonists, many historians, poets, editors, and clergy (whose published sermons were a large and staple part of the seventeenth-century national "literature") recognized the inevitable literary modifications imposed by the exigencies of settlers' lives; yet with a cisatlantic pride and sense of mission they were reconciled to their "plaine" Muse, their "new true stile," their "plain simplicitee" (*Quest*, pp. 7, 8 ff.). The eighteenth-century growth of wealth, education, and urban centers fostered more sophisticated literary aspirations, including imitations of Pope and the Augustans; but the founding of the American nation prompted not only a renunciation of British "turgidity" and imagery but also a disparagement of such native growths as florid orations and the "Indian vocabulary" (*Quest*, pp. 53–60). Moreover, between the Revolution and Civil War national literary confidence expanded with John Pickering's and Noah Webster's lexicographal stabilization of an American linguistic usage and idiom as found in the popular discourse of daily activities, and even some of the Transcendentalists espoused a cisatlantic diction nourished by American occupations and experience (*Quest*, pp. 130–34, 183–87). In the latter half of the century the journalistic humorists with their varied dialects and unabashed colloquialism further helped to pave the way toward the indigenous art of *Huckleberry Finn* (*Quest*, pp. 312–15).

By the twentieth century, therefore, there was less and less argument about the existence or the literary respectability of an American style and idiom. The exaltation of Whitman and the triumph of Twain—although neither of them founded a school or specified stylistic principles much beyond the former's espousal of organic cadences in a poem and the latter's advocacy of founding on fact—implied for most American writers that the native idiom was a rich and flexible instrument for their imaginative use. To be sure, Sherwood Anderson (as is noted later) echoed the seventeenth-century colonial writers in pronouncing his style that of a "crude woodsman" and admonished his compatriots to prefer a native stylistic crudity and its correlative honesty above polished transatlantic models; and Faulkner somewhat later, and no doubt disingenuously, apologized for his prose as that of an illiterate farmer whose "demon" accounted for his literary power.[34] Furthermore, though Williams and Olson, as previously noted in this essay, with their Objectivism and Objectism respectively, argued that a basic attention to "things" was an integral part of any authentic national utterance, the mystics and visionaries such as Frank and Crane, while not indifferent to objects, could point to the transcendental emphasis of Emerson and Whitman as an equally valid national focus. Moreover, those who considered the nation to be essentially a federation of regional cultures could defend the rhetoric of Faulkner and Wolfe as in part derived from a tradition of Southern oratory and hence indigenous. It would seem, therefore, that Frost was justified in supposing that an American style must be regarded pluralistically. As he wrote Untermeyer: "About all we can do is write about things that have happened to us in America in the language we have grown up to in America."[35]

A conspicuous exemplar of Frost's pluralistic and generic assumption is Hemingway. That he had some concern for an indigenous American literature is indicated by his oft quoted dictum in *Green Hills of Africa* (New York, 1953 ed.): "All modern American literature comes from one book by Mark Twain called *Huckleberry Finn.* . . . it's the best book we've had. All American writing comes from that. There was nothing before. There has been nothing as good since" (p. 22). On what grounds Hemingway made this dubiously sweeping appraisal is not clear. Did it rest on the novel's characterizations, its social and moral implications, or its disenchanted humor? From Hemingway's own literary practice one may assume that he saw in Twain's work the first impressive coalescence of a distinctively indigenous style—a style based on close observation, replete with colloquial Midwestern idiom and cadences, and free of genteel or traditional cant. It was a reportorial style shaped in part by

Midwestern or Far Western journalism in which both authors were for a time involved. Indeed, in comments in *Green Hills* on the satisfactions felt by a writer, he asserted that the greatest challenge came in attempting to project his prose into a "fourth and fifth dimension" (pp. 26–27); and with journalistic detachment he stated that, since writers "are forged in injustice," civil wars are especially valuable to them (p. 71).

To Hemingway the writer seems to be essentially a skillful verbal gamesman striving, like Poe, for "effect." Hence his pronouncement in *Life* (January 10, 1949): "No writer worth a damn is a national writer or a New England writer or a writer of the frontier or a writer of the Renaissance or a Brazilian writer. Any author worth a damn is just a writer." In the "hard league" he played in, he found that the "ball parks . . . are all good" and that "There are no bad bounces" (p. 101). With substance and implication the mere grist of technical proficiency, an American style to Hemingway was apparently whatever a writer moulded by the American milieu could effectively devise. His own experience (familial, vocational, regional) led him to a distrust of such abstracts as courage, honor, pride, pity, and sacrifice, which Faulkner in his Nobel Prize speech stressed as the basis of his own writing. Hemingway's style is no doubt closer to the common American idiom than that of his Mississippi contemporary; but an English author could have more readily written any of Hemingway's novels than *Absalom, Absalom!*.

American poets were scarcely more successful than the novelists in defining a native style. Both Pound and Williams, while acknowledging Whitman's liberating influence in transcending English metrical patterns and idiom, considered the elder poet's verse structurally lax and insisted on tighter linear coherence and form. Toward this end Williams sought to give "measure" to Whitman's style by the transformation of his line into three "variable feet"; but he used his triadic line only sporadically and, as is noted later, he finally conceded it to be a negligible innovation. Pound's attempts to inaugurate new poetic modes were directed, like those on Imagism, to English writers as well as American. Though often more irregular than Whitman in his use of the poetic line in *The Cantos*, he relied heavily on iterative motifs and images to ensure a greater coherence. Thus, like

Crane's "logic of metaphor," Pound's and Williams's prosodic reforms had only incidentally a national focus. Yet at times, as Mike Weaver has shown in his *William Carlos Williams: The American Background*, Williams did try to align American poetic practice with the cultural imperative expressed in his *In the American Grain:* to return the American mind and imagination to their cisatlantic origins. Accordingly, he advocated stripping words of their accrued associations and giving them a fresh correspondence with indigenous reality. As a means of projecting the elemental as opposed to the traditional, he urged a greater use of colloquial language and especially that of minority races such as the blacks, whose jazz rhythms he thought could be incorporated into poetry. Furthermore, he stressed the gulf that existed between "standard English" and an autochthonous American speech "in pronunciation, in intonation . . . , in metaphor and idiom, and the whole fashion of using words."[36]

Though many twentieth-century authors apparently recognized the need for an indigenous mutation in the nation's literary style, usually, like MacLeish, they could provide few clues to how it was to be achieved or what its configurations or characterizations would be. As MacLeish wrote in 1941, the new world now in the making in America requires a "revolutionary change in structure" differing from the forms of older cultures; but except for citing Twain as an example of the mastery and communication of "the American experience," he provided no help to those authors who might wish to be involved in this "revolutionary change."[37] A few years later Eliot was probably on sounder critical grounds in asserting that such evolving forms have their inception in the rich soil and diversity of regional cultures rather than in nationally oriented prescriptions and exhortations since a nation completely unified culturally will "cease to produce any culture."[38] Indeed, the durable American writers would generally seem to be those who, free from obsequiousness to foreign modes and sensitive to their native environment, use the patterns and tones of the language where their sensibility has been formed. What common characteristics in poetic style do Williams, Frost, Roethke, Robert Lowell, and Gary Snyder have that would justify the conclusion that there is an American poetic style? What common characteristics in prose do Hemingway, Faulkner, Saul Bellow, Norman Mailer, and Cather have that would justify the conclusion that there is an American fictional style? It would seem that an American style most substantially emerges as an integral aspect of one of the diverse cultures in a "nation of nations." It is, as Emerson in 1843 said of a national literature, a "generic result" (*Quest,* p. 159).

Notes

1. B. T. Spencer, *The Quest for Nationality* (Syracuse, 1957), p. 27. Hereinafter in reference to concepts of nationality before 1912, this volume will be cited as *Quest*.
2. *Ibid.*, pp. 6–18, 25–32, 39–60.
3. T. Dreiser, *Letters*, ed. Robert Elias (Philadelphia, 1959), I, 216; W. Frank, *Salvos* (New York, 1924), pp. 96–98, 109–10; E. L. Masters, *Whitman* (New York, 1937), pp. 312–13.
4. For the source of Williams's language, see page 108 in the chapter on Williams in this book, which is devoted to his attempt to redirect his compatriots to the "ground" of American experience, to the "local," and to indigenous "things" as the proper source of American culture and ideas.
5. W. Stevens, *Collected Poems* (New York, 1954), pp. 27, 34, 36–37.
6. E. L. Masters, *Spoon River Anthology* (New York, 1916), p. 194.
7. John Dos Passos, in *The New Republic*, October 14, 1916, pp. 269–71.
8. Zona Gale, *Portage, Wisconsin and Other Essays* (New York, 1928), pp. 106–8, 109, 152.
9. Howard Nemerov, *New and Selected Poems* (Chicago, 1960), pp. 97–98.
10. J. S. Vierick, *The Candle and the Flame* (New York, 1912), pp. xii, xv, 125.
11. H. L. Mencken, introduction to E. W. Howe's *Ventures in Common Sense* (New York, 1919), pp. 9, 12–13.
12. E. A. Robinson, *Selected Letters*, ed. Ridgely Terrence (New York, 1940), pp. 121, 128; R. Frost, *Letters . . . to Louis Untermeyer* (New York, 1963), p. 132.
13. T. Dreiser, in *The Seven Arts*, February 1, 1917: 378; T. Wolfe, *Thomas Wolfe's Letters to His Mother*, ed. J. S. Terry (New York, 1943), p. 143.
14. W. Faulkner, *Selected Letters*, ed. Joseph Blotner (New York, 1977), p. 354.
15. W. Stevens, *Letters*, ed. Holly Stevens (New York, 1966), pp. 495, 518, 859.
16. *Ibid.*, pp. 568, 571, 613.
17. *American Writers Congress* (New York, 1935), p. 16. Foreword by Waldo Frank.

18. J. Freeman and N. Arvin, in *The Writer in a Changing World*, ed. H. Hart (New York, 1937), pp. 20–21, 36, 38.
19. See J. F. Lynen, *The Pastoral Art of Robert Frost* (New Haven, 1960), pp. 130–31; R. L. Cook, "Robert Frost's Asides on His Poetry," *American Literature* 19 (January 1948): 355.
20. Amy Lowell, *The Craftsman* 30 (July 1916): 343–44.
21. Sinclair Lewis, in *The New Republic*, August 19, 1936, pp. 36–37.
22. V. Lindsay, *Adventures While Preaching the Gospel of Beauty* (New York, 1914), pp. 16–19, 171–73.
23. Norman Rosten, *Return Again, Traveler* (New Haven, 1940), pp. 21–22; Randall Jarrell, in *The Nation*, May 8, 1948, p. 512.
24. Henry James, *Autobiography*, ed. F. W. Dupee (New York, 1956), pp. 46, 422, 424.
25. Edith Wharton, *A Backward Glance* (New York, 1934), p. 186.
26. K. Fearing, see *Poetry* 57 (January 1941): 266.
27. R. H. Pearce, "Whitman and Our Hope for Poetry," in *Historicism Once More* (Baltimore, 1969), pp. 330 ff. See also C. A. Brown, "Walt Whitman and the 'New Poetry,' " *American Literature* 33 (March 1961): 33 ff.
28. B. Tarkington, in *Literature in the Making*, comp. Joyce Kilmer (New York, 1917), p. 40.
29. A. MacLeish, *Poems, 1924–1933* (Boston, 1933), p. 88.
30. J. C. Ransom, in *American Review* 2 (January 1934): 298, 302; R. P. Warren, in *American Review* 8 (December 1936): 142, 143, 148, 149; A. Tate, in *Virginia Quarterly Review* 21 (Spring 1945): 263, 266, 269.
31. W. Stevens, *Letters*, pp. 228–29; *Poems by Wallace Stevens*, ed. S. F. Morse (New York, 1960), p. vii.
32. W. Stevens, *Opus Posthumous*, pp. 111–12, 118.
33. T. S. Eliot, *To Criticize the Critic* (New York, 1965), p. 54.
34. W. Faulkner, *Faulkner at the University*, ed. F. L. Gwynn and Joseph Blotner (Charlottesville, Va., 1959), pp. 159–60.
35. R. Frost, *Letters . . . to Louis Untermeyer*, p. 88.
36. Mike Weaver, "An American Measure," in *William Carlos Williams: The American Background* (Cambridge, U.K., 1971), pp. 67, 76, 80, 87.
37. A. MacLeish, in *Yale Review* 31 (Autumn 1941): 62, 64, 71, 73–75.
38. T. S. Eliot, in *Sewanee Review* 53 (July–September 1945): 337.

AN AMERICAN
LITERATURE AGAIN:
POSTWAR
CONSIDERATIONS

THE OLD PROBLEM OF a national American literature manifestly
will not die. Since the days of the Hartford Wits scarcely a native
author or critic of first, second, or third rank has left unrecorded
his convictions on the subject, and now a few of them have
confidently disposed of it. Yet they have scotched the snake, not
killed it. Persistently it slithers its way back into the area of
critical discussion, especially when American participation in
foreign wars expands the national pride and makes self-conscious
the national culture. The renaissance of the controversy during
the 1940s thus repeats the pattern established during and after
the Revolution, the War of 1812, and World War I.

In the uneasy years of peace since 1945 with American culture more sharply than ever outlined against that of Eurasia,
national self-consciousness has scarcely abated; and the prospect
of a long ideological conflict has intensified the search for cultural
unity as an instrument of national strength. Lest American literature fatally play the dilettante in an oasis of irresponsibility,
authors with tastes and histories as diverse as those of Van Wyck
Brooks, Archibald MacLeish, Lewis Mumford, and Bernard
DeVoto have become, with their allies, what Karl Shapiro in his
"Essay on Rime" calls "messengers of the official muse,"[1] what
Allen Tate terms "our young pro-consuls of the air,"[2] or what
James T. Farrell more bluntly calls "ideological policemen."[3]
The issue of a proper expression of nationality was never more
important, either for civilization or for American literature. Per-
haps amid the manifestoes and rejoinders that persist in this

little war, there is room for a brief inquiry into the way in which literature becomes American.

So long as there are both nations and literature, nationality will be reflected in literature; for nationality in its broadest sense is a group consciousness, involving masses of attitudes and sentiments that can scarcely be ignored as legitimate constituents of literary expression. Yet nationality involves also a political structure, an historical development, a racial convergence, a geographical extension, a social arrangement. The question for the critic, and perhaps for the poet and novelist, is: How does nationality get transposed into literary modes? Are certain aspects soluble; are others irreducible? Fearing a spurious embodiment of Americanism in literature, some nineteenth-century Anglophile critics such as Edward Everett Hale argued that a national literature is neither more desirable nor more attainable than a national mathematics or astronomy.[4] But an argument that literary and mathematical symbols are analogous rests on a dubious assumption; for Valley Forge and x in diverse fashion stand for something other than themselves. On the other hand, certain aspects of nationality (for instance, a scheme of social security) are with difficulty convertible to the mode of communication to which the writer of fiction as opposed to history, to use an Aristotelian distinction, has accustomed himself. Surely literary communication can never attain a mathematical purity; but surely also it cannot be sustained merely by the quick energy afforded by political controversy.

In earnest answer to such questions the proponents of an indigenous American literature for generations have played endless variations on a few simple themes: An American literature should exploit the American past (the Indians, the heroic warriors, the triumphs in battle); it should convey the range, the grandeur, the romantic beauty of the American landscape; it should cultivate the lore of the nation's naive social strata (the tall tale, the cowboy ballad, the racy anecdote); it should express the virile Western spirit of a youthful and self-reliant people; it should enhance a political ideal (individual liberty or natural rights); it should proclaim the diversity of America through regionalism and local color; it should catch the actual life of the nation through a depiction of manners, surfaces, behavior. For all these proposals much has been and can be said. Yet no wide and lasting agreement has been reached; emerging in momentary triumph, each school has in turn found itself engulfed by a succeeding wave of critical fashion. It would be impertinent, therefore, to assume that one at length has found a definitive solution. But one may at least attempt to clarify the nature of the problem involved; one may at least hope to identify phantoms. Some help is afforded, I think, by laying on the table the old assumptions and turning to the process of reading itself. For as Milton remarked that "a wise man like a good refiner can gather gold out of the drossiest volume, and that a fool will be a fool with the best book, yea or without a book," so perhaps the American incidence of any work, like its wisdom, may be measured at last only in terms of a given reader. Perhaps a book is in effect American or non-American, depending upon the nature and level of response.

The most elementary, or possibly the primary, mode of comprehension of a novel or poem I judge is the sensory. By this I mean that "images" become the extent of the reader's awareness. Although such a mode is rarely found in purity, some readers undoubtedly respond largely within its limitations. For such readers an American work must be one that emphasizes the American scene or the events of American history. Such a view coincides with Ellen Glasgow's judgment, in *A Certain Measure*, of the Americanism of her own fiction: "Because I have painted an actual scene, my novels are fundamentally American in conception." Indeed, she felt her "actual scene" was more authentic than that of the "severely regimented realism" of which "Mr. Howells was still the acting dean." Today much of the reading of James T. Farrell and William Faulkner, with their bizarre and brutal situations, no doubt ends with sensory impressions that both authors may well have intended as only initiatory to more complex states of mind—to what some would call imagination. On this level Faulkner and Farrell are perhaps as thoroughly American in their writings as authors can be, for their manifold perceptions are of American objects and people. In this sense our literature has been American since colonial days. The oaks and elms of Anne Bradstreet, the honeysuckle of Philip Freneau and the gentian of William Cullen Bryant, and the mining camps of Bret Harte form for certain readers the most relevant basis for Americanism in literature. As Allen Tate has said of Hemingway, Dreiser, and Faulkner, such authors "have made us at home physically in our country."⁶ Yet for the sensory reader *For Whom the Bell Tolls* must be chiefly a Spanish novel (as in effect it has been for the majority, I think), because his reading has not carried him beyond the images of its Spanish world.

Few proponents of Americanism in literature, however, are content to allow it to rest on this plane; and, in fact, readers have confined themselves rarely to a merely perceptual comprehension of the world's body. They have cherished the epigram, the teasing implication, or even the blatant moralism; they have conceived of meaning in literature as an ideational or ethical derivative. Since James Fenimore Cooper's insistence that the "only peculiarity that can, or ought to be expected [in an American literature] is that which is connected with their [Americans'] distinctive political opinions," many have felt that some unique American quality or idea is the only proper measure of the Americanism of a book. As Cooper thus defended before a sensitive, nationalistic public his own use of foreign scenes, so Julian Hawthorne later skillfully elaborated this point of view in behalf of his father;⁸ and thus William Dean Howells apologized for his expatriate friend, Henry James.⁹ All assumed a "frame of reference," a representation of interlocking values and concepts peculiar to America, above the level of simple perception.

A statement by Allen Tate that the "American novel has had to find a new experience" here becomes pertinent.¹⁰ That in a certain sense Americans do have new experiences is undeniable: The sight of a copperhead or cottonmouth, the descent in an express elevator in the Empire State Building, attendance at a county fair or a court day or a national convention—these, viewed as units or wholes, are uniquely American experiences. Moreover, as has been said, on a perceptual level the representation of such experiences may constitute a literature legitimately termed "American." Yet something much more complex usually has been in the minds of those for whom American literature is marked by a "new experience," and the view has been reiterated enough to merit some scrutiny.

The precursor of such a view I judge to be the Rousseauistic

St. Jean de Crèvecoeur, who in his famous third chapter of *Letters from an American Farmer* affirmed that the "American is a new man, who acts upon new principles; he must therefore entertain new ideas, and form new opinions."[11] Whitman elaborated this pronouncement in the following century, projecting it as the *sine qua non* of a sound and autochthonous literature that should be interfused with and expressive of the whole life of the nation. And more recently, MacLeish restated this thesis: Our failure to create an American literature lies in our inability to fashion an idiom commensurate with the new experience of American life. Our essential literary problem, he said, is to create a form appropriate to "a revolutionary change in structure . . . the adaptation of an art of letters developed in Europe to the experience of life in a country geographically, meteorologically, socially, psychologically, and otherwise unlike the country and the life of Europe."[12] In these words we approach that ill-defined abstraction "the American mind." That there do exist complexes of religion, tradition, and social practices that differentiate certain long-established nations (say, Japan and Denmark) is undeniable; that there are certain habits, tastes, and acquired responses (for instance, table manners, or the liking for Coca-Cola) that may serve for a time to identify one as an American resident is likewise certain. But to find underlying these superficial habits a unique and homogeneous national mind molded by climate, race, and epoch (which MacLeish, following Taine, has posited) has proved difficult indeed. To find it reflected in American literature and to trace the organic relation between an American idiom and American meteorology seem more difficult still.

Any one of a thousand representative poems or novels by American authors would serve to show the nature of "new experience" reflected in our literature. Robert Frost would afford ready examples, with his authentic New England scenes: the mending of walls, the making of axe helves, the lone burials and lonely terror of New England farms. So would Theodore Dreiser's *An American Tragedy*, or Tate's "Ode to the Confederate Dead," or MacLeish's "American Letter." Do these works have in common a new American experience? Or do they not by their very diversity suggest the heterogeneity of American attitudes?

But, to be more specific, one may examine a poem by some poet who is frequently regarded as thoroughly American in fashioning "an idiom commensurate with the new experience of American life," say Carl Sandburg. Among his many representations of Midwestern life on prairie and in Chicago one finds, for instance, "Caboose Thoughts":

> It's going to come out all right—do you know?
> The sun, the birds, the grass—they know.
> They get along—and we'll get along.

In preceding lines Sandburg tells of the discouraging, rainy days when letters do not come; of the "caboose and the green tail lights" fading "down the right of way like a new white hope." Then turning to American scenes and persons, he reaches a "hotel girl in Des Moines":

> We took away the money for a prize waltz at a
>   brotherhood dance.
> She had eyes; she was safe as the bridge over the
>   Mississippi at Burlington; I married her.

Then, after finding Pike's Peak "a big old stone . . . something you can count on," the poet repeats the opening lines of faith in the future.[13]

Certainly here on the level of simple perception one finds a series of localized American experiences and hence in one sense an American poem. But if one reads the poem for its ideas, its "climate of opinion," surely no peculiarly national or even sectional mind emerges. Reduced to its fundamental implications, the poem expresses a complex of habits and beliefs that are very old and very prevalent: a secular faith in man's future derived from nature, a romantic delight in festivity yielding place to stable affection, a mingling of susceptibility to mechanized conveniences and elemental natural beauty, and so on. If the aggregate of these qualities makes some American minds, it is nevertheless lacking in as many others; and it is found as frequently under a different group of particulars elsewhere in the world. Moreover, I should find it impossible to say how Sandburg's idiom can be traced to an American meteorology. That there have been sectional interests and modes of thought that have settled into temporary regional cultures, such volumes as the Southern agrarians' *I'll Take My Stand* and Perry Miller's *New England Mind* leave little doubt; but the mobility and the breadth of the American scene have scarcely allowed at once enduring and unique national attitudes. Even though John Dewey in pronouncing the pragmatism of C. S. Peirce essentially "American in its origin" was undoubtedly validly recognizing a major strain in the national mind—a "new spirit . . . unlike that of old-world charity and benevolence"—he admitted that it might not yet "mark the attainment of a distinctive culture" or a "new civilization."[14]

Perhaps, then, by way of summary, one could risk this generalization: As the reading of literature moves away from particular, "historical" perceptions to an awareness of concepts and qualities, literature with difficulty retains its national flavor or distinction. To remark such a tendency is not to espouse a disembodied universality. John Crowe Ransom has properly reminded us that attitudes and feelings do not exist by themselves but are always "toward" something;[15] and a century ago Emerson asserted that American literature must develop through a treatment of the particular objects and events of the national scene: the meal in the firkin, the milk in the pan, the stump speech, the camp meeting.[16] But Emerson's objects were merely the vehicles; they were the media for the Over-soul. One need not accept Emerson's metaphysic to grant the virtue of his insight. Recent literary criticism, sharpened by the inquiries of naturalistic psychology and semantics and enriched by anthropological studies of myth and symbol, also confirms the inherence of multiple meanings and allusions in the particulars of a literary work. In André Gide's *Counterfeiters* the novelist Edouard has summarily stated the issue: "It is true that there is no psychological truth unless it be particular; but on the other hand there is no art unless it be general. The whole problem lies just in that—how to express the general by the particular—how to make the particular express the general."[17] Or in Dewey's terminology: The subject matter of a work is not necessarily its subject. It was Whitman's failure to make this distinction, I judge, that led to his fear that Shakespearean kings would turn American republicans into English royalists, while at the same time his ideal American, Lincoln, was devoting himself to Shakespeare, only to become more assuredly democratic. Indeed, if we had really unique national experiences, perhaps we could not communicate them to the world.

Most often within the last century, however, the touchstone for Americanism in literature has not been found in the representation of new experiences or concepts, but rather in the embodiment of the American character. As to what the essential and distinguishing trait of the American character is, there has been little unanimity. One recalls easily enough the varied, casual assumptions: individualism, love of liberty, the pioneer spirit, distaste for tradition and convention, activity, materialism (and its opposite, idealism), optimism, and so on. Now it would be perverse to say that these qualities do not exist in appreciable measure in America—that, indeed, some of them, such as the love of liberty and a penchant for activity, have not flourished here, owing to certain favorable conditions, rather than in other nations. As realities they form legitimate and inevitable centers for our books. Yet most of them have been abundantly present in past ages and literatures. If Shelley's "Ode to the West Wind" had been written in America, one no doubt would find scores of comments to the effect that "here breathes in unmistakable fashion the youthful, determined, and progressive spirit of a pioneer nation." In other words, the method of this species of literary nationalism is to assert a priori an ideal American character and then illustrate it by arbitrarily selected works.

The additional difficulty with such criteria, however, is that unless the catalogue of dominant national characteristics is made so extensive as to become meaninglessly contradictory, the accepted canon of American literature would be immeasurably diminished. Sherwood Anderson, for instance, declared that all genuine American literature is marked by crudity.[18] But, then, are Willa Cather's *Death Comes for the Archbishop*, Nathaniel Hawthorne's *The Scarlet Letter*, and Marianne Moore's lyrics not American? Louise Bogan supposes that "a tough mysticism" is an ineradicable element in our poetry.[19] But does not this mysticism inhere as much in the English poetic tradition during

the past century and a half? And if it is a definitive trait of
American character, what of Twain or Sinclair Lewis? To
Howells "the more smiling aspects of life" seemed "the more
American" (in contrast to Russian somberness) and should de-
termine the tone of our fiction.[20] Should we, then, exclude Poe,
Ambrose Bierce, and Thomas Wolfe as not representative?
Henry Seidel Canby, cautiously aware of defining too simply
the American tradition, proffers a group of traits, "intensely
American," that have dominated American life more than that
of other countries and that "spell in outline the name of our
country when it . . . expresses itself in literature": expansiveness (Edwards's "hell itself became expansive"!), egalitarianism,
humanitarianism, and youthfulness.[21] Yet one must ask if E. A.
Robinson reflects especially the first and last, if Emerson and
Thoreau the second and third. Does Ellen Glasgow? or Hawthorne? or Melville? or Hemingway? Surely few readers leave
the books of these authors confirmed in the attitudes specified
by Canby. Indeed, in his notes to *New Year Letter* W. H. Auden
remarks that the dominant atmosphere of American literature
is loneliness, and elsewhere Mark Van Doren has found Whitman one of the loneliest of writers.[22] Here again may be dubious
generalization; but it serves to illustrate the fact that for almost
every quality asserted to be dominantly American, an antithetical trait can be found permeating our standard literature
from colonial days to the present.

Paradoxically, it would seem that as we have grown into
national maturity, we have been modified increasingly by international currents; our political union, involving many racial
strains, has not been accompanied by the cultural homogeneity
of older isolated nations. Our era of development, our geographical position, our economic resources, and our racial diversity
have given us, of course, special national problems to be attacked
with special techniques. But the influence of these techniques
has not been so formative and persistent as to justify most of
the confident formulations of the American mind and character
and of their subsequent reflection in literature. American minds
and characters have been about as diverse as those of modern
man; and from decade to decade they have found diverse expression. Indeed, it was the perennial indulgence of foreign travelers

in easy national formulas that led Mark Twain at the end of the century to protest in the name of outraged common sense:

> There isn't a single human characteristic that can safely be labeled "American." There isn't a single human ambition, or religious trend, or drift of thought, or peculiarity of education, or code of principles, or breed of folly, or style of conversation, or preference for a particular subject for discussion . . . or any other human detail, inside or outside, that can rationally be generalized as "American." . . . There is no American temperament.[23]

The Lincolnian character is American; but so are the Harding character and the Van Buren character; otherwise, each would not have been approved by the electorate. American readers have always had aesthetic needs too divergent and subtle to be satisfied by a literature ready-made to any formula of national character. Those incompatible poems, "A Psalm of Life" and "Thanatopsis," even today share popular favor. There is room for William Faulkner and William Saroyan, for MacLeish and Jeffers, for Odets and O'Neill within the national mind. For whatever is written and read here must be *ipso facto* a part of what the national mind really is. As *The Nation* bluntly asserted soon after the Civil War, "Just so far as America is American, the literature of America will be American."[24]

There is a third level of reading, however, upon which the Americanism of a work must be determined: broadly speaking, the metaphorical and the symbolic. Transcending sensory images, transcending explicit qualities and concepts, the reader's imagination may venture beyond the precise clarity of object or formula into a maze of elusive associations, into shadowy personal or communal memories. The snake becomes sin or treachery or fear; the whale becomes nature or evil; the bridge becomes the future; the sea becomes mystery or eternal peace. Objects and persons in a story or poem exist in their own right for those who prefer so to take them; but they also involve associations which throw a flickering light into the obscurer corners of life and nature.

For the American writer who wishes to suggest the wide

range and quality of human experience, a major problem, I judge, is the availability of rich symbolic counters. They cannot be arbitrarily fashioned by an author, however fecund his imagination. They must be shared by his community. Hence *Moby-Dick*, written though it was with a remarkable fusion of Melville's marine experiences, of his reading of Shakespeare, and of his probing of the question of evil, no doubt long failed to secure an attention commensurate with its insight partially because it employs symbolic objects too far removed from the stretches of the American continent. Mark Twain was closer to the long known and felt aspects of American life—the country graveyard, the Sunday school, the river—and hence America understood him as the Elizabethans understood Shakespeare. Therefore, it is natural that the availability of adequate symbols should have been the concern of many who for a century and a half have pondered the problem of creating an American literature. Halleck's lament, more than a century and a half ago, over the lack of historical associations, folk backgrounds, and traditions, was perhaps not merely the aberration of an excessive romanticism.[25] The problem was in Hawthorne's mind when, in the Preface to *The Marble Faun,* he declared poetry and romance inhibited in a country where there was "no shadow, no antiquity, no mystery, no picturesque and gloomy wrong."[26] It was in Henry James's mind when he remarked, "It takes so many things . . . such an accumulation of history and custom . . . to form a fund of suggestion for a novelist."[27] In listing all the advantages of the English novelist in this respect, James was not indulging in expatriate snobbery. He was rather asserting the necessity of a body of stable associations if literature is to express sensitively for a nation the human scene. If there are few classics in American literature, perhaps a major factor in our poverty lies in a dearth of adequate symbols.

Objects, persons, and places used metaphorically and symbolically, of course, do not usually or primarily convey unique American experiences or qualities or concepts. The compulsion to employ American backgrounds lies not in national pride but in the nature of the communicative process. The oft repeated admonitions against the use of the nightingale in American poetry ought not to be posited on the fact that the bird is Old

World, but that it is not New World; never having seen it as a familiar object, pondered its habits, or wondered at its song through generations, the American reader is likely to find it a symbolic blank. It can have for us only a kind of derived (or what Tolstoy scornfully called "poetic") signification. But have we a bird to substitute? Perhaps not; at least not to convey what the nightingale expressed to Shakespeare and Keats. Even our eagle is scarcely a genuine symbol; for it is almost as rare in American experience as the nightingale. (Franklin suggested the turkey as a more representative national bird!) And so with most of our natural objects and creatures. The buffalo is almost as literary as the dragon. In our vast and swiftly changing landscape few flora and fauna are available for long, if at all, as national referents. We read of them for their novelty; and novelty and symbolic meanings are scarcely compatible.

In the poverty of national associations in nature, American authors have frequently turned for symbols to products and structures omnipresent in American life: the bridge of Hart Crane, the plane of Faulkner, the train of Wolfe, the steel of Sandburg. Indeed, it must be admitted that an American mythology, a final and almost unquestioned assumption of the real and valuable, is chiefly to be found in this world of commerce and industry and engineering. Whether these objects and this world are too much at the mercy of our restless economy to act as stable referents for substantial literature remains to be seen. Thus far our most enduring metaphors and symbols in America have not been exclusively American. For generations the nation found the crucial periods of its life bound to and interpreted by a religious tradition; or it found a secular fund of meaning in domestic activities and objects. Hence Emily Dickinson could employ the terminology of church and home—the crucifixion, sacraments, and household business—as the vibrant heart of her poems. And Mark Twain, as strange as it may seem, did much the same thing, like the poetess finding in the rituals of salvation and in domestic habits not so much his primary subjects as his metaphorical or symbolic media.

Literature may become American, then, on this plane not by seeking to express a new experience, but by expressing or exploring the far reaches of human consciousness through objects

primarily American in memory, through "felt objects," and by
eschewing objects foreign to the recurring associations of the
American people. It is on this level, too, that one may speak
most relevantly of an American style. Like the unique particulars
of our scenery, there is obviously an American vernacular that
may distinguish our literature from all others. But beyond this,
the rhythm and turn of phrase, the tone and inflection of reiterated speech, serve a communicative function. Much of
Frost's understatement, of Hemingway's staccato dialogue, of
Whitman's bravura passages is a further projection of explicit
meaning through the reader's familiarity with or recollection of
the idiomatic implications in the speech of certain classes or
sections of American society. Once again, like American metaphors, they do not convey unique American qualities or ideas
or feelings; they are, in effect, another metaphorical medium.
In this sense there can scarcely be said to be at present or to
have been at any time in the past one inclusive American style.
Rather there are numerous American styles, each ineffectual to
some extent for an appreciable part of the American people who
are deaf to its particular overtones.

What, then, is an American literature? If the foregoing approach to it is valid, it is a complex of several potential responses
on the part of the reader. At present the term is so variously
used, is charged with so many assumptions, that it is all things
to all men. For a century and a half nearly every American
author or critic of note has been a proponent of some kind of
American literature; but an inquiry into their constructions of
the term discloses the fact that many of them have desired
something quite unacceptable to many others. Perhaps now our
first duty is semantic contrition. If we are helpless to fix a single
meaning for the term, we can at least refrain from a sharp or-
thodoxy that would impale on the stake of official Americanism
much that has been sensitively and maturely written within our
borders; we can abjure patterns that would cut too narrowly the
wide and rich fabric of human experience. In Ellen Glasgow's
words: "America, if not the didactic term Americanism, is wide
enough to include the diverse qualities in all the novels ever
written by American novelists at home or abroad."[28] On certain
simple levels of response it would seem that almost every work

since John Smith's *A True Relation* may legitimately be called American; on other levels some of our most powerful figures with difficulty retain their literary citizenship. If the choice lies between a continued loose construction of the term and a doctrinaire list of exclusions, I believe the former is preferable, if not inevitable. A given work may be American for one reader and divorced from national referents for another. One will remain literally within national limits; another will pause lightly and then spring symbolically far beyond.

Whatever an American literature may be, we can expect its presence only as an organic part of American life. Emerson, despite his plea for a self-reliant culture, realized by 1843 that an American literature cannot be created by fiat, but is "a secular and generic result."[29] James Russell Lowell insisted that we want a natural rather than a national literature.[30] And in more recent years, Van Wyck Brooks has seemed to align himself with that century-old position: "The only 'Americanism' that is worth pursuing for literature is a by-product of the process by which genuine men living in this country genuine lives are genuinely expressing their convictions and conceptions."[31] To the extent that Americans become unique creatures, the expression of their conscious life will reflect a peculiar nationality. Inevitably on the perceptual and consequently on the metaphorical plane there will continue to be peculiar national elements; but to enforce nationality on the level of concepts is to narrow and impoverish American literature and to lead it to an ironic betrayal of its own national tradition by making it the ideological lackey of forces to which it should play the imaginative tutor. A national literature may after all be responsible enough if it can use native symbol and native experience to suggest the nature and destiny of man.

Notes

1. K. Shapiro, *Essay on Rime* (New York, 1945), p. 30
2. A. Tate, *The Swimmers and Other Selected Poems* (New York, 1970), p. 92; in *Virginia Quarterly Review* 21 (Spring 1945), 262 ff.
3. J. T. Farrell, *The League of Frightened Philistines* (New York, 1945), p. 11.

4. E. E. Hale, *Life and Letters*, ed. E. E. Hale, Jr. (Boston, 1917), II, 115.

5. E. Glasgow, *A Certain Measure* (New York, 1943), pp. 14, 67.

6. A. Tate, *Essays of Four Decades* (Chicago, 1968), p. 130

7. J. F. Cooper, *Notions of the Americans* (Philadelphia, 1828), II, 101.

8. J. Hawthorne, in *North American Review* 139 (July 1891), 167–69, 177.

9. W. D. Howells, *Life in Letters*, ed. Mildred Howells (New York, 1928), II, 394–96.

10. Tate, p. 130.

11. St. Jean de Crèvecoeur, *Letters from an American Farmer* (New York, 1945), p. 44.

12. A MacLeish, in *Yale Review* 31 (Autumn 1941), 62, 64

13. C. Sandburg, *Complete Poems* (New York, 1970), pp. 93–94.

14. J. Dewey, *Philosophy and Civilization* (New York, 1931), p. 16; Percy Boynton, *The Rediscovery of the Frontier* (Chicago, 1931), pp. 181–82; C. S. Peirce, *Chance, Love and Logic*, ed. M. R. Cohen (New York, 1923), pp. 301 ff.

15. J. C. Ransom, *The World's Body* (Baton Rouge, La., 1968), pp. 116–18, 152–62, 205–6, 215–18.

16. R. W. Emerson, *Works* (Boston, 1888), I, 113–15.

17. A. Gide, *The Counterfeiters*, trans. Dorothy Bussy (New York, 1928), p. 172.

18. S. Anderson, "An Apology for Crudity," *The Dial* 63 (November 8, 1917), 437–38.

19. L. Bogan, in *The New Yorker* 17 (September 6, 1941), 60.

20. W. D. Howells, *Criticism and Fiction* (New York, 1891), pp. 128–29.

21. H. S. Canby, in *The Saturday Review of Literature* 22 (August 31, 1940), 3–4.

22. W. H. Auden, *New Year Letter* (London, 1946), p. 153; M. Van Doren, *The Private Reader* (New York, 1942), p. 70.

23. M. Twain, *How to Tell a Story and Other Essays* (New York, 1897), pp. 189–90.

24. *The Nation* 6 (1968), 7–8.

25. F. Halleck; see N. F. Adkins, *Fitz-Greene Halleck: An Early Knicker-bocker Wit and Poet* (New Haven, Conn., 1930), pp. 44 ff.

26. N. Hawthorne, *The Marble Faun* (Boston, 1888), p. 15.

27. H. James, *Hawthorne* (New York, 1887), p. 43.

28. E. Glasgow, *A Certain Measure*, p. 146.

29. R. W. Emerson, *Works*, XII, 260

30. J. R. Lowell, "Preface" to *The Pioneer* (1843), quoted in B. T. Spencer, *The Quest for Nationality* (Syracuse, 1957), p. 197.

31. V. W. Brooks, *Opinions of Oliver Allston* (New York, 1941), p. 186.

NATIONALITY DURING THE INTERREGNUM (1892–1912)

By 1892 THE IDENTITY of American literature had been generally established on both sides of the Atlantic, as Brander Matthews maintained in an essay on "The Literary Independence of the United States" written in that year.[1] A decade later William Dean Howells ventured to say that in both demand and supply the American spirit in literature was such that if any common ideal with the English was to be approached, they must come to us.[2] "Directly, or indirectly, American Literature, both Preferred and Common, is now among the standard securities," declared the critic Percival Pollard, soon thereafter. The question, he added, is whether the Preferred is really Common and the Common merely water.[3]

Paradoxically, however, with their sense of independence, American authors in the 1890s felt themselves at the end of an era—a *"Dichterdaemmerung,"* as John Hay called it, when the great constellation of literary stars had passed, leaving "an hour or two of dubious twilight" before the literary dawn should break.[4] In 1900 E. C. Stedman also spoke of the period as a "twilight interval" or an "afterglow"; young Edwin Arlington Robinson in a sonnet lamented his "barren" era as a "changeless glimmer of dead gray"; and in reviewing Robinson's poems in *Outlook* Theodore Roosevelt remarked that the "twilight of the poets" was "especially gray" in America.[5] Earlier, however, Stedman had prophetically referred to the *fin de siècle* decline as an "interregnum,"[6] a term also favored by the poet-novelist Charles Leonard Moore when, in 1910, he proclaimed that this "period of comparative dullness and poverty" seemed to be

49

drawing to a close. These past twenty years of wandering in the desert, Moore reminded his readers, had borne out Aldrich's prophecy in 1891 that during the next two decades American poetry was to have a hard time.[7]

Although fiction scarcely passed through the same twilight interregnum, it too had "gone soft," as Ellen Glasgow said in deploring the whole American literary scene as a vast kinder-garten.[8] The same comparison occurred to Walter Blackburn Harte, who confessed that "To read one's contemporaries in the department of imaginative literature, in this country at least, is almost tantamount to sentencing one's mind to a life-time of the sucking-bottle."[9] The remedial counteragent, he thought, must be the infusion of "great Titanic imaginings," and this conviction was increasingly expressed in the 1890s and early 1900s by those who, like Whitman a generation earlier, felt the gulf between American experience and the gentility that served as the arbiter for publication at the end of the century. In these days Owen Wister was asking if American fiction "must be perpetual tea-cups,"[10] and in her novel *The Aristocrats* Gertrude Atherton created as one of her characters a popular American author who confessed that he "nearly starved trying to be a man" and that he had discovered "to be great in American literature you've got to be a eunuch."[11]

For this general literary malaise numerous analyses and cures were proffered, pointing variously in philosophical, economic, moral, or aesthetic directions. Inevitably they involved an as-sessment of the American writers' relation to their national mi-lieu—that is, the liabilities imposed and assets conferred peculiarly by their being Americans. Probably the most sub-stantial considerations of the question during the interregnum were Hamlin Garland's *Crumbling Idols* (1894), Frank Norris's *Responsibilities of the Novelist* (1903), Henry James's *American Scene* (1907), and, for the American drama, Percy MacKaye's *Playhouse and the Play* (1909). Excepting perhaps *The American Scene*, these analyses and briefer explorations by scores of other authors and critics were designed to infuse a new brightness into the twilight imagination by reassessing constancy and change in the national experience. As an inescapable prerequisite of this renaissance, it was generally assumed, American writers must come to terms with the realities of their native milieu. Consonant with this design three major versions of nationality were proposed: the continental, the veritist, and the regional.

I

On the purely literary plane the aspiration to treat the continental—the broad scope, impulse, and the norms of the national life—sprang from a weariness with nearly a generation of local color. American life, wrote Richard Hovey in 1892, is healthy, strenuous, and interesting; but our literature languishes under the fetish of local color and the sway of dialect and etiquette—under the reigning dictum that "to be American is to be local."[12] A few years later Ellen Glasgow, beginning her long career as a novelist, explicitly renounced the "little vessels of experience" as too trivial a mode for her treatment of Virginian life;[13] and Gertrude Atherton, chagrined by the failure of American letters to reflect the audacity, energy, and genius of the American race, scoffingly redefined localism as "Littleism."[14]

In a more comprehensive and positive sense, however, the aspiration for a continental literature at the turn of the century was a reaffirmation of the antebellum desire of Emerson, Thoreau, and Whitman for an utterance consonant with the New World temper and scene. Their dismissal of the graceful and courtly muses of Europe in favor of the untamed, the Titanic, the choral reflection of what they called the "American genius" or the "tremendous idea"[15] acquired during the interregnum a new relevance. Thus, in his attempt to deliver the American theater from an imitative Bohemianism, Percy MacKaye based his plea on Emerson's "The American Scholar" as a document "revolutionary for all time." The American drama, he asserted, for "indigenous confidence and growth . . . demands the American Scholar" or "man thinking." In Emersonian tones MacKaye remarked the diversity of American life:

. . . . if we shall look around us with fresh eyes, and if,

with fresh vision, we peer into that Yankee past which
produced us, and beyond to the horizon of cosmopolitan
promise which is our destiny to come, surely in this America we shall discover, in riches, more than the raw stuff of
our bank accounts; in art, more than a mere standing-place
whence we may crane our pigmy necks toward Rome and
the Old World; in prophecy, more than the *bourgeois* hope
of imitation and self-disguise.

Renouncing Ibsen, as Whitman might have done, as the diag-
nostician of a "corroded society," MacKaye instead pleaded for
a drama "fused by the American Spirit—one nation," and breathing a "New World optimism, based in the heritage of the land
itself."[16]

Although antebellum writers could provide the traditional
motifs for the continental conception of the American genius at
the end of the century, new shadings of interpretation and emphasis were inevitable. The frontier had virtually disappeared,
an agrarian society had moved appreciably toward urbanism and
industrialism, and the Spanish-American War gave a new imperial focus to the traditional view of America's manifest destiny
among nations. Moreover, from abroad Rudyard Kipling, rather
than Walter Scott or Madame de Staël, was setting a new tone
and direction for American literary nationalists. In fact, the realistic novelist Judge Robert Grant went so far as to declare
Kipling, by reason of his virility and "deep, simple, sham-
detesting sympathy with common humanity," the best literary
exponent of Americanism. Kipling's scorn for the "dainty, ex-
clusive, elegantly romantic," said Grant, "is of the essence of
the American idea."[17] To Jack London, however, Kipling's
strength lay in his being the most honest chronicler of Anglo-
Saxon imperialism in an age of nationalism, commercialism, and
democracy;[18] but young Owen Wister merely asked why no
American Kipling was "saving the sage-brush for American literature."[19]

This new continental nationality, fused from Emerson and
Kipling, so to speak, probably found its most articulate and
influential spokesman in Theodore Roosevelt. Concerned for
what he called a broad Americanism and a "full and ripe literary

development in the United States," he deplored in the 1890s the parochial spirit that exalted the small community at the expense of a great nation. In his scorn for transatlantic modes and opinions, he directed his sharpest attacks at the expatriates as overrefined weaklings whose effeminate delicacy would not allow them to "play a man's part among men."[20] As a corollary of this Rooseveltian temper, the dominant note of the new continentalism became manliness, and its sounding board became the West. "Stand up and show what man you are," wrote Frederick Knowles in his hortatory lyric "To the American Poet" in 1901. Virtually the poet laureate of the Rooseveltian creed, Knowles conceived of Democracy as no "virgin fair, but a Western Titan . . . / Huge-legged, low-browed, and bearded as of old"; and viewing America as "Mated to the Millennium—Time's last heir," he scoffed at the "metre-mongers [who] haunt the shades" while "Fame crowns the Golden Gate and Palisades."[21]

Among the novelists the same masculine norm was invoked in the name of Americanism. Although Frank Norris could scarcely alter the sex of "the muse of American fiction," he could admonish future novelists that she was "no chaste, delicate, superfine mademoiselle . . . but a robust, red-armed *bonne femme* who rough-shoulders her way among men and among affairs, who finds a healthy pleasure in the jostlings of the mob, and a hearty delight in the honest, rough-and-tumble, Anglo-Saxon give-and-take knock-about that for us means life." This muse, he added, is "hail-fellow-well-met," a "Child of the People" with "a new heaven and a new earth . . . in her face . . . with an arm as strong as a man's and a heart as sensitive as a child's."[22] Even James Lane Allen, a novelist close to the genteel tradition, in the late 1890s concluded that for a "full portrayal of American civilization" the masculine must be reasserted to include the "tremendous fling and swing that are the very genius of our time and spirit"; for to leave out the unrefined is to ignore "most of the things . . . truly American."[23] But it was no doubt Owen Wister who most contagiously represented the manly nationality during the interregnum. Dismayed by what he called the "shapeless state" of American codes and manners, he saw in the cowpuncher, as he said, "the manly, simple, humorous, American type which I hold to be the best we possess and our hope

in the future."[24] In the character of his Virginian, Wister wrote
Justice Holmes, he "set out to draw something like genius—the
American genius; and in rededicating *The Virginian* to Roosevelt
in 1911, he remarked that if the book "be anything more than
an American story, it is an expression of American faith."[25]

What Allen called the feminine principle in American literature, however, also had its continental implications. In the
American girl rather than in the strong man of industry or of
the plains, authors as diverse as Maurice Thompson and Henry
James found the redemptive American type.[26] American woman
"is all that is left to art," Henry Adams advised George Cabot
Lodge, adding that if he were beginning his literary career he
would drop the American male as a cheap and simple mechanism
in favor of the complicated American woman.[27] With a similar
conviction Judge Robert Grant, determined to write "a significant novel of American scope," sought to achieve his aim by
focusing his *Unleavened Bread* on the character of Selma White,
whom he described as "so forbidding" yet "so true to the American scene."[28]

Yet it was Henry James, of course, who during the interregnum extensively portrayed the American girl as the "heiress
of all the ages" and through her sought to catch the finest impulse
of America's development. Sketching in 1892 a character for a
light comedy, he conceived of a representative American
woman, "intensely American in temperament—with her free-
doms, her immunity from traditions," yet with a sense of the
past that keeps her from being vulgarized. Intent on representing in this girl the "unmistakableness and individuality of
her American character," James sustained his concept through
The Wings of the Dove and *The Golden Bowl* by portraying his
heroines, as he said, as "intensely American."[29] Thus with his
heiresses he explicitly revealed, as Wister had done with his
manly heroes, a belief not only in an "American genius" but also
in its redemptive qualities for the world.

The larger testament of James's insistent concern with the
character and imaginative range of his native land, however,
came in his *American Scene* in 1907. Earlier he had prefigured
his own literary relation to America by the term "dispatriation"
to indicate a detachment of viewpoint as opposed to a severance

of interest.[30] From this transatlantic perspective he discerned American types "yearning for their interpreter," not only that of the American girl but also that of the American business-man—an epic figure, he thought, too occult for an outsider to treat but yet *"the* magnificent theme *en disponibilité"* whose "romance of fact . . . puts to shame the romance of fiction."[31] During and after his visit to America in 1904–5 James's most frequent attitude seems to have been not so much one of ex-patriate renunciation as of "dispatriate" bewilderment. The "largest and straightest perception" awaiting him, he reported, was that of a new richness in places formerly felt to be impov-erished—of "a greater depth of tone." Convinced, for the time at least, that young societies might be even more interesting than old ones, he probed with new interest, but without any definitive answer, what meaning might "attach to such a term as the 'American character'" in view of the vast racial amalgam; and he found large intellectual and aesthetic margins in the society as he did in the baffling vastness of the country. The "American way," he could but confess, was a "new and incal-culable thing," but the very incalculability seemed to him to offer the American author "his liveliest inspiration." Indeed, he concluded, the romantic essence and complexity of Europe had increasingly diminished, and "American civilization . . . had begun to spread itself thick and pile itself high."[32]

II

Of this Jamesian concern to comprehend "American civili-zation," the veritism of Garland's *Crumbling Idols* is in many ways the antithesis. Veritism, said Garland, rests on the pos-tulate that "the sun of truth strikes each part of the earth at a little different angle," and hence "each locality must produce its own literary record, each special phase of life utter its own voice."[33] Thus he could call veritism another name for Ameri-canism because it expressed not a continental norm but the locally unique.[34] The logic of such a doctrine, of course, impelled American literature toward an increasingly smaller focus; centripetal in impulse, it moved American fiction from nation to region to city and finally to neighborhood or family.

Moreover, veritism was temporally as well as spatially disjunctive. It made flux its axiom and emphasized discontinuity. "The business of the present," Garland wrote, "is not to express fundamentals, but . . . its own minute and characteristic interpretation of life."[35] Drawing upon H. M. Posnett, H. A. Taine, and Herbert Spencer—from whom he derived his emphasis on, respectively, the provincial, the environmental mutation, and the doctrine of Progress—he dismissed the past as "a highway of dust."[36] The veritist, he said, rather looks to the future as "an optimist, a dreamer" who by "delineating the ugliness and warfare of the present" becomes the agent of social change. To "write of those things you know most, and for which you care most," he advised American writers, is to be a veritist and to meet the "test of a national literature" by creating something that could have been written in no other time and place.[37]

The conversion of a writer from the continental to the veritist mode of nationality Frank Norris illustrated through his poet Presley in *The Octopus*. At first conceiving, as Roosevelt and Wister did, the conquest of the West to be the unsung national epic, Presley aspired to write the "diapason" song of an "entire people"—of "a new race . . . —hardy, brave, and passionate"; but touched by the sufferings of the exploited ranchers and convinced that brutal economic forces were more real than the pioneer's dream, he renounced poetic tradition and wrote from the heart, as Garland would have him do, a "comment on the social fabric."[38] Although Norris continued to lament that the empire builders of the West had been commemorated only in the ignoble dime novel rather than in a Homeric epic, he also espoused the veritist position that fiction must "search for the idiosyncrasy . . . that distinguishes the time or place . . . from all other times and places . . . the specialized product of conditions . . . in that locality."[39] Norris in effect comprehended both modes of nationality in devising what he termed his "big epic trilogy" on wheat, which, as he wrote to Howells, "would be modern and distinctively American."[40]

Somewhat earlier, both Stephen Crane and Dreiser had made similar shifts toward veritism. Early in the 1890s, Crane wrote, he had abandoned the "clever Rudyard Kipling style" and developed a literary creed focused on "nature and truth," which he discovered was the same as that of Howells and Garland.[41] Though Dreiser scarcely aspired to write an American epic, he was for a time in effect a young Presley, viewing Chicago as a city of romance and America as an idyllic land of promise. Under the influence of the Chicago school and of authors as diverse as Machiavelli, Balzac, and Herbert Spencer, he came to feel that a genuine national literature could no longer rest on the "purely imaginative American tradition" of rural America that had degenerated into the genteel misrepresentations of *Scribner's, The Century,* and *Harper's;* it must rather reveal the real forces determining the national behavior—Darwinian forces that involved the craft and jungle brutality of city life such as he found in Pittsburgh.[42] It is not surprising, therefore, that Reedy's *St. Louis Mirror* in 1901 should have said of *Sister Carrie* that "its veritism out-Howells Mr. Howells and out-Garlands . . . Mr. Garland."[43] By the end of the interregnum Mencken was supporting veritism as the most valid mode of nationality by acclaiming Dreiser as the "man of tomorrow" for his searching portrayal of the "American mind" and "American types." *The Financier* (1912) he pronounced to be "wholly accurate and wholly American," and Edgar Lee Masters found in the same novel final proof that Dreiser comprehended the "facts of American life" better than any other American writer.[44]

Although Garland supposed that his veritism would have regional application, especially in the West, its very emphasis on the changing social surfaces inevitably made it the mode for portraying a competitive urbanism rather than a cohesive regionalism. Whereas, a century earlier, fiction had often been subtitled "an American tale," now Norris's practice of adding "A Tale of San Francisco" or "A Tale of Chicago" to the title was not uncommon. With the interregnum, indeed, the city novel evolved as an integral phase of the national literature. The most literature-conscious city in America during the period, Chicago provided with its swift expansiveness and its "crude juice of life," as Moody phrased it, not only an ideal subject but also the matrix for the veritist mode, as the experiments of H. B. Fuller, Garland, George Ade, Robert Herrick, Norris, Dreiser, and lesser figures show.[45]

III

Between the continental ideal of Roosevelt and local impetus of veritism, however, regionalism maintained its century-old claims. Fundamentally these claims rested on the premise that, culturally speaking, the region, section, or province was the homogeneous unit in America; or, as Josiah Royce defined the "province" in 1902, as a part of the nation "which is, geographically and socially, sufficiently unified to have a true consciousness of its own unity, to feel a pride in its own ideals and customs, and to possess a sense of its distinction from other parts of the country." As an apologist for "a wholesome provincialism," Royce found it compatible with both a proper nationalism and cosmopolitanism.[46] On the same assumption that the nation is a union but not a unit, Frank Norris concluded that it may foster *a* great American novel, but that *the* Great American Novel is "mythical like the Hippogriff."[47] And the aging Mark Twain, like Hawthorne before him, finding every native novelist becoming a "foreigner, with a foreigner's limitations, when he steps from the State whose life is familiar to him," declared it impossible for the American writer to "generalize the nation. . . . There isn't a single human characteristic that can safely be labelled 'American' "; for any American peculiarity will disappear, he said, if you "cross a frontier or two, or go down or up in the social scale. . . . There is no American temperament."[48]

Upon such assumptions the regionalists plumbed their native areas, relying on what Twain called the "slow accumulation of *un*conscious observation—absorption." Generally indifferent to the labels "realist" and "romanticist," they often worked in both modes, as did James Lane Allen and Mary E. Wilkins. Holding to the older organic concepts of society and literature rather than to the social Darwinism that underlay veritism, they were concerned with the cultural constants in their region and often ventured, unlike the veritists, into the past and hence into the historical novel. Thus Ellen Glasgow, dissociating herself from the "local color school" in the belief that "literature, like life, must spring from roots," felt impelled to return to her "own place and soil" to write her series of novels depicting the "history and manners" of Virginia, since they "could grow and flower . . . in no other air."[49] With a similar conviction that veritism undervalued the total regional culture, Kate Chopin wrote of the Creoles, and Sarah Orne Jewett, aligning herself with the regional tradition of Harriet Beecher Stowe, proposed to reveal not the changing surfaces but the substratum of New England provincial life.[50] In California Jack London judged that Norris's *Octopus* had at last succeeded in encompassing "the spirit and essence" of the "great, incoherent, amorphous West"; and in turn Norris himself concluded that to catch the "huge conglomerate West" was to come as close to nationality as an American could.[51]

Thus throughout the interregnum the continentalists, veritists, and regionalists, searching anew for a mode that would best comprehend their distinctive culture and scene, helped to provide direction and motive and substance for much of the memorable writing of the next two decades. By 1912 Ezra Pound, as a skeptical continentalist, had concluded that Whitman was "America's poet," that he was to America what Dante had been to Italy, and that "his message is my message."[52] Moreover, feeling himself one of those "Who bear the brunt of our America / And try to wrench her impulse into art," Pound saw latent forces in his country which would effect a Risorgimento that would "make the Italian Renaissance look like a tempest in a teapot."[53] Closer to the veritist tradition, before 1912 William Carlos Williams had abandoned Keats and begun writing of a locale that led to his *Paterson* poems, Vachel Lindsay had begun his campaign for a regenerated American art through his gospel of the "New Localism," and Percival Pollard had pointed out the rich possibilities in such common American materials as the letters of "a young girl in the State of New York whose lover was convicted . . . of having drowned her."[54] Among the journalists during the same years Francis Hackett, Floyd Dell, and H. L. Mencken had introduced fresh, trenchant standards on behalf of what Dell called "a growing youthful body of American literary taste."[55] It was in this atmosphere that Charles Leonard Moore in 1910 correctly prophesied that the interregnum was ending and that America's literary recovery would first be recognized through a new belief in poetry.[56]

Notes

1. B. Matthews, *Americanisms and Briticisms* (New York, 1892), pp. 26 ff.; *Cosmopolitan* 13 (July 1892): 343 ff.
2. W. D. Howells, in *North American Review* 172 (January 1901): 151.
3. P. Pollard, *Their Day in Court* (New York and Washington, 1909), p. 458.
4. J. Hay, *Addresses* (New York, 1906), p. 94.
5. E. C. Stedman, *An American Anthology: 1787–1900* (2 vols.; Cambridge, Mass., 1900), p. 28; E. A. Robinson, *Collected Poems* (New York, 1937), p. 93; T. Roosevelt, in *Outlook* 80 (August 12, 1905): 913–14; T. Roosevelt, *Letters*, ed. E. E. Morison *et al.* (8 vols.; Cambridge, Mass., 1951), IV, 1145.
6. E. C. Stedman, *Poets of America* (Boston and New York, 1888), p. 457.
7. C. L. Moore, *The Dial* 48 (May 1, 1910): 307–9.
8. E. Glasgow, *The Woman Within* (New York, 1954), p. 103.
9. W. B. Harte, *Meditations in Motley* (Boston, 1894), p. 80.
10. O. Wister, *Roosevelt: The Story of a Friendship* (New York, 1930), p. 29.
11. P. Pollard, *Their Day in Court*, pp. 123–24.
12. R. Hovey, in *Independent* 44 (November 3, 1892): 1546–47.
13. E. Glasgow, *The Woman Within*, pp. 97–98.
14. G. Atherton, in *North American Review* 178 (May 1904): 772–75, 779.
15. Cf. B. T. Spencer, *The Quest for Nationality* (Syracuse, 1957), pp. 171–80, 223–30.
16. P. MacKaye, *The Playhouse and the Play* (New York, 1909), pp. 91–92, 94–95, 98–99, 102–4, 114, 117.
17. R. Grant, *Search-Light Letters* (New York, 1899), pp. 169–70.
18. J. London, *Revolution and Other Essays* (New York, 1910), pp. 223–24, 225, 230, 232, 234.
19. O. Wister, *Roosevelt: The Story of a Friendship*, p. 29.
20. T. Roosevelt, in *Forum* 17 (April 1894): 198–201.
21. F. L. Knowles, *On Life's Stairway* (Boston, 1901), pp. 5–6, 21–22, 25, 34–35, 47–48.
22. F. Norris, *The Responsibilities of the Novelist* (New York, 1903), pp. 208–10.
23. *Atlantic Monthly* 80 (October, 1897): 434–36. Cf. also Grant Knight, *James Lane Allen and the Genteel Tradition* (Chapel Hill, N.C., 1935), pp. 114–15.
24. O. Wister, *The Virginian* (New York, 1911), p. xi; *Owen Wister Out West*, ed. Fanny K. Wister (Chicago, 1958), p. 246.
25. O. Wister, *Owen Wister Out West*, p. 16; *The Virginian*, p. 7.
26. Cf. M. Thompson, *Chap-Book Essays* (Chicago, 1896), pp. 248–50.

27. H. D. Carter, *Henry Adams and His Friends* (Boston, 1947), pp. 544–45.
28. R. Grant, *Fourscore* (Boston and New York, 1934), pp. 219–20, 282–83.
29. H. James, *Notebooks*, ed. F. O. Matthiessen and K. B. Murdock (New York, 1955), pp. 128–30, 131, 175, 185–86, 310.
30. Cf. Edna Kenton, "Henry James in the World," *Hound and Horn* 7 (April–June 1934): 508–9.
31. Cf. *Public Opinion* 24 (April 28, 1898): 532–33; Edith Wharton, *A Backward Glance* (New York, 1934), p. 176.
32. H. James, *The American Scene* (London, 1907), pp. 52–53, 121, 123, 138–39, 357, 365–66.
33. H. Garland, *Crumbling Idols*, ed. Robert E. Spiller (Gainesville, Fla., 1952), p. 22.
34. H. Garland, *Roadside Meetings* (New York, 1930), p. 252.
35. H. Garland, *Crumbling Idols*, pp. 24, 54, 57, 75.
36. H. Garland, in *Forum* 16 (October 1893): 166.
37. H. Garland, *Crumbling Idols*, pp. 29, 35, 45–46, 52–53.
38. F. Norris, *The Octopus* (New York, 1901), pp. 9–10, 307, 371, 394–95.
39. Cf. *World's Work* 5 (December 1902): 2904–6; W. E. Martin, "Two Uncollected Essays by Frank Norris," *American Literature* 8 (May 1936): 190–98.
40. W. D. Howells, *Life in Letters*, ed. Mildred Howells (2 vols.; New York, 1928), II, 103.
41. Cf. Stephen Crane, *Sullivan County Sketches*, ed. Melvin Schoberlin (Syracuse, 1949), p. 19; John Berryman, *Stephen Crane* (New York, 1950), pp. 53–55.
42. T. Dreiser, *A Book About Myself* (London, 1929), pp. 1, 69–70, 376–77, 412, 422, 426, 457–58, 490–91; *Letters*, ed. R. H. Elias (3 vols.; Philadelphia, 1959), I, 211–12.
43. St. Louis *Mirror* 10 (January 3, 1901): 6–7.
44. T. Dreiser, *Letters*, pp. 1, 113, 115–16, 123; Bernard Duffey, *The Chicago Renaissance* (East Lansing, Mich., 1954), p. 158.
45. Cf. W. V. Moody, *Some Letters*, ed. D. G. Mason (Boston and New York, 1913), pp. 30–31; B. Duffey, *The Chicago Renaissance, passim*.
46. J. Royce, *Race Questions/Provincialism/and Other American Problems* (New York, 1908), pp. 61 ff.
47. F. Norris, *The Responsibilities of the Novelist*, pp. 87–89; Ernest Marchand, *Frank Norris: A Study* (Stanford, 1942), p. 31.
48. S. L. Clemens, *How to Tell a Story and Other Essays* (New York, 1897), pp. 186–87, 188–89, 190, 197.
49. E. Glasgow, *A Certain Measure* (New York, 1943), pp. 43, 67; *The Woman Within*, pp. 97–98, 129, 171, 192, 195.
50. Cf. D. S. Rankin, *Kate Chopin* (Philadelphia, 1932), pp. 141–44; S. O. Jewett, *Deephaven* (Boston and New York, 1894), preface; *Letters*, ed. Richard Cary (Waterville, Me., 1956), pp. 64–65.
51. F. S. Foner, *Jack London: American Rebel* (New York, 1947), pp. [507], 508; W. E. Martin, in *American Literature* 8 (May 1936): 190 ff.

52. Cf. Herbert Bergman, in *American Literature* 27 (March 1955): 56–61.

53. E. Pound, *Patria Mia* (Chicago, 1950), pp. 21, 22, 24, 42–43, 63, 64; in *Poetry* 1 (October 1912): 7; H. Monroe, *A Poet's Life* (New York, 1938), p. 260.

54. W. C. Williams, *Autobiography* (New York, 1951), pp. 56–70; E. L. Masters, *Vachel Lindsay* (New York, 1935), pp. 222–27; H. Garland, *Companions on the Trail* (New York, 1931), pp. 462–66; P. Pollard, *Their Day in Court*, pp. 9–11.

55. F. Dell, *Homecoming* (New York, 1933), pp. 194–95.

56. C. L. Moore, in *The Dial* 48 (May 1, 1910): 307–9.

PART TWO

Eight Ways to Nationality

GERTRUDE STEIN, NON-EXPATRIATE

All things are breathing.
Can you see me.
Hurrah for America.[1]

The Context of Nationality

AMONG GERTRUDE STEIN'S oft reiterated declarations or dicta, such as "When this you see remember me," is the following: "After all anybody is as their land and air is. Anybody is as the sky is low or high, the air heavy or clear and anybody is as there is wind or no wind there. It is that which makes them and the arts they make and and [sic] the work they do and the way they eat." In repeating this statement she made only slight variations. In "What Are Masterpieces" she added that she was "an American" who had lived half her life in Paris, "not the half that made me but the half in which I made what I made." In *Everybody's Autobiography* she shifted the phrasing to note that "everybody is as their food and weather is" and that American college football players and red Indians move alike. In *Wars I Have Seen* she shifts the pronoun from "anybody" and "everybody" to "every one" and more specifically includes the mountains and rivers and oceans, the rain and snow and ice, as formative indigenous influences on "their way to act their way to think and their way to be subtle . . . any American knows that."[2]

The sense of diversity in all such national qualities, Stein remarked in her last years, had been impressed upon her even as a child in Vienna, where she had a Czech tutor and a Hungarian governess; and this sense was subsequently intensified by the various ethnic strains that had converged in the California of her school days. Here she learned that "Germans are as they are and French and Greeks and Chinamen and Japs," and that though people may develop, they do not change. Every nation, she concluded, "has a way of being of being that nation that makes it that nation," and any important person "in the development of that nation has to be some way somehow like that." Throughout her life she was intent on discovering the indices that showed the way a nation had of "being that nation," whether it was the dogs, which "resemble the nation that creates them," or distinctive foods and colors and houses.[3]

In her preoccupation with "The Psychology of Nations or What Are You Looking At"—to use the title of one of her "plays"—she often found her most revealing clues in the servant class. Though in *The Making of Americans* she had consistently attached the epithet "german" to the central family of Herslands in the manuscript version, it is through the female servants, whether Irish or Mexican or German, that national diversity is most explicitly projected; and in the servant girls of *Three Lives*, as Michael Hoffman has observed, German frugality is contrasted with Irish freehearted impulsiveness. Though such contrasts were Stein's normal mode of disclosing dominant national traits, she occasionally noted salient correspondences. Both Spain and America, she observed, are "abstract and cruel," and they are the "only two western nations that can realize abstraction," which Spain expresses by ritual and America by "disembodiedness, in literature and machinery." Similarly, in contrast to England where "the dead are not dead because they remain connected with others living," both Spain and America "make them alive and they make them dead"; and, indeed, Mark Twain's ability to "make a dead man dead" seemed to her "a great American thing to do."[4]

In her more frequent employment of cultural contrasts, however, France and England served as the dominant foils in Stein's attempts to define American nationality. French life, she discovered, could afford a proper stimulus to the American imagination because "the french and the Americans do not have the sense of going on together," whereas "living in England does not free the American the way living in France frees him. . . . England to an American English writing to an American is not in this sense a foreign thing." Unlike the Americans, she said, the French do not glamorize or worry about the twentieth century, for they are wholly concerned with their "daily life." Always aware of the "earth," they paint it but do not "poetize" it. Rather they are committed to "logic and fashion," and with the English they will civilize the twentieth century and "make it a time when anybody can be free, free to be civilized and to be."[5]

Though Gertrude Stein felt that England was too much like America to provide stimulus and perspective for cisatlantic writers, she repeatedly pondered the contrasting effects of the geography of the two countries on their cultures. As an island culture England may well need to absorb the similar culture of the Greeks, she remarked to Bertrand Russell, but "America needed essentially the culture of a continent which was of necessity latin." Indeed, America's continental expanse seemed to her to have determined much of the national psychology and behavior. In answer to her own question of why "Americans [are] different from others," she emphasized their mobile homelessness and their pioneer experience and heritage. Because "waiting is a part of earning a living and there is no waiting in an American," she somewhat abstrusely argued in writing of Grant, Americans can succeed (that is, earn a living) only because they "are part European." And if she could find a distinctive restlessness nurtured by the empty American continent, she could also understand American religion as lacking a sky such as European religion had. In asserting that Americans had only air and not a sky above them, she apparently intended a metaphor to suggest a confident or even defiant egalitarianism in which "heaven" has disappeared and there is "no over all" and "Each one is all." In her attempts to define the national character, however, Stein did not ignore the more generally acknowledged traits such as pragmatism: Americans "know what they are . . . by looking at what they do." Thus George Washington, observing America's geographical uniqueness, "began a novel . . . the great American novel"; he did "do what a novel is."[6]

Yet it was attachment to freedom, the corollary of uncircumscribed physical space, that Stein finally stressed as primarily and emphatically American and accordingly judged both Presidents Roosevelt atypical because "They do not feel America to be a very large country around which anybody can wander." In general she accepted this influence of American space as a positive one. The pioneer experience had necessitated and bred optimism, she argued; but after the economic depression of the 1930s she began to fear that her country would "never be so young again" since, lacking the old pioneer venturesomeness, Americans would increasingly be content to "feel themselves employed and not potential employers." Viewing the mid-twentieth century as the crucial period for America since the Civil War, she warned that Americans "have to fight a spiritual pioneer fight or we will go poor as England and other industrial countries."[7]

The ultimate interpretation of American nationality that emerged from Stein's lifelong concern with her country was thus not merely a conceptual one but an affective one as well—an affirmative acceptance of her cisatlantic heritage. More ingenuously and explicitly than her venerated Henry James, she not only recognized the "complex fate" of her nativity but also confidently assimilated and examined it. "It made me wonder a lot about what it is to be an American," she said after speaking at New England colleges and observing that those that had been "made to make missionaries were more interesting than those that had been made to make culture." Repeatedly she attached the epithet "American" to herself to explain her behavior or tastes, such as her indifference to African sculpture because its primitiveness seemed not "savage" enough; or, in expressing her love for France and the French people, she felt impelled to add: "but after all I am an American, and it always comes back to that . . . one's native land is one's native land."[8]

In her early novel *Things as They Are* (1903) Adele, the narrator who generally reflects Stein herself, observes that she and her two friends are "distinctively American"; Helen is the "American version of the English handsome girl," and Sophie's "long angular body . . . betrayed her New England origin." Though Adele alludes to James's Kate Croy in *The Wings of the Dove*, in her staunchly American loyalties and attitudes she herself rather resembles his Isabel Archer or Henrietta Stackpole in *The Portrait of a Lady*, convinced as she is that "no passion [is] more dominant and instinctive in the human spirit than the need of the country to which one belongs"—a passion that Gertrude Stein admitted as her own. In the fog and soggy streets of London Adele, like James's Henrietta, felt nostalgic for the "clean blue distance" and the "clean-cut cold" of her native land. In New York, on the other hand, she rejoiced in the functional simplicity of the "undecorated houses" and the elevated railway. With a more personal involvement in Boston she "steeped herself in the very essence of clear eyed Americanism" and with native pride observed both the "passionless intelligence of the faces" about her and also the "ready intercourse, free comments and airy persiflage all without double meaning" in the streetcars. Such, indeed, was the national consciousness of the James-Stein heroine of the early 1900s.[9]

In *The Making of Americans* (1906–8) Stein's concern with the national character found its most sustained and extended utterance. From the experience of her California girlhood she attempted to depict "the new people made out of the old" and the creation of a national "tradition" in "scarcely sixty years." The epic quality of her fictive record emerges not only from its extensive interweaving of the lives of the Dehning and Hersland families through three generations in the late nineteenth century but also from her expressed conviction—and one alien to the expatriate temper—that it is "a rare privilege" to be "a real American" involved in the creation of a new culture such as the book cumulatively portrays. Though her ultimate focus of reference may be that of universal psychological types (such as dependent-independent), these very types are integrally related to their Western milieu. Thus Julia Dehning at eighteen "showed in all its vigor, the self-satisfied crude domineering American girlhood that was strong inside her" yet did not "attain quite altogether that crude virginity that makes the American girl safe in all her liberty." And on Julia, as on many a Jamesian heroine, her culture had impressed a "moral idealism, the only form of culture the spare American imagination takes refuge in." Even the dull, hopeless red and green shades of Julia's living rooms Stein correlates with the "ethically aesthetic aspiration of the spare American emotion."[10]

The psychological concern of *The Making of Americans* thus constantly veers toward social psychology—toward hypotheses concerning American mores and ethical and religious attitudes underlying American behavior: "In American teaching marrying is just loving"; religion in the West can be like "eating and sleeping," or like "washing" or "believing," "like breathing," or "like loving"; education can be redirected, as by the Herslands and Wymans, so that California children will have "american training" for outdoor living and thus be "brought up american." Such hypotheses, however, persistently suggest an imaginative flight beyond clinical observation, as does the memorable conclusion to her description of Western college life: the "american mind accustomed to waste happiness and be reckless of joy finds morality more important than ecstacy [*sic*]. . . . To our new world feeling the sadness of pain has more dignity than the beauty of joy." Thus there remained for Gertrude Stein during her first decade in France a sense of a distinctively "western morality" and a "new world humanity." And there was also, more concretely and affectively, a recollection of the "real country living" experienced by the Hersland children in contrast to their father, the urban-oriented fortune seeker who felt himself "as big as all the world" around him—a "real feeling of wind blowing in the country" and of fruit trees and vegetable gardening, of ploughing and haymaking.[11]

Thus in Gertrude Stein's work over almost half a century, both her persistent resort to the concept of nationality and her especial concern with the formation and values of the national character are evident. Convinced of the ineluctable impress of one's native land, she happily affirmed her own American heritage. "Our roots can be anywhere and . . . we take our roots with us," she said after her American visit. "The essential thing is to have the feeling that they exist." Though America was her "well-nourished home," it was "not a place to work," she had written earlier in *transition*—a judgment that she further explained by asserting that though America is the oldest country and the mother of modern civilization, one wishes to be born in the country that has "attained" and to live in the countries that are "attaining." In conjunction with her more famous pronouncement that "America is my country and Paris is my home town," she affirmed the need of "every one who makes anything inside themselves" to have both their native civilization and also one "that has nothing to do with them." Or, in a later version in *Paris FRANCE:* "Writers have to have two countries, the one where they belong, and the one in which they live really. The second one is romantic, it is separate from themselves, it is not real but it is really there." Hence, residing in Paris she became a European, as she said, only "for the purposes of daily living." On the more profound level of cultural alienation from her native land, she was surely justified in disclaiming expatriation: "For one thing, for all the time I've been in France, I have never been called an expatriate and that is the thing I am proud of. I proved you could be a good American anywhere in the world." And so she did.[12]

The Correlative of Style

Beyond the evidence of Stein's non-expatriated mind in her own substantive remarks, however, lies the subtler confirmation of the impress of her native land and air on her aesthetic theory and the modes of her writing. It was on the level of style in the most comprehensive sense—a projection of felt experience through linguistic forms and structure—that she saw her own work as indubitably American. Thus *The Making of Americans* seemed to her "an essentially American book" not primarily because of its California setting and its developing New World characters but rather because of its attempt to express "something strictly American . . . a space of time that is filled always filled with moving." Proceeding beyond the use of idea and image and even myth, therefore, she sought through such stylistic devices as the enlargement of paragraphs to recreate the innermost sense that an American has of "what is inside this space of time."[13]

To correlate Stein's style with defensible conclusions about the American psyche, however, becomes a difficult endeavor for several reasons: the difficulty of validly establishing any nation's distinctive character, the appreciable changes in her own style during nearly half a century, and the intuitive and often whimsical or simplistic nature of her dicta on America. Moreover, she implies for herself a partial release from the nationalistic determinism that she so generally perceived in other artists such as

Picasso; for in reviewing her life in the United States and abroad she makes a distinction between "the half [of her life in America] that made me" and "the half in which I made what I made." Thus she posits a "freedom inside yourself" which life in an alien culture permits, while, "in your own civilization you are apt to mix yourself up too much with your civilization." In reiterating her contention that writers "interested in living inside themselves" need a country "to be free in," Stein is surely implying that there are aspects and qualities of her work that do not bear the stamp of their author's American nurture. It is therefore not judicious to assume that her resistance to expatriation permitted her to achieve some impersonally pure national style. Indeed, it may be said of her style, as she said of the bias of one of her character types in *The Making of Americans:* "In a way it is a personal thing for them, in a way it is a family affair in them, in a way it is a way of living in a national way for them, in a way . . . of the local way in them, in a way . . . their kind in men and women have in being in living."[14]

Although Gertrude Stein declared that "any nation's literature is a homogeneous thing" throughout its history, she made virtually no observations on the presence or nature of this homogeneity in such major antebellum authors as Emerson, Thoreau, Melville, and Whitman. Indeed, so far as explicit comments are concerned, the authentic national mode in her view was rather embodied in the varied realism of Twain, Howells, and Henry James; and of these it was James who took up where English literature left off because "it had no further to go." His "disembodied way of disconnecting something from anything . . . was the American one," she said, and this way "had a future feeling." In fact, she came to recognize him as the only nineteenth-century American writer who "felt the method of the twentieth century"; and despite her insistence in the Toklas autobiography that in her formative years she had neither read nor cared for his work, the point of view, structure, and characterizations of her early *Things as They Are,* as Michael Hoffman has convincingly argued, attest to James's strong influence. Later her recognition of his brilliant fictional strategies—his ability to write simultaneously both "what you are writing" and "what you are going to be writing"—prompted her fantasy of him as a "general," though as a general, she concedes, "he was a European." Yet far more cogent than this capricious portrait is her tribute to his creation of a "whole paragraph" structure that "was detached what it said from what it did, what it was from what it held, and over it all something floated."[15]

Stein's relationship to other Americans, forebears and contemporaries, in the "homogeneous" national literature generally eludes firm or substantial definition. Undoubtedly the psychological and philosophical views of her preceptor William James left their deep imprint upon her—both his earlier concept of consciousness as an entity that determines character types (implicit in *The Making of Americans*) and his later idea of the unpredictable "stream" of consciousness (implicit in *Tender Buttons* and the portraits).

Although her psychological emphasis and stylistic patterns thus owe much to the brothers James, her early settings and characters also reflect current trends among the naturalists. "I have to content myself with niggers and servant girls and the foreign population generally," she wrote after completing *Three Lives;* yet in treating such characters she was generally indifferent to the humanitarian concern that motivated much of the naturalists' fiction, and she dispensed with their heavy reliance on quotidian data and colloquial idiom in favor of an exploration of states of mind or psychological types. Apparently, therefore, she was indifferent to "Melanctha" in *Three Lives* as an innovative projection of the Negro into American fiction, for she rather valued the book as a "noble combination of Swift and Matisse." Moreover, she declared that since her "very simple and very vulgar" materials would not "interest the great American public," she could "never write the great American novel." (She was later willing to pronounce Wilder's *Heaven's My Destination* to be "*the* American novel.") Thus, though in the early 1900s she had affiliations with the naturalists and felt that American "life needed a clean and resistant realism," she also realized that both her literary purposes and the American temper required larger dimensions than realism encouraged. There was also the need to "move around," she observed, and this moving involved "feeling romantic." Hence she spent the early part of her life, as she said, escaping the nineteenth century with its reliance on science and technology, its belief in progress, and its ultimate literary creed nurtured by a positivistic philosophy. It may be that, as Allegra Stewart contends, Gertrude Stein's "romanticism" finally brought her in "Doctor Faustus Lights the Lights" close to "an authentic American tradition as expressed by Emerson, Thoreau, and Whitman"—a tradition that fused "Oriental and Occidental spirituality"; but if so, her affinity with the three nineteenth-century figures must be nonderivative and hence illustrative of her view of the inherent homogeneity of national literatures. Her admission of any significant indebtedness to their works is not a matter of record.[16]

If Stein found little of a "usable past" in American letters before 1900, she nevertheless deduced from her own comprehensive observation of American behavior and attitudes the qualities that characterized the national imagination and issued in a distinctive national style. Primary among these traits was the American proclivity toward abstraction. To Bertrand Russell she eloquently asserted the "disembodied abstract quality of the american character" and cited automobiles and Emerson as typical American "products." Later, in her *Lectures in America*, she correlated this abstractionism with the absence in her native land of that "daily island life" that had held English literature close to the earth and the emotions. Accordingly, in "all persistent American writing" she found "a separation from what is chosen to what is that from which it has been chosen," and she asserted that Washington Irving, Whitman, and James (among others) showed that what "makes what American literature" is this lack of "connection with that from which it is choosing."[17]

The validity of Stein's generalized insistence on the American penchant for such "disembodiedness" is indeed dubious. One may suspect that she has prejudicially posited the Hawthorne-James tradition as the authentically American one and has casually dismissed the strong empirical strain of Irving's genre pieces, of Whitman's extensional richness and devotion to identity, of Twain's principle and practice of "founding on fact," of Dreiser's massive naturalism. Her own graduate training and experiments in psychology had of course instilled in her an ultimate concern for the generalized "what" rather than the concrete "it." Later in Europe her predilection for the abstract was attested by her especial affinity for Spanish landscapes and art and culture—an affinity that arose, as she said, "because I was expressing the same thing in literature" and because Spaniards and Americans, unlike other Europeans and Orientals, "do not need religion or mysticism not to believe in reality as all the world knows it . . . and that is why there are skyscrapers and American literature and Spanish painting and literature." Hence, too, her admiration for Picasso's cubism, for if it properly concerned itself with "visible things," it nevertheless projected a "visible world" not as everybody sees it but as an intuited essence or rhythm, or as what Mabel Dodge praised as "the 'noumenon' captured" in *The Making of Americans*. Similarly in her portraits, as Stein explained, she had "tried to tell what each one is without telling stories," and in the early plays she had likewise dispensed with narration in order to evoke the "essence of what happened." Accordingly in *Geography and Plays* the "essence" of France is presumably suggested by a collage of aphorisms such as "To be afraid is not near sighted," or "One special absence does not make any place empty"; and America is even more tenuously adumbrated by "Pow word, a pow word is organic and sectional and an old man's company," or by "America key, america key."[18]

The complex relationship of Stein's style to Continental aesthetics during the two decades following 1910 has already received thoughtful treatment by several critics, including Edmund Wilson, Donald Sutherland, and J. M. Brinnin. Only one aspect of that relationship is relevant here: the extent to which Stein's residence abroad diverted her from the native influences that she so assiduously delineated and explicitly embraced. At least one tendency would seem persistently clear: Whatever she did in her cumulative experimentation she always related to the American mind. Thus if she was drawn toward abstraction (as she was from the beginning), she assured herself and others that Americans are generally so inclined. Viewing America as the creative founder of twentieth-century culture, she accordingly construed her innovations in style to be the prophetic vehicles and agents of the inclusive mutation initiated by her country. Thus the patterns in the lines and quarter sections of the landscape observed during her plane flights across the States, she said, "made it right that I had always been with cubism and everything that followed after."[19]

Although her notorious *Tender Buttons* (1914) scarcely impresses most readers as a distinctively American product, Stein has essentially provided from time to time the critical assumptions for arguing that the work is actually a complex of stylistic tendencies markedly cisatlantic. At its center lies its use of the word as, in her view, it was transformed by New World experience. After *The Making of Americans*, as Michael Hoffman has discovered from an autobiographical statement in one of her unpublished essays, she felt a new sense of the creative possibilities inherent in her native language. Indeed, as she said, she found herself "plunged into a vortex of words, burning words, cleansing words, liberating words, feeling words, and the words were all ours and it was enough that we held them in our hands to play with them; . . . and this was the beginning of knowing; of all Americans knowing, that it could play and play with words and the words were all ours all ours." In her later lectures in America she further observed that though England and America had the same words and grammatical construction, they had "come to be telling things that have nothing whatever in common." The English language, made as it was "to tell the story of the soothing of living every minute," had proved uncongenial to the restive temper of the New World; hence "in American writing" the old English words began to reflect a new "consciousness of completely moving, they began to detach themselves from the solidity of anything" and to have a "different pressure put upon them." Sensing this verbal liberation, Emerson, Whitman, Hawthorne, and Twain, she asserted, had all shown that the old words could be pressed and shaped into doing what was needed. In *Tender Buttons*, therefore, Stein was at least indulging a native propensity to play with words, to make them move in any and every direction, and to enjoy "the feeling of words doing as they want to do and as they have to do when they live where they have to live." Americans could adapt their linguistic heritage to their needs, she later observed in *Wars I Have Seen*, only by choosing words they liked best, "by putting words next to each other in a different way . . . , by shoving language around." Sherwood Anderson therefore seems justified in the early 1920s in viewing Stein as "an American woman of the old sort" creatively living "among the little housekeeping words" in "her word kitchen in Paris."[20]

How far the verbal play of *Tender Buttons* can be translated into paraphrasable or discursive or subliminal meanings reflecting an American genesis or influence is not easily established. During this cubistic phase of her writing her reiterated intention was to strip words of their overtones and associations and to treat them as plastic entities, as colors on her palette, and therein she dissents from the linguistic assumptions of contemporary symbolists and of Joyce and Eliot. As early as 1920 Richard Aldington had traced this autotelic word play to its cisatlantic source. Asserting that *Tender Buttons* constituted with "The Raven" and *Leaves of Grass* one of the "three impingements of American genius upon the mind of Europe," he characterized Stein's style as that of the new "American calculated facetiousness"—a conclusion in which most readers are inclined probably to concur. Yet assuming psychic processes involving a complexity and depth far beyond "calculated facetiousness," Allegra Stewart has recently argued that the diction and verbal patterns of *Tender Buttons* were media to the unconscious through which she attained profound insights into the nature of reality and the self. Through an awareness of the root meanings of key words (such as the seven in "A Caraffe") and through meditations generated by these words, Stewart learnedly argues, Stein was enabled to touch the mythic and ritual depths of human experience and to achieve flashes of "subliminal intuition." The "tender buttons," in effect, are the "living words [that] seem to put forth like green buds in the spring," and, like all vegetation, contain "the secret force of life." In this essentially mythic reading of *Tender Buttons* the American quality of the work is found to lie in its reassertion of the Emersonian quest for the authentic self and in the process of "denudation" whereby Stein achieves the transcendence of an "Emersonian transparent eyeball."[21]

Between these alleged American matrices of "calculated facetiousness" and "subliminal intuition" one may also perceive in *Tender Buttons* that "naivety of vision," with its collages of objects and its consequent paratactic style, which Tony Tanner has convincingly shown to be a persistent characteristic of American

writing. According to this version of a cisatlantic mode Stein
sustains the "innocent eye" of Emerson, Thoreau, and Whitman,
with its simple delight in discrete objects that achieve coherence
chiefly through the naive "wonder" in the mind of the observer.
Though this "wonder" did not necessarily involve Jungian insights or archetypes such as Stewart finds inherent in *Tender
Buttons*, it did involve the responses of what Stein called "human
nature," with its impure concern for the self and identity as
revealed in the context of memory and time. This context Stein
renounced more decisively than did the Transcendental exponents of the "innocent eye." Great literature, she insisted, is the
product rather of the "human mind" liberated from the contingencies of "human nature" and from the sense of identity and
localization imposed by valleys and hills. On such assumptions
she could prophesy that America, with its vast flatlands, would
produce a civilization capable of releasing the "human mind"
from "local assertion" and of nurturing thereby a literature that
would express "the way the earth is and looks." In the impersonality and objectivity of *Tender Buttons*, therefore, she may
well have felt her writing to be distinctively American in its
projection of the literary mode of that future civilization where
pure reality is revealed by the "human mind" unalloyed by facts
or meaning or a sense of time.[22]

In addition to the abstract perspective and the liberated
diction (but related to these two aspects), Stein remarked a third
distinguishing element: a new feeling for space-time induced by
American experience. "It is singularly a sense for combination
with a conception of the existence of a given space of time," she
wrote in explaining the genesis and style of *The Making of
Americans*, "that makes the American thing the American
thing . . . "; it is "something strictly American to conceive a
space that is . . . always filled with moving . . . ," and as an
"American," she testifies, she "felt this thing, and . . . made a
continuous effort to create this thing in every paragraph." Because Americans unlike the English have "no daily life at all,"
she further explained in *Narration*, they want everything to be
"exciting, and to move as everything moves." This "vitality of
movement" she supposed she had projected in her portraits and
in *Four in America* by a kind of cinematic process—by a "con-

tinuous succession of the statement of what that person was until I had not many things but one thing." Thus through the slight phrasal variations in a series of sentences, comparable to the changing images in successive frames of a film, and by ignoring what a character does or says in favor of disclosing "the intensity of movement" inside him, she sought to create a "continuous present" untainted by distracting associations and memory. Through this "more and more listening to repeating," she asserted, she allowed each of her characters to become a "whole one" for whom she had achieved a "loving feeling" and a "completed understanding."[23]

In place of the old Aristotelian reliance on a causally sequential plot, Stein therefore proposed the assumption of a "continuous present" as the corollary of a twentieth-century culture nurtured primarily by her native land. As "an American," she said, she had gradually discovered "that anything that everything has a beginning and a middle and an ending," and that "American writing has been . . . an existing without the necessary feeling of one thing succeeding another thing." In the 1920s she had asserted that "composition" is based on the "thing seen," which changes from generation to generation, and she later added that "the business of Art . . . is to live in . . . and to completely express that complete actual present." Her emphasis on the reality of the continuous present was therefore neither pragmatic nor humanitarian but rather epistemological in origin. Knowledge to her was "what you know at the time . . . you really know anything," and hence "knowing has not succession" since it is always contingent on the "time you are knowing it." Her addiction to the present participle in *The Making of Americans*, she explained, was an aspect of her effort to escape the assumption that meaning resides in beginning and middle and ending and to posit it in the only valid matrix of knowledge—that of the continuous present. And this sense of the present seemed to her, as did the penchant for abstraction and the transformation of English diction, essentially an "American thing."[24]

The Final Phase

Although during the first third of the century Stein made a continuous attempt to comprehend the American mind and to disclose its distinctive voice both by critical analysis and literary experiment, the final dozen or so years of her life were marked by a more inclusive involvement and synthesis. Even in the late 1920s, before she made her single return to the States, her concern for dispassionate abstraction had begun to yield, as Virgil Thomson has observed, to the more "visceral" and emotional vein of "Patriarchal Poetry" (1927) and *Lucy Church Amiably* (1927), a "Novel of Romantic beauty" (as she calls it), which occasionally resorts to such whimsical American-oriented word play as "Atchison Topeka and Santa Fé when this is not the month of May." Moreover, in *Stanzas in Meditation* (1932) she moved from the still lifes and household objects of *Tender Buttons* to pastoral imagery and landscapes—to manifold and specific animals, flowers, birds, and trees, and to human relationships often described in ethical terms. With the Toklas autobiography (1932) she had for the first time, she said, "felt something outside me while I was writing"; and soon therafter in *Four in America* (1933) she had again turned to the history and characters of her native land as the matrix of an entire book.[25]

Coming as it did following her shift toward romanticism and extroversion, Stein's visit to America induced an almost rhapsodic involvement with a culture and people and landscape upon which she had reflected for over thirty years from abroad. Her "Meditations on Being About to Visit My Native Land" (1934) reveals a mingling of childlike eagerness with small anxieties and concerns that her country will not be "really different," that she will prove to be "a good American," and that she can "see and talk to and listen to Americans as they come and go." With her triumphal lecture tour her hopes and expectations were so superlatively realized that she could pronounce "everything" to be "wonderful" and could express the desire "to stay in U.S.A. for ever." Entranced by the cultural differences among the various states, by the landscapes as viewed from the air, and especially by the wooden houses and their windows ("the most interesting thing in America"), she confessed on her return to Paris that she was already "homesick for America," and that, indeed, she was "married; I mean I am married to America, it is so beautiful." So contagious was her enthusiasm in these years that Thornton Wilder, after reading *The Geographical History of America* (1935), felt impelled to write her from Vienna: "Yes, I'm crazy about America. And you did that to me, too." In view of such warm and ingenuous responses on Stein's part, it is difficult to concur in John Peale Bishop's indictment of her as an "emotional invalid."[26]

Delighted during her visit that America was not merely the same country she had left a generation earlier but that, in fact, "now it's more so," Stein inevitably tended to reconsider many of the national traits that she had with more detachment discovered in her youth and had later assessed from her Parisian perspective. Yet the late 1930s and the 1940s bred fears that her compatriots were losing something of their former individualism and initiative, as evidenced by the fiscal policies of the New Deal and the rise of an "employee mentality," which her fictional GIs Brewsie and Henry find displacing the distinctive American propensity "to pioneer." But as Whitman had found a reassuring integrity and humanity in the soldiers of the Civil War, so did Stein in the GIs of the 1940s; and if in her later romantic vein she glossed the brutal and gross aspects of American army life, she perhaps did so, like Whitman, in order to disclose and reaffirm what she deemed to be the more durable and positive traits of the national character. Prominent among these were an independence of mind, a tolerant and skeptical common sense, and an interest in disputation that impels the GIs to "just keeping on thinking and talking" and to admit that "we dont think we know that all America is just so." Stein's occupation forces probe the American character—its hubris, its evolution, and its current liabilities; and their discussions, she confessed in a postcript entitled "To Americans," "made me come all over patriotic. . . . I was always in my way a Civil War veteran, but in between, there were other things, but now there are no other things."[27]

Yet, on a level of perception and understanding below that

of the GIs' discussion of the American character and destiny lay Stein's own rich fund of responses and reflections accrued through two generations of experience with American persons and things. Hence the reiterated fascination that American voices held for her in the last years of the war: the radio Voice of America, with its broadcasts beginning with "poetry and fire" and modulating to "modesty and good neighborliness," thereby revealing the conduct of the war itself; or, in the soldiers' responses to her persistent inquiry about their native state and occupation, the tonal diversity of regional and urban voices whereby the sound not only of Colorado but also of Chicago, Baltimore, and Detroit could become "music to the ear." The "thing I like most," she declared, "are the names of all the states. . . . They make music and they are poetry." Indeed, after World War I she had projected a long book or poem about how each state differed from the others—how each had "its own character, its own accent" like the ancient French provinces, and yet was American. The delight afforded by the talk of the "GI Joes," however, involved beyond its "music" a linguistic pride. They had completed the necessary transformation of the English tongue, she said; they had not merely possessed their language but had also dominated it, and in making it "all theirs" they had both "become men" and also "become more American." Surely implicit in these responses to the music and poetry and vitality of the GI vernacular is an almost complete reversal of Stein's linguistic views during the cubistic period. Words are no longer merely plastic entities to be liberated from time and memory in behalf of a pure expression of the "human mind"; "human nature," with its involvement with identity and the local has finally reasserted itself, and Stein's writing, despite earlier dicta, is no longer indifferent to "meaning" and "remembering," to "beginning" and "ending."[28]

Even at the end of her life, therefore, Gertrude Stein not only retained her belief in the ineluctable imprint of nationality but also affirmed the native roots of her own writing. Because "a nation is even stronger than the personality of any one," she concluded, "it certainly is so nations must go on, they certainly must." Such a concession to nationality seems to some of her critics to have led her to an "uncritical patriotism"; but Mary

Ellen Chase, visiting with her in England in 1936, perhaps more validly construed her attitude as a belief in "some stout American dream, massive, like herself, rather than sentimental, but to her, clearly real and even possible of fulfillment." No doubt much of her final view of the essential national character is contained in her admonitions at the end of *Brewsie and Willie:* avoid being "yes or no men," "learn to express complication," and "go as easy as you can." It was, indeed, her adherence to such maxims that enabled her to resist a modish immersion in the expatriate temper during her decades abroad. Incisively and persistently probing the phenomena of American history and experience, she fashioned an organically national literary style and aesthetics the pervasive influence of which on her country's literature is a matter of record.[29]

Notes

1. G. Stein, *Geography and Plays* (New York, 1968), p. 392.
2. G. Stein, *Geography and Plays*, p. 419; *What Are Masterpieces* (Los Angeles, 1940), pp. 61–62; *Everybody's Autobiography* (New York, 1937), p. 198; *Wars I Have Seen* (New York, 1945), p. 250.
3. G. Stein, *Wars I Have Seen*, pp. 5, 8; *Painted Lace* . . . (New Haven, 1955), p. 72; *Paris FRANCE* (London, 1940), pp. 33–36.
4. G. Stein, *Geography and Plays*, p. 416; M. J. Hoffman, *The Development of Abstractionism in the Writings of Gertrude Stein* (Philadelphia, 1965), pp. 69, 100–102; G. Stein, *The Autobiography of Alice B. Toklas*, in *Selected Writings,* ed. Carl Van Vechten (New York, 1946), p. 76; *Picasso* (Boston, 1959), pp. 12, 16, 18; *Everybody's Autobiography*, pp. 110, 270; *Painted Lace* . . . , p. 316.
5. G. Stein, *What Are Masterpieces*, pp. 64, 68; *Paris FRANCE*, pp. 2, 22, 24, 43.
6. G. Stein, *Selected Writings*, p. 126; *Four in America* (New Haven, 1947), pp. 10, 16, 30, 32, 167, 169, 195.
7. G. Stein, *Painted Lace* . . . , p. 74; *Everybody's Autobiography*, pp. 105, 233; *Brewsie and Willie* (New York, 1946), p. 113.
8. G. Stein, *Everybody's Autobiography*, p. 239; *Selected Writings*, pp. 53–54; *Wars I Have Seen*, p. 132.
9. G. Stein, *Things as They Are* (Pawlet, Vt., 1950), pp. 4, 54–55, 75.
10. G. Stein, *The Making of Americans* (New York, 1966), pp. 3, 14–15, 22, 31.
11. *Ibid.*, pp. 68, 110–112, 118, 132–133, 240, 280, 438.
12. See J. M. Brinnin, *The Third Rose: Gertrude Stein and Her World* (Bos-

ton, 1959), pp. 276, 339; *transition*, No. 28 (Fall 1928), quoted in G. A. Harrison, *Gertrude Stein's America* (Washington, 1965), p. 68; W. G. Rogers, *When this you see* [*sic*] . . . (New York, 1948), pp. 45, 46; G. Stein, *Paris FRANCE*, p. 2; *What Are Masterpieces*, pp. 61–62, 64, 68; *Wars I Have Seen*, p. 56.

13. G. Stein, *Selected Writings*, pp. 225–26.

14. G. Stein, *What Are Masterpieces*, pp. 61–63; *Paris FRANCE*, pp. 2–3; *The Making of Americans*, p. 718.

15. G. Stein, *Narration* (Chicago, 1935, 1969), p. 3; *Lectures in America* (New York, 1935), pp. 52–54; *Selected Writings*, p. 65; M. J. Hoffman, *op. cit.*, pp. 32–36; R. Bridgman, *The Colloquial Style in America* (New York, 1966), pp. 165 ff.; G. Stein, *Four in America*, pp. 127, 137–39.

16. See M. J. Hoffman, *Personalist* 67 (Spring 1966): 227–32; E. Sprigge, *Gertrude Stein: Her Life and Work* (New York, 1957), pp. 57–58; J. M. Brinnin, *The Third Rose*, p. 338; M. J. Hoffman, *The Development of Abstractionism in . . . Stein*, pp. 80–86; G. Stein, *Wars I Have Seen*, pp. 44, 48, 80; Allegra Stewart, *Gertrude Stein and the Present* (Cambridge, Mass., 1967), pp. 143–44.

17. G. Stein, *Selected Writings*, p. 126; *Lectures in America*, pp. 46–47, 50, 51, 53.

18. G. Stein, *Picasso*, pp. 15–18, 38; *Selected Writings*, p. 99; D. Gallup, ed., *The Flowers of Friendship: Letters . . . to . . . Stein* (New York, 1953), p. 52; P. Meyerowitz, ed., *Gertrude Stein: Writings and Lectures* (London, 1967), p. 75; G. Stein, *Geography and Plays*, pp. 28, 41, 44.

19. D. Sutherland, preface to Stein's *Stanzas in Meditation* (New Haven, 1956), pp. v ff.; E. Wilson, *Axel's Castle* (New York, 1959), pp. 241 ff.; J. M. Brinnin, *The Third Rose*, pp. 130–65; G. Stein, *Everybody's Autobiography*, pp. 191–92.

20. M. J. Hoffman, *The Development of Abstractionism in . . . Stein*, p. 154; G. Stein, *Narration*, pp. 13–15; *Wars I Have Seen*, p. 239; S. Anderson, introduction to Stein's *Geography and Plays*, pp. 7–8; in *The New Republic* 32 (October 11, 1922): 171.

21. F. W. Dupee, "Gertrude Stein," *Commentary* 33 (June 1962): 521; R. Aldington, in *Poetry* 17 (October 1920): 35–37; A. Stewart, *Gertrude Stein and the Present*, Chap. 3, especially pp. 91, 107, 112–13, 132; B. F. Skinner (in *Atlantic Monthly* 153 [January 1934]: 50–57) and Francis Russell (*Three Studies in Twentieth Century Obscurity* [Aldington, U.K., 1954], pp. 76–77) also link the style with Miss Stein's experiments in automatic writing but ignore the questions of its wider American provenance.

22. T. Tanner, *The Reign of Wonder* (Cambridge, U.K., 1965), pp. 190 ff; G. Stein, *What Are Masterpieces*, pp. 83–86; *The Geographical History of America . . .* , introduction by T. Wilder (New York, 1936), pp. 8, 14, 51, 54, 114. See also J. M. Brinnin, *The Third Rose*, pp. 135, 142, 156 ff., and D. Sutherland, preface to *Stanzas in Meditation*, pp. x–xi, xiv; R. Bridgman, *Colloquial Style in America*, pp. 11–12.

23. G. Stein, *Selected Writings*, pp. 225–26; *Lectures in America*, pp. 170–72, 173, 176–78, 183, 184–85, 224; *Narration*, p. 6; T. Tanner, *Reign of Wonder*, pp. 192–93; G. Stein, *The Making of Americans*, pp. 291–92.

24. G. Stein, *Narration*, pp. 20, 23–25; *Selected Writings*, pp. 453, 455–57; *What Are Masterpieces*, pp. 17, 26, 27; P. Meyerowitz, ed., *Gertrude Stein: Writings and Lectures*, p. 65. A somewhat similar exhortation to live in a nonsequential present came from Emerson in "Self-Reliance" in his exaltation of the rose, which makes no reference to former roses, while man lives time-bound by past memories and future prospects. Cf. Riverside edition of Emerson: *Selections*, p. 157.

25. G. Stein, *Bee Time Vine . . .*, ed. V. Thomson (New Haven, 1953), pp. 251–52, 256, 258, 270, 272; *Lucy Church Amiably* (New York, 1969), p. 35; *Stanzas in Meditation*, pp. v–vi, xii, 22–25, 36–37; *Lectures in America*, p. 205.

26. G. Stein, *Painted Lace . . .*, pp. 255, 256; *Everybody's Autobiography*, pp. 182–85; W. G. Rogers, *When this you see* [*sic*] *. . .*, pp. 123, 130–34, 152; D. Gallup, *Flowers of Friendship*, pp. 305–6; J. P. Bishop, *Collected Essays* (New York, 1948), p. 387.

27. W. G. Rogers, *When this you see* [*sic*] *. . .*, pp. 130–31; G. Stein, *Painted Lace*, pp. 71–72; *Brewsie and Willie*, pp. 11, 63–65, 82, 96, 97, 113, Chap. 8 *passim*; *Wars I Have Seen*, pp. 251, 252.

28. G. Stein, *Wars I Have Seen*, pp. 155–56, 201, 246, 249–50, 259; *What Are Masterpieces*, pp. 83 ff; *The Geographical History of America*, pp. 8, 54, 69, 114, 174.

29. G. Stein, *Wars I Have Seen*, pp. 132, 156; F. Russell, *Three Studies in Twentieth Century Obscurity*, p. 70; M. E. Chase, in *Massachusetts Review* 3 (Spring 1962): 513–14; G. Stein, *Brewsie and Willie*, pp. 113–14.

POUND:
THE AMERICAN
STRAIN

I

WHATEVER MIGHT HAVE BEEN the court's verdict on Ezra Pound as an American, had he come to trial in the late 1940s in Washington, his biographers and literary contemporaries have consistently affirmed not only the propriety of the epithet but also, from a cultural point of view, its ineluctable pertinence. To his long-time friend and literary associate Wyndham Lewis, his Americanism seemed to be of "primary significance." "Pound is—was always—is, must always remain, violently American," Lewis wrote in 1949, seeing in him a composite of the gait of Tom Sawyer, the "manly candour" of Whitman, the "tough guy" of Hemingway, and the "strenuousness" of Theodore Roosevelt. "The universality in his work is conscious but it overlies an ineradicable Americanism," a friend and biographer, Patricia Hutchins, wrote fifteen years later—a view akin to Donald Davie's conclusion a year earlier that Pound was "thoroughly aware . . . of himself as indelibly American."[1]

From the time when he envisioned a literary career for himself, Pound was aware that his native land would have a bearing on his literary aspirations, and this relationship he frequently assessed over some sixty years. Admitting himself in 1917 to be an "Amurkun" author, he spoke thereafter of the "virus, the bacillus of the land in my blood, for nearly three bleating centuries"—of the "blood poison" that he and Eliot had.[2] In his mid-twenties, contemplating his expatriation from the philistine texture of American life, he resolved to "suffer, or enjoy, his exile, gladly," realizing that "it would be about as easy for an American to become a Chinaman or a Hindoo as for him to

86

acquire an Englishness, or a Frenchness, or a European-ness
that is more than half a skin deep."[3] Some twenty years later,
though disgusted with American publishers' failure to support
him and others who wished to take over literary leadership from
"dying England," he asserted that he was neither expatriated
nor embittered; and in 1937 he could more specifically add, "I
do not think that I have ever abandoned the frontier." "I don't
have to *try* to be American. Merrymount, Braintree, Quincy,
all I believe in or by," he insisted in 1939; and soon thereafter,
despite his long sojourn abroad, he still professed that "curious
letch of Americans to *try* to start a civilization there or rather
to restart it." Indeed, Pound's biographer Charles Norman was
merely sustaining the persistent consensus when in 1960 he
wrote, "Pound was and has remained, American to the core."[4]

Yet beneath this confident consensus, one suspects, inhere
not only shifts in Pound's own attitude but also a vast heterogeneity and even inconsistency of premises, a semantic disjunction of assumptions and implications—historical, temper-
amental, racial, cultural. Is Pound to be considered American
because his imagery is that of "the unfettered West," as an early
review in *Punch* implied, or because of his "transatlantic brio,"
to use Douglas Goldring's descriptive phrase? Was he, as Wyndham Lewis said in 1910, a "cowboy songster" whose distinctive
voice echoed "the staccato of the States"? Does his nationality
lie chiefly in his "frank, open democracy of manners," as John
Gould Fletcher supposed?[5] Or was he, with his nearly three
centuries of American ancestry, drawn close to the racial exclu-
siveness of the Native Americans? Were the texture and temper
of his imagination distinctively fixed by his cisatlantic origins?
How, indeed, as an author was he "American to the core"? Much
of the clue to the Americanism of his mind (as distinct from his
political acts) may be found in his conception of what an American
literature should be and in the distinctive elements of nationality
(or absence thereof) in his poetry.

II

In proclaiming himself an "Amurkun," Pound found the defensive base for his assertion in a putative national culture of a hundred years earlier rather than in that of his own day. To live in Crawfordsville, Indiana, he discovered at twenty-one, was to live in an alien world—to be held "in durance" among "ordinary people [who] touch me not," and hence he longed for his "kindred . . . / Flesh-shrouded bearing the secret," who "know, and feel / And have some breath for beauty and the arts." In his early poems America remained a "mass of dolts," the American "L'Homme Moyen Sensuel" disguising his materialism with a "stale" moralism.[6] At the beginning of World War I America seemed to him like England if from the latter the two hundred most interesting people were removed. By the end of the war his contempt for the American people and their literary arbiters had so deepened that he resolved to revert to the "unconcern" that he had felt for the States before 1911–12; he would never return to America except "as [to] a circus." The crowds of "vigorous unwashed animality" sweeping along Eighth Avenue—Letts, Finns, Algerians, and the like—seemed to him "the America of tomorrow" and confirmed him in his view that art could never rest on or be responsible to the masses. Lacking a knowledge of the classics—the "antiseptics against the contagious imbecility of mankind"—America seemed to him to have been reduced to a cultural blank between the "anemia of guts on one side [the professors] and the anemia of education [the Kreymborgs and Bodenheims] on the other."[7] By the later 1920s in *Exile* he quoted with manifest approval the judgment of the American intelligentsia that his native land was "*the* most colossal monkey house . . . yet seen," and he traced the "drear horror of American life" to the "loss of *all* distinction between public and private affairs" and the "tendency to mess in the affairs of others" by those who had established no order in their own life and thought.[8]

The only America he could respect was that of the high tide

of American civilization as reflected in the Jefferson-Adams letters. Here was the authentic American Paideuma—the "mental formation, the inherited habits of thought, the conditionings, aptitudes of a given race or time." In this ideal American age (1760–1830) an innocent and vital liberty seemed to him to have prevailed, and literature was related to the total life of the nation, including the organization of government. To this American civilization rooted in the cultures of both France and England and thereafter shattered by the Civil War, Pound could and did give his positive loyalty.[9] To speak of him as an American in a sociopolitical context is to recognize his major allegiance to his own synthetic version of the antebellum era in American history and to the Paideuma that he extrapolated from it.

Despite his crescendo of denunciation of twentieth-century American dolts and their philistine milieu, however, Pound in every decade felt a renewal, however briefly, of confidence and faith. In England in 1912 he proclaimed his "country, . . . almost a continent and hardly yet a nation," to be a fusion of idealism and materialism—and basically the latter; to the essential character of this incipient nation Whitman sounded the "keynote": "a certain generosity; a certain carelessness, or looseness . . . ; a hatred of the sordid . . . , a desire for largeness." Hence in correlating the archetypes in the Greek Pantheon with various nations, he discovered America in Artemis: "among us, perhaps because we are a young and inexperienced people, there remains a belief in this type—a type by no means simple—and likewise a belief in affection; in a sort, intimate sympathy which is not sexual."[10] "To return to America is like going through some very invigorating, very cleansing sort of bath," he wrote after his visit to the States in 1910; the country may contain evil, he admitted, "but the odour of the rottenness is not continually obtruded upon one," and many Americans, like naive grown children, are "innocent and unconscious of its existence." Nor could he fail to note affirmatively at this time the vigorous poetry of New York's architecture and the pagan crowds—"eager, careless, with an animal vigour." From such scenes he could feel ambivalently a sense of inherent national power: "One knows that they are the dominant people and that they are against all delicate things."[11]

Although most of Pound's comments on the past and present
of American letters are marked by a sense of outrage and contempt, he never entirely lost his hope for a Risorgimento, which,
as he boldly proclaimed in 1912, would "make the Italian Renaissance look like a tempest in a teapot."[12] Underneath all his
restive search for a satisfying literary environment, T. S. Eliot
wrote of Pound in 1946, "the future of American letters was
what concerned him most."[13] The American literature for which
he contended, however, was primarily not an autochthonous
expression but rather a redemptive agent in the preservation of
the finest values evolved by Western civilization. Rooted as his
mind was basically in the cultural premises of the eighteenth
century and the Enlightenment, he continued to project the
axiomatic belief of such Americans as John Adams and Crèvecoeur
that the arts traveled westward with empire and that America
was destined to complete the great circle. Like the eighteenth
century, too, he inclined to construe literature not in a merely
narrow belletristic sense but as an expression of the full intellectual scope of man. The arts, said Pound during World War
I, must be placed ahead of the church and scholarship as the
"acknowledged guide and lamp of civilization."[14]

Accordingly in 1930, convinced that "European civilization
[is] going to Hell," he was indignant that his literary countrymen
should "waste 5 or 10 years of American time" in importing
"frippery" and discussing outmoded theological questions instead of "getting on with the work fast enough to have a bearable
civilization ready to take on when Europe collapses." Literature
has degenerated, he insisted, through its fragmentation and its
failure to exist "in a full world," as did Adams and Jefferson.
Culture and literature must extend beyond the "penumbra."
Hence in response to John Crowe Ransom's request for an essay
for the newly established *Kenyon Review*, Pound felt impelled
to ask:

> . . . are you ready for a revival of American culture con-
> sidering it as something specifically grown from the nucleus
> of the American Founders, present in the Adams, Jefferson
> correspondence; not limited to belles lettres and American
> or colonial imitation of European literary models, but active

in all departments of thought, and tackling the problems which give life to epos and Elizabethan plays?[15]

If, therefore, Pound was concerned throughout his life to try "to wrench her [America's] impulse into art," as he phrased it in "To Whistler, American" in 1912, he might justly claim himself not only to be a protagonist of historical American values but also to be a proponent of the organic and socially redemptive literature that was actively espoused in the decade 1910–20. In a sense Pound projected more widely and critically the conjoined assumptions of Vachel Lindsay that one might through preaching the gospel of Beauty create the golden city of Springfield. In such a view literature was conceived of as socially imperative not so much through its explicit arguments as through its more subtle imaginative fusing of a sensibility with values that would give direction to the national will and thereby reshape all aspects of American life and ultimately the world at large—a messianic hope embraced by Brooks, Frank, Randolf Bourne, and many others, including most of the editors of the little magazines. Pound's inclusive and ultimate literary concern, therefore, like that of many of his American literary compatriots, was for a "new civilization," and toward this end he could assert in the early 1930s that if literature devoted itself merely to traditional forms to the neglect of causes, it would remain "silly bric-a-brac." Commenting in the early 1960s on his apparent shift from an early concern for form to a later one for ideas, he repudiated the dichotomy by describing technique as the "test of sincerity": A thing must be worth getting the technique to say.[16]

Though Pound thus recurrently and increasingly viewed American literature as a function of the American Paideuma, occasionally before the 1920s he allotted to all art an autotelic exemption from all sociopolitical bonds. "Are you for American poetry or poetry?" he asked Harriet Monroe when she projected her magazine, *Poetry*. "The latter is more important," he asserted, adding that "poetry is an *art* . . . not a pentametric echo of the sociological dogma printed in last year's magazine." Even when he admitted that "American poetry" should be "boosted," he implied by the nationalistic epithet only a poetry whose distinction lay in an art that would not disgrace its cisatlantic origin rather than in one that would peculiarly reflect it. American poetry is simply poetry written in America. To Williams during World War I he expressed his longing for the day when American artists could stay at home and perfect their art without becoming involved in civic campaigns and propaganda. At that time among native American poets only Eliot seemed to him to have properly prepared himself for the arduous art of poetry through training and modernizing himself.[17] Consonant with his eighteenth-century predilections was his insistence in his twenties on "a universal standard which pays no attention to time or country." This standard, he felt, could best be comprehended in the metropolis, whereof "all great art is born," and since America had no literary capital and no worthy literary tradition, her poets must be *au courant* with the literary affairs of Paris and London. "A care for American letters," he declared in 1915, "does not consist in breeding a contentment with what has been produced, but in setting a standard for ambition." For this standard, or what he called figuratively an "absolutely clear palette," Pound by his thirtieth year had begun to formulate the "tradition" later expounded in *Guide to Kulchur*—those authors whose style was permanently and universally valid, such as Dante, Villon, and Heine, as opposed to Milton and Francis Thompson, who were "poison." At this time he could not see that a concept of "American literature" had any more validity than that of an "American chemistry, neglecting all foreign discoveries."[18]

After the war, however, this pure poet who should transcend nationality as scrupulously as the chemist seemed to Pound less and less either a possiblity or a desideratum. When Margaret Anderson, editor of *The Little Review*, disapproved of the "intellectual poetry" of Marianne Moore, Pound argued in defense of Miss Moore and Mina Loy that the "arid clarity . . . of le tempérament de l'Américaine" in their poems is "not without its own beauty," and he praised them because "without clamors about nationality [they] have written a distinctly national product, they have written something which could not have come out of any other country."[19] Soon thereafter the sanction of the indigenous appeared in his praise of Robert McAlmon's presentation of "the American small town in a hard and just light" and in the "American spoken language." In remarking that the "universal must exist somewhere under the American crust" of such portrayals, Pound was admitting to the literary foregound the obscure native setting and the colloquial idiom. Hence in the early 1930s his encouragement to the editor of *Hound and Horn* to stick to his wish for "a STYLE out of America," and his satisfaction in a development in American verse that had issued not only in a divergence in style from the British but also in a superiority that would make a British number of *Poetry* appear to be an act of "American chauvinism."[20]

In his efforts to determine the character and future of American literature Pound's speculations were most effectively crystallized by the diverse art and example of Whitman and James. The latter, he felt, had "put America on the map. Given her local habitation and a name." As another expatriate James could serve as a model, as Pound realized even in 1912, who had both understood and depicted all that is fine in American life. Protesting the popular inclination to term James a European because he felt a "hustling and modern America" that had no tolerance for her finest literary craftsmen, Pound could understandably ask if a man is less an American citizen "because he cares enough for letters to leave a country where the practice of them is . . . well-nigh impossible, in order that he may bequeath a heritage of good letters, even to the nation which has borne him."[21] But beyond furnishing Pound a justification for his own expatriation James conferred a larger benefit through his "research for the significance of nationality," as Pound phrased it, and through his depiction of "race against race, immutable; the essential Americanness, or Englishness, or Frenchness." Through James's acute sense of national differences Pound was impelled toward a cultural pluralism—to what in the 1960s he called the "struggle to keep the value of a local and particular character, of a particular culture in this awful maelstrom, this awful avalanche toward uniformity." James had devoted himself, Pound approvingly wrote, to the great labor "of making America intelligible." In his writings Pound found half of the American idiom and "whole decades of American life," and he felt that no Englishman could know how good his New York and New England are. Even in the Jamesian style he found a trait more integrally related to the American mind than free verse, which he admitted also to be "*un*-English": "I'll tell you a thing that I think is an American form, and that is the Jamesian paren-thesis. . . . That I think is something that is definitely American. The struggle that one has when one meets another man who has had a lot of experience to find the point where the two expe-riences touch, so that he really knows what you are talking about."[22]

For Whitman Pound's admiration was less firm and constant; indeed, it involved reconciliation with a literary progenitor he could neither wholly repudiate nor wholly accept. Hence his varied and at times inconsistent notations on the elder poet form a kind of dialogue whereby he sought to fix his own stance as an American writer. As a "grown child" / Who has had a pig-headed father," Pound in a series of assessments in his twenties concluded that he had "detested" Whitman long enough, and he must swallow the "nauseating pill"; hence he modulated his disgust into a qualified acceptance—for the most part an ac-ceptance of Whitman as pioneer and seer rather than as artist. The only way to enjoy him, he once said, is to concentrate on his meaning and to ignore his language. Although in 1909 Pound affirmed Whitman's "deliberate artistry," two years later, ad-mitting that to "all purposes" he had never read him, he con-demned him as "too lazy to learn his trade . . . he was no artist, or a bad one.—*but* [*sic*] he matters." As Pound explained to Floyd Dell, he "mattered" because he was "*America*. The feel of the air the geomorphic rythm [*sic*] force." The others who tried to be American had not lain "naked on the earth," he added, but "bathed with their clothes on, & the clothes were 'made abroad.' " This praise of Whitman for his "rythmic inter-pretations of his land & time" he repeated in *Patria Mia* (1912): "He was the time and the people (of 1860–80); that is, perhaps, as offensive as anything one can say of either."[23]

Yet whatever flaws of crudity and lack of restraint Whitman may have had, Pound concluded that in the development of American literature he was to his country what Dante was to Italy—the "first great man to write in the language of his people." He "broke the new wood" in preparation for the next century, "the time for carving." Primarily to fix his own place in a viable native poetic tradition springing from "one sap and one root," Pound consented to "commerce" with Whitman—to become "mentally," as he said, a Whitman who had "learned to wear a colar [*sic*] and a dress shirt." For him Whitman's great value was that he was a man "to know," not one whose "tricks" (style and structure?) were to be mastered and imitated. It was his "message" that Pound vowed to make his own and to "see that men hear it."

What that message was he never explicitly defined. In the context of the vow it would seem to be "all the old beauty," with which he would "scourge America." Clearly to Pound the message was not Whitman's cosmic sense, which seemed a fake, nor that "horrible air of rectitude with which Whitman rejoices in being Whitman." No doubt it involved the projection of the "national *timbre*," which he felt Whitman "established," as he said in *Patria Mia*, by his reflection of an unself-conscious "America . . . proud of a few deeds and of a few principles." He was the "American keynote" to that "generosity" and "largeness" and "willingness to stand exposed" that Pound in 1912 attributed to the national character. This was the Whitman in whom he felt the American abroad, if ever likely to forget his "birthright," could find "reassurance." It was no doubt this birthright, this keynote, this *timbre* that Pound persuaded himself in later years he, too, was espousing and for which he was willing to "stand exposed."[24] In later decades as his quarrel with Americn acts and policies intensified, his feeling of identity with and veneration for Whitman deepened. In the 1930s his faults seemed "superficial"; he was artist enough to be included among the immortals. Evidently not so much with Whitman the poetic evangel and innovator as with the isolated septuagenarian did he come to feel bonds and affinities beyond mere "commerce." At any rate, in Cantos LXXXI and LXXXII he reverted to Whitman—in the former to praise him for the "first heave" in breaking the pentameter, and in the latter to reassure himself through parallels in Whitman's career as a poet largely unacknowledged or misunderstood by the nation he addressed. Only through phrases and motifs echoing from "Out of the Cradle," apparently, did he feel that he could convey the accrued depth of his kinship with the aging Whitman, "exotic, still suspect, / four miles from Camden / 'O troubled reflection / O Throat, O throbbing heart'."[25]

In his effort to define his role as an American poet Pound's references to other American writers were only occasional. His "Commission" reflects Thoreau's *Walden* as well as Whitman's 1855 "Preface": his "songs" were designed for the "lonely and unsatisfied," the "enslaved by convention," the "bourgeoise . . . dying of her ennuis." From Frost, whom he encouraged and whose poetic honesty he applauded, he apparently learned nothing. Nor in the half century of his uneasy friendship with Williams did he find in the latter's principle of localism or in his opposition to the infusion of economic panaceas into poetry sufficient validity to follow Williams's counsel or example.[26] Nevertheless, in his own pronouncements over a period of sixty years on the proper nature of American literature, Pound did shift emphasis if not basic principles.

Although he decried the notion that American authors "ought" to write about their country or that it was inherently interesting because American, that it could serve as a proper *donnée* for worthy poetry and fiction he seems never to have doubted. Hence in 1913 he praised Frost (and later Williams) for "rendering American life with sober fidelity." His main desideratum was technical: the fixing of the native scene or quality with precision and in natural speech. Yet, given his pervasive dissatisfaction with the crudity of American life, he expected that this objective precision would be framed by a didactic and often satiric intent. The honorific tones and hues with which aesthetic distance allowed him to educe the life and values of Provence or Homeric Greece were rarely permissible for the depiction of American experience, even for the era of the Adamses and Jefferson. In the attempt "to disentangle our national qualities," he said in the 1920s, American writers must go beyond James to register the national folly with "a vast co-ordination and synthesis . . . without the soft tender hand," or what he later called the "Kate Douglas Wiggin touch." The great function is to "portray" rather than instruct, he explained, but the portrayal must be done by those who are "superlatively *aware*."[27] Hence the America of the Wilson-Hoover era seemed to him to afford plenty of literary opportunities for a native Flaubert, though its subject matter was closer to that of Dostoevsky's *Idiot*. The advent of World War II intensified Pound's feeling that the "superlatively *aware*" author cannot help portraying America as a land of idiocy—indeed that such portrayal is the very proof of authorial awareness and literary maturity. Perverted by "goddam colleges *and* subsidized reviews," American letters, he felt, had sunk into a "dryrot." The corruption of words and language in the dominant literary figures and publications of America, he proclaimed from Italy in 1942, had issued in "dung heaps of perfumed pus"—the ultimate issue of a diseased economy, government, and people.[28]

III

From Pound's temperament and behavior and from his explicit statements about America and her literature one can undoubtedly derive a complex of interrelated traits and attitudes suggesting an "ineradicable Americanism"; to reach a similar conclusion through a scrutiny of his belletristic modes is more difficult, for its involves the question not only of what Americanism is and how it leaves its authentic impress on poetry but also of how far one in reading Pound's poems can achieve a "pure" aesthetic response unalloyed by the controversial and vivid image of their author. Indeed Pound cumulatively affords strictures on if not a refutation of Eliot's doctrine of the impersonality of mature poetry; his creative mind was no neutral "filament of platinum" acting merely as a catalyst and dissociated from "the man who suffers," as "Mauberley" and *The Cantos* abundantly show. The existential Pound is indubitably and avowedly present in his poems. The very rhythm of a poem, he believed, should correspond exactly to the shade of the emotion expressed, and hence a poet's rhythm is interpretative and ultimately "uncounterfeitable."[29] Would Pound's verse, had it remained unknown and were now suddenly discovered as the work of an anonymous author, betray not only through explicit statement and allusion but also through its rhythms, its idiom, its temper, and its ideological implications an "ineradicable Americanism" as an aspect of his unique self?

Although in his late twenties Pound praised Frost for his "natural cadences," he evidently was not content like Frost to allow the patterns, inflections, and stresses of colloquial Amer-

ican discourse to assert such a dominant influence on the movement and tone of the poetic line. Indeed, while praising Frost's
naturalness, in *Poetry* he was urging American poets to fill their
minds with the finest cadences, preferably of foreign origin.[30]
In effect Pound set an example for such a procedure, and until
the 1920s through translations and varied experimentation he
relied on classical, Provençal, and Chinese modes and rhythms
rather than on the patterns and intonations of his native speech,
although in *Lustra* such poems as "Commission" and "Salutation
the Second" echo America indirectly through Whitman: "But,
above all, go to the practical people / go! jangle their door-bells!"

The sound and texture of American speech reasserted themselves, however, especially after Pound left England, and were
increasingly incorporated into his work. Many of his letters,
especially those in which he speaks of himself as "old Ez," might
pass for extracts from some Southwestern or Western humorist,
with their contrived misspellings, their drawl, their coinages,
their innuendoes, and their inherent profanity. But it is in the
later Cantos that he became most distinctly an American voice
with an easy virtuosity which no English contemporary did (or
probably could) approach. "(Pistol packin' Jones with an olive
branch)" he wrote in Canto LXXX, in the midst of Chinese
ideograms, Italian dialogue, and classical allusions; or later in
the Canto: "and the jambe-de-bois stuck it up / at an angle, say
about 140 degrees / and pretended it was a fiddle / while the 60
year old bat did a hoolah," or "young nigger at rest in his wheel-
barrow / . . . addresses me: Got it *made*, kid, you got it made."
Would "Whitcomb Riley be still found in a highbrow anthology"?
Pound ambiguously asked in the same Canto, giving a directive
answer, perhaps, as Noel Stock has observed, in *The Confucian
Odes* (1954) where he echoes Riley's "Knee-Deep in June" with
"Yaller bird, let my corn alone, / Yaller bird, let my crawps
alone / . . . I wanna go back whaar I can meet / the folks I used
to know at home." Or in *Thrones*, Canto 99, Pound abandoned
Hoosier dialect to project Confucian wisdom on a normal colloquial level: "And if your kids don't study, that's your fault. / Tell
'em. Don't kid yourself, and don't lie."[31] In hundreds of other
instances Pound's recourse to the distinctive patterns and diction
of native speech reflected an "ineradicable Americanism" not

only in the articulation of his thoughts but also in making viable the wisdom of ancient cultures.

With the more constricted use of the word and the principle of Imagism, however, his Americanism is more difficult to establish. To William Carlos Williams, who believed that poetry more than any other literary form "carries the mark of any race that uses it," Pound's poems seemed to convey above all a "love for human communication and what it can do for the world"; and this trait, he added, "shows his [Pound's] distinct American origin. Where but in America would you expect the naked word itself to work such miracles. [*Sic*.] Pound was born in Idaho and has never forgotten it. By talking too much he has gotten himself jailed." But surely this faith that through the "naked word" would emerge a new intelligent view of our lives that could remake the world is not peculiarly American, as Williams asserts; nor is the principle of Imagism, which was one of its corollaries. In his stress upon identifying the word with the thing it named and in his belief in the redemptive power of the direct and objective treatment of the thing, Pound admittedly had European preceptors or allies rather than disciples (for example, T. E. Hulme and Ford Madox Ford). Yet in assuming that names are the consequences of things, he may well have inclined to such nominalism because it is consonant with, if not peculiar to, the pragmatic and empirical strain in American thought in which he was nurtured. The sights and sounds and actions of the external world for Pound as for Whitman precede and form the "vortex" of ideas; they are not the mere illustrative contingencies (objective correlatives) of an antecedent reality in subjectivity or emotion. Priority, therefore, as Pound said in his well-known Imagist creed, must go to the "direct treatment of the 'thing' whether subjective or objective," with the "viewy" and the "descriptive" left respectively to the philosophic essayist and the painter.[32]

Although the Imagist movement was centered in England, Pound might well have been inaugurator rather than mere ally had he in his "pact" with Whitman based his allegiance on the latter's literary principles and practice rather than on his "message." For Whitman in his preface of 1855 had not only repudiated metronomic verse but had vowed to hang no curtains between himself and reality: "What I tell I tell for precisely what it is"; and, in effect, in some sections of "Song of Myself" and in his Civil War vignettes he had composed small Imagist poems. In *The Reign of Wonder* Tony Tanner has recently ventured to link the Transcendentalists, Symbolists, and Imagists in a sequential "belief in the intense suggestiveness of separately perceived objects." Though Tanner's inclusion of the Symbolists may need further validation, and though Pound's concentration on and exaltation of the factual, objective world were secular and affective rather than cosmic in intent and implication, his massing of discrete particulars often resembles passages of the Transcendentalists and their followers for whom a sense of wonder suffused all objects and held them together in mystic unity. In both, the "precision" of the senses provided the initial and basic stage (or what Pound called a vortex) toward some sort of epiphany, whether archetypal emotion or the intuition of the Over-soul.[33]

This emphasis on the concrete image, moreover, determined not only the sensory orientation but also the very structure of a poem. To the question of how coherence and form could emerge from the observed and discrete minutiae of experience, Pound gave his answer in his *Guide to Kulchur* and elsewhere in his figure of the rose pattern in the iron filings: The dead filings are driven into a "forma" not by a direct contact with the magnet, he said, but "Cut off by a layer of glass, the dust and filings rise and spring into order." To Hugh Kenner the poetic act in Pound is therefore the "electrification of mute experiential filings," which take dynamic form not as directly illustrated concept but as the expression of deeply felt values, the magnet being analogous to Eliot's catalytic strip of platinum, the glass to the separation of the suffering man and the creative poet. Yet this method, in which explicit authorial unity and comment are eschewed and meaning emerges from the juxtaposition of objects and actions, has been shown by Tanner to be peculiarly the predilection of American authors from the Transcendentalists to Salinger and Hemingway. Their style, he argues (following Eric Auerbach's terminology), has been consistently *paratactic:* in other words, "the syntax which puts things next to each other without trying to relate them."

The Cantos, Tanner might have said had he treated Pound,
are the culmination of a century of paratactic writing in America,
its "endless amazing particulars" held together by no explicit
formal scheme or forma. Such were Pound's iron filings with the
magnet under glass. Like Whitman's epic "Song of Myself,"
Pound's epic might be described in Tanner's words as "a powerful flow of unstated association." Or, as Gertrude Stein said
in her disparagement of memory and narrative plot in favor of
a "verbal still life": American writing has been an escaping not
an escaping but an existing without the necessary feeling of one
thing succeeding another thing of anything having a beginning
and a middle and an ending." Could not *The Cantos*, indeed,
go on forever—despite Pound's profession of a Dantean structure
culminating in "Thrones" as a kind of "Paradiso"? Perhaps in
their ellipses, their paratactic juxtapositions, and their fusion of
past and present *The Cantos* are more "ineradicably American"
in style than Pound himself realized.[34]

Yet, given the paratactic style, two interrelated questions
remain: Does a "forma," a rose pattern, emerge from the iron
filings, and is the pattern an American one? Numerous critics,
including F. R. Leavis, have regarded *The Cantos* as essentially
a game with no interesting patterns or urgent philosophy;
D. S. Carne-Ross concludes the "general impression" to be
"chaos"; Northrop Frye can find no "sense of an enveloping body
of vision," no "great epic image of life" emerging from Pound's
"pastiche of harangue and exempla"; Allen Tate, with reiterated
praise for their rambling conversational mode and "distinguished
verse," nevertheless has judged them not to be "about anything." As *The Cantos* developed, however, surely Pound abandoned his early view expressed in "The Serious Artist" (1913)
that "art never asks anybody to do anything, or to think anything,
or to be anything." Most good literature, he declared a decade
later, has been didactic and may continue to be, though it should
exclude "crankism."[35] By the 1930s that "gross mismanagement"
in governmental affairs had reached the stage which he felt
should draw the author into public comment and away from the
problems of formal composition to which normally he should
"stick . . . as hermetically as an inventing chemist in his labo-
ratory." Richly drawn as they were from classical, Chinese, Ren-

aissance, and American history, Pound's juxtaposed characters and incidents were not mere disinterested "ideas in action"; rather they were designs consciously calculated to affect political action and give order to society. No longer were cultural norms merely implicit, as they were in most of his earlier poetry. Hence in replying in 1940 to Pound's statement that "everything he's written has economic implications," Williams argued that of late a blatant propaganda in *The Cantos* was subverting the proper function of poetry, that Pound's economic concepts were worthless in his "poetic quantum," and that if they "ever clarify themselves . . . it might be the end of him."[36] Increasingly in *The Cantos* the rose pattern proved not to emerge from a forma under glass but to be shaped by an obtrusive conceptual magnet.

The nationalistic relevance of *The Cantos*, therefore, must involve Pound's views of the economic structure of the good society and the character of the political leader. That his attacks on "usura," his resistance to monopoly capitalism, and his emphasis on the government's monetary responsibility to its citizens were an expression of Americans' traditional revolt against tyranny he persistently reiterated. His own grandfather's concern for monetary reform, he felt, was a reflection of a larger native movement embodied in Jackson and the Populists. Usura or the private control of money seemed to him to have finally evolved a "capitalist society [that], in its last vile chancrous phases, has set no value whatsodamever on fine perception or on literary capacity." Hence, in his attempt to write an epic poem, which "crosses the Purgatory of human error and ends in the light," Pound declared that he had had to understand error, a major element of which was economic: "Usury spoiled the Republic." Even the assassination of Lincoln he could trace to an American "usorocracy." Yet if his economic attitudes had their American prototypes, much of his immediate and specific program was inspired by an Englishman, Major C. H. Douglas, the evangel of Social Credit. Indeed, the fact that Pound relied chiefly on Douglas, Alfred R. Orage, Silvio Gesell, and other European writers for his analysis and cure of contemporary politicoeconomic ills, combined with his subsequent praise of Mussolini and the corporate state, suggests that his obsession with usury was so mixed with foreign alloys as to be a negligible counter in his "ineradicable Americanism."[37]

His vision of an American society, however, with such *aristoi* as Jefferson and Adams as the exemplars and rulers, is more solidly a part of a New World political tradition—a preromantic tradition, to be sure, which belonged to the eighteenth century as Henry Adams understood and wrote of it. Pound's fondness for and espousal of the Enlightenment has been frequently remarked: Its ideal of liberty, its conception of rational order, its Deistic cosmology were all involved in his praise of Adams and Jefferson in the American Cantos. The sanity of their civilization, he declared, rests on the Encyclopaedists; and, in turn, the best definition of a national American culture (or Paideuma) is to be found in Jefferson's letters. Herein, perhaps, lay the paradox of Pound's cosmopolitan Americanism. In the century preceding the romantic concept of the nation as an organically unique and autochthonous growth, the eighteenth-century American stressed the ideal of an America that would be the culmination and sublimation of past cultures rather than a repudiation of them; the "new man" in America, as Crèvecoeur phrased it, would "complete the great circle." It was in the furtherance of this dream, one may suppose, that Pound turned to China and Greece and the Renaissance to consolidate for American culture the Confucian idea of the leader, the rich humanism of the Greek Paideuma, and the bold color of the Renaissance. Tate has written acutely of Pound's cosmopolitan curiosity, with its essential disrespect for myths and the supernaturalism of local cultures; he finds him "a typically modern, rootless, and internationalized intelligence." A similar description might be made of many an eighteenth-century American, especially of those whose cultural affinity was with France.[38]

From the perspective of nationality the rose that emerges from the iron filings of *The Cantos* is not ultimately the economic obsession, which is too explicit and conceptual; the magnet, in other words, is not "cut off by a layer of glass" but exerts the naked force of Pound's personal bias. The pattern that emerges from the filings of many cultures is that of an ordered community, humane and devoted to the arts and governed by leaders whose self-knowledge is a prerequisite to their control of public affairs. The pattern, with its frequently aberrant configurations, essentially traces Pound's eighteenth-century search for a redemptive world "Kulchur" for America. A reactionary idealist,

a political innocent, with no "negative capability" for compre-
hending the texture and substance of everyday American life,
he screened out the barbarism of past and current tyrannies and
emerged with a naive abstraction: the state as "public conven-
ience." With this Thoreauvian conviction he marched almost
alone to the music of a different drummer—the strains of liberty
that he heard from the Founders and that compelled a civil
disobedience no more extreme than that in Thoreau's famous
pamphlet. To the extent that Thoreau's individualistic revolt
against representative government reflects an authentic and recurrent native position, to the extent that the American tradition
itself provides for conscientious (however misguided) protest
against compromise, political or aesthetic, Pound may be considered to be in the American grain.[39]

To the degree that Pound failed as an American artist, it may
be argued that his failure came not from his paratactic focus on
things but basically from his apostasy from Whitman's principle
that the great poet does not argue or moralize: "He knows the
soul." Indeed, in the very issue of *The New Freewoman* to which
Pound contributed "The Serious Artist," the editorial "Views
and Comments" (presumably by Ford) observed that the soul
is a thing, a province of art to make a chart of: "a poet concerning
himself with concepts is a sad spectacle; so ill-employed, busily
propagating illusions. . . . Hence, art comes as a flail to concept-
based morality." Though Whitman may have imposed his ego
on the phenomenal world, it was a representative and intuited
self rooted in native experience such as all other Americans
might "assume"; the ego that Pound imposed, messianic and
authoritarian, moved toward such obsessive concepts as Social
Credit, "propagating illusions." Yet in the last years the vanity
and excesses were "pulled down," and even the humiliating
stringencies of the Pisan imprisonment and the long confinement
at St. Elizabeth's did not extinguish his concern and hope for
America. In the 1950s in Washington he could advise young
writers to "stay in America—it's nearly all that's left." Still con-
tending in the next decade that his Italian broadcasts were non-
treasonable arguments for a "Constitutional point," he nevertheless
admitted that his "method of opposing tyranny was wrong over
a thirty year period." The violent affirmations of the enlightened

civilization of the Founders in *The Cantos* and the Italian broadcasts softened in the 1960s into a "nostalgia" for an "America that isn't there anymore"—into an acceptance of the difference between an "abstract Adams-Jefferson-Adams-Jackson America and whatever is really going on." As he grows older, he says, he "feels more American all the time" and would like to spend a part of each year in the States. "There are so many things which I, as an American, cannot say to a European with any hope of being understood. Somebody said that I am the last American living the tragedy of Europe." In his own mind, therefore, Pound remained ineradicably American. If one assesses not only his individualism, his mobility, his experimentalism, his evangelical desire to "make it new," but also his concern for American leadership in the arts and politics and his American idiom and style, there is much evidence to justify his claim. Nor can one, even conceding the gravity of some of his excesses, quite concur in the judgment of one of Pound's friends as reported by Mina Loy in the 1920s, that he "brought from America the faults of America and none of its virtues."[40]

Notes

1. Wyndham Lewis, in *Quarterly Review of Literature* 5 (1949–50): 137 ff.; Patricia Hutchins, *Ezra Pound's Kensington* (London, 1965), p. 13; Donald Davie, *Ezra Pound: Poet as Sculptor* (New York, 1964), p. 21.
2. Cf. W. C. Williams, *Selected Essays* (New York, 1954), p. 8; E. Pound, *Letters 1907–1941*, ed. D. D. Paige (New York, 1950), pp. 123, 124, 158.
3. E. Pound, *Patria Mia* (Chicago, 1950), pp. 64–65.
4. E. Pound, *Letters*, pp. 256, 322, 346; Noel Stock, *Poet in Exile: Ezra Pound* (New York, 1964), p. 210; Charles Norman, *Ezra Pound* (New York, 1960), p. 230.
5. Cf. E. Mullins, *This Difficult Individual, Ezra Pound* (New York, 1961), pp. 39, 61, 72–73, 89–90.
6. E. Pound, *Personae* (New York, 1926), pp. 20–21, 235, 238, 243.
7. E. Pound, *Literary Essays*, ed. T. S. Eliot (London, 1954), p. 372; Margaret C. Anderson, *My Thirty Years' War* (New York, 1930), p. 168; E. Pound, *Imaginary Letters* (Paris, 1930), pp. 4–5; *Letters*, pp. 128, 144, 148.
8. E. Pound, *Impact* (Chicago, 1938), p. 221; in *Exile*, No. 1 (Spring 1927), p. 92; No. 2 (Autumn 1927), p. 35.

9. E. Pound, in *Exile*, No. 4 (Autumn 1928), p. 51; *Impact*, pp. 4, 7–8, 151, 167, 169, 173–74.

10. E. Pound, *Patria Mia*, pp. 21–22, 55–56, 73. Clark Emery in *Ideas into Action* (Coral Gables, Fla., 1958), p. 112, notes that Artemis is both "cruel and kind" and suggests the "dual nature of change."

11. E. Pound, *Patria Mia*, pp. 26–27, 32, 33, 55.

12. E. Pound, *Patria Mia*, pp. 24, 42–43; H. Monroe, *A Poet's Life* (New York, 1938), p. 260.

13. Cf. *Poetry* 48 (September 1946): 327; or W. Sutton, ed., *Ezra Pound* (Englewood Cliffs, N.J., 1963), p. 18.

14. Cf. B. T. Spencer, *The Quest for Nationality* (Syracuse, 1957), pp. 16–17, 22; E. Pound, *Letters*, p. 48.

15. E. Pound, in *Hound and Horn* 4 (Fall 1930): 115, 116; *Impact*, pp. 175–76, 179–83; *Letters*, p. 319.

16. Cf. W. Wasserstrom, *The Time of the Dial* (Syracuse, 1963), Chap. 1, *passim*; E. Pound, *Impact*, pp. 222, 227, 238, 240; in *Paris Review*, No. 28 (1962), p. 21.

17. H. Monroe, *A Poet's Life*, p. 259; E. Pound, *Letters*, pp. 40, 123.

18. E. Pound, *Letters*, pp. 9–10, 24; in *Poetry* 5 (February 1915): 227–33.

19. *The Little Review Anthology*, ed. Margaret C. Anderson (New York, 1953), pp. 187–89.

20. E. Pound, in *The Dial* 72 (February 1922): 192; 73 (September 1922): 336; in *Hound and Horn* 4 (Summer 1931): 571–72; *Letters*, pp. 231, 232, 234.

21. E. Pound, *Letters*, p. 138; *Literary Essays*, p. 302; *Patria Mia*, p. 48; *Pavannes and Divisions* (New York, 1918), p. 244.

22. E. Pound, *Literary Essays*, pp. 296–98, 302; in *Little Review Anthology*, pp. 226–28; in *Paris Review*, No. 28 (1962), pp. 26, 43.

23. E. Pound, "A Pact," *Personae*, p. 89; C. B. Willard, "Ezra Pound's Appraisal of Walt Whitman," *MLN* 72 (January 1957): 19–26; H. Bergman, "Ezra Pound and Walt Whitman," *American Literature* 27 (March 1955): 56–61; G. T. Tanselle, "Two Early Letters of Ezra Pound," *American Literature* 34 (March 1962): 114–19; *Patria Mia*, p. 38.

24. H. Bergman, pp. 60–61; E. Pound, *Personae*, p. 89; C. B. Willard, pp. 19–26; E. Pound, *Patria Mia*, pp. 62–64.

25. Cf. C. B. Willard, "Ezra Pound's Debt to Walt Whitman," *SP* 54 (October 1957): 573–81; R. H. Pearce, "Ezra Pound's Appraisal of Walt Whitman: Addendum," *MLN* 74 (January 1959): 24–27; *The Continuity of American Poetry* (Princeton, 1961), pp. 85–91.

26. E. Pound, *Personae*, pp. 88–89; W. C. Williams, *Selected Essays*, pp. 8, 9, 106, 237–38.

27. E. Pound, *Polite Essays* (Norfolk, Conn., n.d.), pp. 69, 72; in *The New Freewoman* 1 (September 1, 1913): 113; in *The Dial* 73 (September 1922): 336 (November 1922): [549], 554; 74 (March 1923): 279.

28. E. Pound, *Impact*, p. 238; *Letters*, p. 325; E. Mullins, *This Difficult Individual, Ezra Pound*, pp. 209–11.

29. Cf. T. S. Eliot, "Tradition and the Individual Talent," *The Sacred Wood*

(London, 1928), pp. 53–57; cf. D. Davie, *Ezra Pound*, pp. 74 ff.; E. Pound, *Pavannes and Divisions*, p. 103.

30. E. Pound, in *The New Freewoman* 1 (September 1, 1913): 113; H. Monroe, *A Poet's Life*, p. 299.

31. Cf. E. Pound, letters Nos. 240, 257, *Letters*, pp. 226, 242–43; Pisan Cantos, pp. 77, 83, 84, 88 in *The Cantos*; *Thrones* (New York, 1959), p. 57; cf. Noel Stock, *Ezra Pound . . .*, pp. 3–4; L. S. Dembo, *The Confucian Odes of Ezra Pound* (Berkeley and Los Angeles, 1963), pp. 3, 32–34, 90.

32. W. C. Williams, in *The Pound Newsletter*, No. 8 (October 1955): 8–9; D. Davie, *Ezra Pound*, pp. 56–59; E. Pound, *Pavannes and Divisions*, pp. 95–97, 99.

33. T. Tanner, *The Reign of Wonder* (Cambridge, U.K., 1965), pp. 87–93; J. Kennedy, in *The Pound Newsletter*, No. 10 (April 1956), pp. 11–12.

34. E. Pound, *Guide to Kulchur* (Norfolk, Conn., n.d.), p. 152; cf. Hugh Kenner, "The Rose in the Steel Dust," *Hudson Review* 3 (Spring 1950): 66 ff., 76, 77, 80–81; T. Tanner, *Reign of Wonder*, pp. 11, 12, 30, 79, 194, 197; D. Davie, pp. 219–20, 239–40.

35. Cf. Peter Russell, ed., in *An Examination of Ezra Pound* (New York [1950]), pp. 21, 67, 150; N. Frye, in *Hudson Review* 4 (Winter 1951–52): 627–31; E. Pound, *Literary Essays*, p. 46; in *The New Freewoman* 1 (October 15, 1913): 161–63; in *The Dial* 74 (March 1923): 279.

36. E. Pound, in *Hound and Horn* 3 (July–September 1930): 576; W. C. Williams, *Selected Essays*, pp. 237, 238.

37. Cf. Noel Stock, pp. 180–93, 212, 219; E. Pound, *Polite Essays*, p. 101; *Impact*, pp. 15 ff., 20–22, 26, 190.

38. Cf. D. Davie, *Ezra Pound*, pp. 135–37, 164–66, 170–73; E. Pound, *Impact*, 169, 177; A. Tate, in *An Evaluation of Ezra Pound*, pp. 70–71.

39. E. Pound, in *Exile*, No. 1 (Spring 1927), p. 88.

40. *The New Freewoman* 1 (October 15, 1913): 166; E. Pound, in *Paris Review*, No. 28 (1962), pp. 45, 50; C. Norman, *Ezra Pound*, pp. 273, 444.

DR. WILLIAMS'S
AMERICAN GRAIN

I

ALTHOUGH MOST AMERICAN WRITERS since the turn of the century had accepted American literary independence as an accomplished fact—a status only to be further consolidated, not to be won—not so William Carlos Williams. For more than fifty years he persistently maintained that American writers have neither understood their New World heritage nor created the distinctive idiom that would at once clarify and express it. As "ex British colonials" we are "an ignorant crew," he wrote Henry Wells in 1950, and with difficulty we try "to stand on our feet."[1] "Our enemy is Europe, a thing unrelated to us in any way," his protagonist earlier asserts in *The Great American Novel* (1923), insisting that we still need to free ourselves and "learn the essentials of the American situation" and damning with one word, "England," those "Concordites" (Thoreau, Emerson, and Holmes!) who but superficially charted the nation's literary emancipation a century ago. From this point of view as a "beginner" and a "United Stateser,"[2] through essay and poem, through letters and through drama, through preface and through novel, for more than five decades, he probed the nature of an indigenous American literature more zealously than any other major writer since Whitman. Williams was not an intellectual, and it was "unfortunate for him that he must engage in theory at all," Karl Shapiro has written, validly noting that his performance is greater than his theory.[3] Yet with all the muddle and contradiction that any critical reader of Williams must concede, there are throughout both his poetry and his criticism a tonic diagnosis and a sustained conviction that have made him one of the inescapable forces in twentieth-century American writing.

Primary in Dr. Williams's prescription for the vitalization of

American literature has been the local. As early as 1913, convinced that he was "not English," he began to "look at poetry from the local viewpoint."[4] This principle he continued to espouse in editing *Contact* during the 1920s, praising Joyce for his exemplary immediacy with his locale—an immediacy which seemed to him to preclude a reliance on foreign precept and outmoded usages.[5] In the 1920s this buoyant localism, as Williams termed it, was more than a literary device: As envisaged by its exponents (H.D., Margaret Anderson, Marsden Hartley, *et al.*) it involved not only an aesthetic but also ultimately a whole cultural regeneration. As the city depends on the country, and as the river flows to the sea, Williams wrote to Horace Gregory as late as 1944, so local cultures are the origin and measure of general ideas; the poet, therefore, by living locally becomes "the agent and the maker of all culture."[6] To this view and its aesthetic implications Eliot was regarded as the malevolent reactionary. His *Waste Land* Williams construed as a damaging blow to the emergent and confident localism of the 1920s, and in his view Eliot remained throughout succeeding decades the "worst possible influence in American letters."[7]

Williams's concept of the local, as he from time to time took pains to make clear, had little in common with the local color or regional doctrines dominant in American literature in the late nineteenth century. To be sure, he could praise Wallace Gould's poems of Maine, for they showed that "man can be a poet anywhere under any circumstances" if he will only take the land at his feet and use it, that "poetry is made by the hands of the poet out of nothing" and not out of the brains of Frenchmen, Englishmen, or dead Greeks; but he was careful to distinguish Gould from those "'chance, lovely singers' who pipe up and do conventional ditties in Wyoming or Texas or Delaware or Nebraska, taking in the ready scenery of the place."[8] Indeed one of the true values of art, he felt, was its deliverance of the object from the sentimental and associational into its own character.[9] Hence his aversion to the repetitious use of sonorous American place names, a weakness that he charged even to Thoreau and Henry Adams as well as to Stephen Vincent Benét in what he called "the John Brown thing."[10]

Ideally, then, Williams would seem to push the poem or the

fiction to the purely objective extreme of the subject-object continuum. His American poetry would be a mass of disclosure of the pure being of discrete particulars. The only human value of anything, he once declared, is "intense vision of the facts"; the poet's aim must therefore be "to be nothing and unaffected by the results, to unlock and flow, uncolored, smooth, carelessly."[11] Hence his admiration for the clear, washed, unassociated language of Marianne Moore's poems, for her "objective" quality, whereby an "apple remains an apple whether it be in Eden or the fruit bowl where it curls"; hence also his dictum that American art should emulate American plumbing by "paying naked attention to the thing itself"; and hence his denigration of the simile, since the greater power of art lies in its discovery of dissimilarities, the peculiar perfection of the thing in question."[12] "The particular thing," he explained in *Kora in Hell*, "say a pencil sharpened at one end, dwarfs the imagination, makes logic a butterfly, offers a finality that sends us spinning through space, a fixity the mind could climb forever . . . a complexity with a surface of glass; the gist of poetry. *D.C. al fin.*"[13]

From such imagistic premises Williams apparently arrived at his dictum in "A Sort of a Song" and in Book I of *Paterson:* "No ideas but in things."[14] Because America was pre-eminently rich in "things" unencumbered by traditional biases and predispositions, Williams had high hopes in the 1920s and 1930s for a renascent native poetry of localism. Hence he could counter Pound's expatriate reflections on the American scene by insisting that though he was "no more sentimental about America than Li Po was about China," nevertheless there is no taboo effective against any land, and where he lived was no more a "province" than he made it.[15] To rely on one's own well-schooled senses, to become "sensuously local," to search through one's own "common sensual relationships," he was convinced, is the *sine qua non* of universal understanding.[16] "This primitive and actual America—must sober us. . . . There is nothing to help us but ourselves," he wrote in 1932, advocating "the objective immediacy of our hand to mouth, eye to brain existence" as opposed to a regionalism that would by its associational and cultural biases taint the purity of the objective revelation.[17] The artist as a man of action and a whole man, he further argued, does not translate

reality into symbols but deals directly with it. Hence his de-
murrer at Babette Deutsch's interpretation of the pieces of a
green bottle amid the cinders in his "Between Walls" as signi-
fying life arising out of death; he had only in mind, he said, an
imaginative picture of loveliness in a "waste of cinders."[18]
Through such an unadorned attachment to sensuous experience
in one's own locale, Williams believed, the poet might best be
received into the understanding of all men, for paradoxically
"the local is the only thing that is universal": "The classical is
the local fully realized, words marked by a place."[19]

II

One would suppose that, with this persistent emphasis on
the deliverance of the local thing from associational and symbolic
impurities, Williams would find a subversion of his literary principles in those romantic poets who, as he remarked of Hart
Crane, were "searching for something inside" instead of striving
"for a sharp use of the materials."[20] Yet in a full chapter in *In
the American Grain* he undertook the feat of reconciling the two
modes by pronouncing Poe to be "American. He was the as-
tounding, inconceivable growth of his locality." It was he who
made the "first great burst through to expression of a reawakened
genius of *place*."[21]

Actually Williams's evaluation of Poe is not radically new:
Poe's search for form and originality, his skepticism of the "natural" in literature, his sensitive revulsion from the crudities of
his milieu, his pathetic allegiances and tortuous idealism have
all been previously acknowledged and explored. The difficulty
that Williams's approach involves is largely the semantic one
imposed by the insistence that "localism" is the essential term
to embrace Poe's efforts to "clear the GROUND" for a literature
that would not be sugared over with foreign precedents or colonial imitation.[22]

In fact, what Williams has done is, by a kind of critical New-
speak, to shift his own established use of the term "local" from
its insistent reference to the sensory contact with the things of
the milieu itself to a diametrically opposite subjectivism in which

"local conditions" have nothing to do with "trees and Indians," but rather with "the soul." In Poe's very language Williams understandably finds a "luminosity, that comes of a dissociation of anything else than thought and ideals," and hence his "locality" must accordingly spring from "the compelling force of his isolation." Poe's purest local expression, he concludes, is to be found in his "best" poem, "To One in Paradise," since this poem most sensitively reflects the New World through the very desperation of the poet in a "formless 'population'" that drove him to terror and to a single pathetic love.[23]

Thus, "locality" has become for Williams the complex of conditions that impel and account for the generalized emotion or ideal of the poem. It is wholly implicit; it is the opposite of the locality of *Paterson*. Inevitably, because of his own previous definitions of the "local" and those of traditional usage, Williams must sustain his apology for Poe as the progenitor of a "juvenescent *local* literature" by paradox: "By such a simple, logical twist ["by flying to the ends of the earth for 'original' material" in contrast to Hawthorne's "willing closeness to the life of his locality"] does Poe succeed in being the more American, heeding more the local necessities . . . by standing off to SEE instead of forcing himself [as did Hawthorne] too close." "What he wanted," Williams explains, "was connected with no particular place; therefore it *must* be where he *was*."[24] Of the poet who fled to the ends of the earth and beyond, Williams paradoxically concludes: "In him American literature is anchored, in him alone, on solid ground."[25] But in this sense, one must ask, can any poet anywhere ultimately avoid being "local"? Are not "Christabel" and *Paradise Lost* also, in the last analysis, superbly local poems?

In pushing the local away from the thing and the milieu into the soul and the "elevated mien" of Poe, Williams not only embraced the sheerest American romanticism but also projected a subjective factor that perhaps always lay at the periphery of his exaltation of the intense vision of fact and the release of the distinctive character of the object. Like Wallace Stevens, he long pondered the proper grasp of a reality somewhere between the green world of primordial being and the blue guitar of the ordering imagination. Even in his early stress on the poet's precise comprehension of his given world, he saw that there must be "the necessary translations," and he asked how in a democracy we could "be at once objective (true to fact)[,] intellectually searching, subtle and instinct with powerful additions to our lives." The answer he found in "invention," which he supposed could allow one both to render what impinges on the senses and also "to ascend to a plane of almost abstract design to keep alive."[26] Hence in "A Sort of a Song," where "ideas" are said properly to emerge only from "things," one is nevertheless admonished "through metaphor to reconcile / the people and the stones. / Compose. . . . / Invent! / Saxifrage [the imagination?] is my flower that splits the rocks."[27] Later in *Paterson*, Book II, there is, in effect, a hymn to "invention" without whose agency, we are told, "nothing is well spaced / . . . . unless there is / a new mind there cannot be a new / line . . . / without invention / nothing lies under the witch hazel / bush." Hence, too, in *Paterson* the "particulars" must expand into the "general," and memories play their part, for "a place is made of them as well as the world around it." In "Shadows" the imagination is conceived as memory added to sight.[28]

The poet, therefore, Williams concluded by the 1940s despite all his encomiums on the objective, is not the mere holder of the mirror up to nature, the perceiver of the *Ding an Sich;* he is a "maker," and his importance lies not in what he reveals of the object but in what he makes through an invention that refines, clarifies, and intensifies the moment in which we live.[29] It is not entirely surprising, therefore, that he should have found a literary virtue in Poe's failure to mirror explicitly and sensuously his milieu, that he should have construed Poe's Americanism rather to reside in a style and temper that springs from "local conditions," and that he should have measured the real character of the New World by Poe's psychic response to it, not Poe's picture of it.[30]

III

Having come, therefore, through his scrutiny of Poe to the view that the local writer is, whatever his donnée, merely one

who is "intimately shaped by his locality and time,"[31] it was
inevitable that Williams should probe these shaping forces
unique to the New World. Although on occasion, reverting to
his earlier "localism" of the discretely realized thing, he could
proclaim that he had no belief in the continuity of history and
that the classic is now and the Greek is in the Preakness, yet
he could not consistently discount cisatlantic historical forces
and perspective.[32] Convinced in the early 1920s that his home
was to be in America and that Europe is "a thing unrelated to
us in any way," he made it the first business of his life to possess
this land that, he said, he felt to be founded for him personally.[33]
The most substantial act of possession is, of course, his series
of historical probes in *In the American Grain* (1925), but the
varying moods and phases of his struggle to understand his "locality" have in fact occupied more than a half-century. Thus in
The Great American Novel (1923) there are preliminary sketches
of characters and ideas that are to appear in the larger work two
years later. Here he is already proclaiming through his narrator
that "the American background is America," that since we need
only learn from ourselves "it would be a relief to discover a critic
who looked at American work from the American viewpoint"
and who had learned the "essentials of the American situation."[34]
For the differences between the "American strain" and the domineering English critical point of view are "epochal," he wrote
a few years later in *transition* (No. 15, 1929), and "Every time
American strength goes into a mold modeled after the English,
it is wholly wasted."[35]

In this process of possessing his country, however, Williams
emerged not with one "America" but actually with three: a kind
of Platonic idea of America historically expressed in the American
dream; a covert America intuited by poets like Poe and Whitman; and finally an existential America, vulgar and recalcitrant
in its temporal pursuits. Of the first or ideal America the purest
vision among the early explorers seems to Williams to have been
that of Raleigh, "that lost man: seer who failed," betrayed and
deserted by the English authorities. Yet by his dream "he became America," so that even now there is "a spirit that is seeking
through America for Raleigh."[36] In the Revolutionary generation
Williams finds this essential idea exemplified by Burr, with his

warm, impulsive love of freedom and delight and his resistance to a repressive closing of windows and building of walls against the humane and joyous.[37] And there was Washington (when not dominated by Hamilton) in whose "flaming center" beneath his taciturnity glowed an image of a republic that we still "labor to perfect."[38] Such are Williams's "heroes" (in Carlyle's terminology), his "representative men" (in Emerson's)—those who most surely prefigured that "beauty of spirit" of which the New World should have been "a great flowering, simple and ungovernable as the configuration of a rose—that should stand with the gifts of the spirit of other times and other nations as a standard to humanity."[39]

Of this quintessential "beauty of spirit" of which America in Williams's Platonic view should have been flowering, however, the Puritan spirit intervened as a mighty and aborting archenemy. Even though the Puritans stamped their character on the land, even though their "tough littleness" was the medium of endurance through which the seeds of the "great flower" might have been projected, through their ascetic fear of "touch" they in fact "produced a race incapable of flower," impelled not toward germination but the tomb; their form was bred of brutality and cruel amputations that left a heritage of the grotesque, the violent, and the mad. Their lack of imagination "became a malfeasant ghost that haunts us all." It is scarcely surprising that Williams with his essentially Hellenistic view of America's cultural destiny, should charge these Hebraic forefathers with a "puritanism" that "breathes still" and, paradoxically, "has turned us anti-American."[40]

Beyond this Hellenistic idea of the "true" America, however, and beneath its current utilitarian and pious surfaces Williams perceives a national psyche induced by a unique New World history: its brutal Spanish conquerors, its massacred aborigines, its ravaged beauty, its "implantation of a partly cultured race on a wild continent."[41] The result has been a terror focally expressed in the "localism" of the visionary Poe and racially embodied in aboriginal ghosts. "History begins for us with murder and enslavement, not with discovery. No, we are not Indians, but we are men of their world. The blood means nothing; the spirit, the ghost of the land moves in the blood, moves the blood. . . . We

are the slaughterers. It is the tortured soul of our world." Or,
again, Williams sees the American, forced by Puritanism into
an inner emptiness, as "Lost . . . an Indian robbed of his world."
Inheriting both the guilt of the conquerers and the deprivations
of the conquered, the American has thus become the split and
fearful soul of which his national literature, if astutely read, is
the reflection, ineluctably pervaded with haunting imagery of
Indians, forests, and the night.[42] America is like a stupid giant
in a folk tale, futilely trying through wealth and generosity to
still a fear that it cannot understand.[43]

Blandly existing on the surface of this psychic terror, however, Williams argues, lies a third America which "is a mass of
pulp, a jelly, a sensitive plate ready to take whatever print you
want to put on it—we have no art, no manners, no intellect—we
have nothing. . . . We have only mass movement like a sea."[44]
Confronted by this mass, Williams felt both hope and despair.
The American people are essentially asleep, he writes in "The
Somnambulists," bound in a spell of conformity and equality,
of "drab tediousness" and the "dull nerve" of a democracy.[45] It
was to this "mass" that he referred bitterly in 1915 after the
apparent failure of the little magazine *Others:* "America has
triumphed."[46] Even the universities, with their particular brand
of knowledge and culture, are a part of the "dry mass," he felt,
that had destroyed Pound and made Eliot what he is.[47] For this
condition as it applied to both the general culture and the artists
therein, Williams's favorite epithet is "maimed." Marveling at
the age-old richness of Rome he can but think of "how maimed
we are" and deplore "our subservience to our crippledom"; or
as the reflective Dora and Lottie suspect in Williams's novel
The Build-up: "America is a maimed environment out of which
nothing wide and broad enough in the artist's experience could
come to stand up against time."[48]

IV

It was from these three interrelated yet distinct
Americas—what may be termed the Platonic, the unconscious,
and the cultural—that Dr. Williams derived his prescriptions

for an autochthonous literature that would at once spring from and be relevant to American conditions. In this literature there is, of course, to be nothing of the literary "enemy," England—a separate race, an alien historical experience, with a dissimilar language. Instead, for the greatest works, there must first be a submersion in the American psyche as it has been formed indigenously through four centuries of violence, of struggle with the wilderness, of the fearful closing of windows on those humane impulses of which it should have been the bright flowering. For this psychic plunge figures as varied as Sam Houston, Poe, and Whitman seem to Williams to have provided examples. Or, as he phrased it in another trope, the authentic American utterance can come only from the writer's descent to the earth, to a level of the elemental native forces of American experience below the alien patterns that have been imposed upon it. To achieve the requisite insight, he wrote, "all have to come from under and through a dead layer." For the primal vision of America one must "sink" to a "Knownothingism": "Know nothing (i.e., the man in the street), make no attempt to know."

In the "new beauty of ignorance that lies like an opal mist over the West coast of the Atlantic" Williams had early seen a kind of naked simplicity of attitude from which a new and honest literature might arise. (His intent here seems akin to Wallace Stevens's counsel to the "ephebe" to "become an ignorant man again / And see the sun again with an ignorant eye," and to Whitman's advice to the poet to "go freely with powerful uneducated persons.") "Those who come up from under," those who have gone back to such "beginnings, . . . will have a mark on them that invites scorn, like a farmer's filthy clodhoppers," he prophesied, but theirs will be the redemptive and authentic voice.[49]

In his attempt to prepare the ground for such a national utterance, it is not surprising that Williams, like Whitman, should have accepted the common and even vulgar strains in American life as a most fertile soil in which to nurture a more vital literary growth than the academic, traditional, and genteel had produced. Hence his praise for the Negro, who in his fearless confrontation of experience achieved an art that "integrates with our lives."[50] Hence, too, his approval of racial fusion whereby, "in the best spirit of the New World," new traits were imparted and old orthodoxies and ancient and medieval views were expelled.[51] To diminish the influx of Eastern and Southern European immigrants, he argued, would in effect sterilize the national mind and rob it of much of its spontaneity. Especially among the immigrant working girls and in the flamboyant and gaudy aspects of American life he perceived an affirmation of national energy that was at once a "declaration of richness" and "the beginning of art."[52]

The generating element of a vital and indigenous literature, however, seemed to Williams to reside not alone in the energy of American society but also in the American language. American poetry, he declared at the time he was working on *Paterson*, must be built on a "distinct, separate language in a present (new era) and . . . it is NOT English." English can never be *real* for us, for both the language and its prosody are accretions reflecting a character that is "NOT *our* character." Hence, American poets must not be diverted to the mode of Dylan Thomas's Welsh-English poems, since theirs is a "different compulsion" that must issue in a "different language."[53] For his own work, Williams felt, the American vernacular, the spoken language, provided the necessary liberation from classical English and the culture involved therewith; in a poem like "The Clouds" it could determine the "rhythmical construction" itself. "From the beginning," he said in his later years, "I knew that the American language must shape the pattern; later I rejected the word language and spoke of the American idiom." As "loose, dissociated (linguistically), yawping speakers of a new language," Americans seemed to him to have the privilege of making new discoveries and opening new worlds; and hence in this bold use of his native idiom he recognized "the fountainhead of what [he] wanted to do."[54]

As the prime agent in this liberation through language Williams fixed on the "word"—a term whose meaning he expands at times into something akin to the "logos." "We have no words," cries his aspiring novelist in *The Great American Novel*. "Every word we get must be broken off from the European mass. . . . Piece by piece we must loosen what we want." Before we can have *le mot juste*, the novelist contends (as if in answer to Pound's contention for *le mot juste),* the "word must be free." By a kind of creative mystique, the self, the word, and the novel are ideally and integrally related: "If I make a word I make myself into a word. . . . One big union." New experiences (like "A moon making a false star on the weathervane in the steeple"), unique in their perceived relationships, merge as a fresh vision of the world and the self and hence as new "words." Cumulatively "a novel must be a progress toward a word," and in time words thus become "the flesh of yesterday." The supreme art of writing, the novelist concludes, is to make all words over and make them new for oneself. One is of course close to Joyce here, and the novelist not surprisingly "as an American" pays tribute to the Irish author for liberating words, freeing them "for their proper uses" and thus helping to destroy "what is known as literature."[55]

Yet the word was not for Williams the only creative agent. After a few early imitative years as a poet he began to adopt the pace and texture of American speech in his verse and to search for a new stanzaic and rhythmic unit, for a new poetic "form without deforming the language."[56] At the heart of the new form, as he says later in *Paterson,* lies the "supple word" that has "crumbled now to chalk," but beyond the word the verse line; for, as the playwright Hubert says (surely echoing Williams) in *Many Loves,* only verse can say "what I am saying beyond the words. / There can never be a play worth listening to except in verse."[57] Hence his aim, he declared, was a new, non-English prosody, which it was the American destiny to invent as an expression of the modern world and which should emerge as the "blossom of a triumphant culture."[58] In designing this new American prosody, however, Williams felt (as had Noah Webster, Emerson, and Whitman before him) that he was really going back to Nature; his new principles, he said at seventy, were really the ancient ones that had long been overgrown with weeds, and he was grateful that a "new country, unencumbered by the debris of the ages" had afforded him the opportunity to discover them.[59]

In his study of the "formal resources of a new cultural concept" and, more specifically, in an attempt to achieve a verse form consonant with the native speech, Williams slowly evolved his principle of "measure" and the "variable foot"—a principle, as both R. P. Blackmur and Williams himself testify, "not easy to teach" or "even . . . apprehend."[60] Free verse, he concluded, although a liberating device, is in the end a confusion in terms, for "no verse can be free." Measure, therefore, is necessary—a recognition not merely of the words but also of *"the spaces between the words"* in a foot that is accordingly not rigid but proceeds in "cadences dictated by the American idiom." This idiom Williams would take "as a constant" and have American poets make "units of it," units composed according to the desired effects. "What I in my American world am proposing," he said, "is that they [native poets] divide their lines differently and see what comes of it."[61] His own practice of this theory, he remarked, was crystallized in Book II, Section II, of *Paterson* in the passage beginning, "The descent beckons"; here he achieved the variable foot, a disciplining of free verse into measure through its three phrasal divisions, or, as he once described it, a quatrain transmuted into a three-line stanza.

As he had praised Poe for his devotion to method, for his concern to detach a form from the inchoate mass and sentiment of American experience, so he at last felt that he had likewise achieved a requisite formal perspective, in part through his writing of *Paterson*, from which he could consider verse coldly and intellectually.[62] Thus to his own satisfaction he had achieved the aim of exemplifying for his countrymen that "modern technique" that in 1932 he had declared "we Americans" are in the act of creating for ourselves.[63] Yet even in the midst of his satisfaction Dr. Williams could but admit that no "measure" could escape the crippling forces of the traumatic age in which we live. Hence his variable feet would be "hunchbacked, limping," he wrote John Holmes in 1952.[64] Already in *Paterson* at the end of Book I he had included John Addington Symonds's comments on Hipponax's mutilated verses, halting and lame in their meter because of the "distorted subjects with which they dealt—the vices and perversions of humanity—," and it is not surprising that he concluded Book V with a restatement that the measure must be danced "Satyrically, the tragic foot." Yet even in the early 1950s he was inclined to admit that he may have overstated the case for the "new measure." After all, he realized, it was not "too big, too spectacular a divergence from the old."[65]

V

In the half century during which he pondered the nature of American literature, Williams conceded and assessed an indebtedness both to Poe and to Whitman for having cleared the ground for an indigenous utterance; and in this double and at times conflicting acknowledgment lie many of the puzzling or unresolved phases of his pronouncements. To Poe the tribute had been focused and tortuous, as previously noted in *In the American Grain;* to Whitman it had been more casual, sporadic, and at times grudging. Perhaps, as Karl Shapiro has written, some of Williams's associates poisoned his mind against the Good Gray Poet; or perhaps, as Whitman often belittled his debt to Emerson lest his own poetry be thought the less "transcendent and new," so Williams unduly minimized his obligations to the poet who is, as Shapiro is surely correct in saying, "his mentor after all."[66] To be sure, in later years Williams named Whitman as one of his "contemporaries" with whom he was constantly in touch, and his earliest poems were admittedly a mixture of the "studied elegance" of Keats and the "raw vigor" of Whitman.[67] In the years between, however, he inclined to say that though Whitman broke through the "deadness of copied forms" of British prosody and made the necessary descent through dead cultural layers into the American earth, he was "not a clear-thinking rebel"; he "had no idea" of the "basic significance" of the free verse he "popularized" and hence could not develop properly the poetic line. To Williams in 1950 Whitman was "an instrument, one thing"; his "own meaning" was that he "cleared decks, did very little else."[68]

Implicit in his alternate tributes to Poe and Whitman is essentially Williams's unresolved debate within himself as to whether his own poems as well as American literature should be nurtured as basically an organic growth or as a contrived effect. Overtly he tends to the latter emphasis; covertly to the former. Until the "underlying mechanism" is established, he argued on the one hand, a poem can never be an "organism"; the "skeleton" must precede "the flesh, the muscles, the brain"—a view he traces to his scientific training. "A poem is a small (or large) machine made of words" with nothing sentimental or redundant about it, he wrote in a similar vein in 1944; or, as he phrased it a few years earlier, a poem is a structure, and a "form is a structure consciously adopted for an effect." Here is Williams in the Poe-Valéry tradition, with the poet the producer and the reader the consumer, a tradition antiromantic in its insistence that the mind must control the poem, driving and selecting among the emotions "as though they were a pack of trained hounds."[69]

Yet in reading Williams's prose and poetry, one can but observe dominantly organic imagery through which the inception, nurture, and final expression of "writing"—as he prefers to call the identity underlying poetry and prose—is conceived.[70] In contrast, moreover, to his conception of the poem as a machine are his dicta that measure is "the rhythmic beat of charged language" and poetry the "flower of action," that "plot is like God: the less we formulate it the closer we are to the truth."[71] When the Williams-like playwright of *Many Loves*, declining to write like a "diluted Shakespeare," aspires toward a new style for poetic drama, he does not conceive of it as a machine but as something, similar "to daily speech" and as "simple as water flowing," that will lift the audience into the empyrean.[72] Or in organic phrasings that echo Whitman's 1855 preface and *Democratic Vistas* Williams can see the mass of American poetry, in contrast to Eliot's small polished achievement, as a "modern bolus": "We're not putting the rose, the single rose, in the little glass vase in the window—we're digging a hole for the tree." Or he can have his American literary apologist in *The Great American Novel*, conscious of the lack of fire and passion in native works, ask: "What is literature anyway but suffering recorded in palpitating syllables?"[73] Here Williams betrays, as he so often does, his essential romanticism, construing literature in the prevailing figures of a plant or an overflow of feeling. But beyond his explicit criticism the Whitman influence is pervasive in his structure and line, in his urban themes, in his epic impulse, in his reverence for the thing, in his gusto, in his dismissal of the academy, and in innumerable further ways.

If Williams looked to the past, to either Poe or Whitman,

however, he did so only to project the future: "My whole intent, in my life, has been . . . to find a basis (in poetry, in my case) for the actual. . . . To discover new laws of the metric and use them." With his acute sense of a world in flux, he constantly played variations on the "new"—on the "new seed that counts in the end," "for nothing is good save the new."[74] To keep poetry alive, he remarked the necessity of a Jeffersonian revolution therein every ten years, for all art is like the Phoenix, continually destroyed and continually reborn, and "nothing stinks like an old nest."[75] Hence American poetry must catch the color and swiftness of the day, embracing "everything we are." Since "we live in bags," our poetry may consist in the fragment, in the improvisation where "attenuated power" draws "many broken things" into a "dance" and gives them a "full being"; or it may be "a fashionable grocery list" treated rhythmically in the American idiom.[76] Speaking specifically of America's cultural dilemma in the face of Europe, he concluded in the 1930s that "the new and the real, hard to come by, are synonymous"; nevertheless "one must be at the advancing edge of the art; that's the American tradition."[77]

Notes

1. *Selected Letters* (New York, 1957), p. 285.
2. *The Great American Novel* (Paris, 1923), pp. 26, 61, 62.
3. Karl Shapiro, *In Defense of Ignorance* (New York, 1960), pp. 144, 149.
4. W. C. Williams, *I Wanted to Write a Poem*, ed. Edith Heal (Boston, 1958), p. 14.
5. W. C. Williams, *Selected Essays* (New York, 1954), pp. 28, 29, 32.
6. *Selected Letters*, p. 225.
7. W. C. Williams, *Autobiography* (New York, 1951), pp. 174–75; *Selected Letters*, pp. 225–26.
8. *Little Review* 6 (August 1919): 37–39.
9. *Selected Essays*, pp. 8–11.
10. *Selected Letters*, p. 262.
11. *Selected Essays*, pp. 71, 72.
12. *Selected Essays*, pp. 16, 35, 125, 143; *Selected Letters*, pp. 122–23.
13. *Kora in Hell* (San Francisco, 1957), p. 82.
14. W. C. Williams, *Collected Later Poems* (Norfolk, Conn., 1950), p. 7; *Paterson* (New York, 1951), p. 14.
15. *Selected Letters*, pp. 139–40.

16. *Contact* 1 (May 1932): 109; *Selected Essays*, pp. 198, 212–13.

17. *Contact, loc. cit.*

18. *Selected Essays*, p. 197; *Selected Letters*, p. 264.

19. *Selected Essays*, pp. 118–19, 132; *A Novelette and Other Prose (1921–31)* (Toulon, 1932), p. 117.

20. *Selected Letters*, p. 186.

21. *In the American Grain* (New York, 1925), pp. 216, 226.

22. *Ibid.*, pp. 216, 225.

23. *Ibid.*, pp. 223, 227, 228–29, 231–33.

24. *Ibid.*, pp. 217, 220, 223, 228.

25. *Ibid.*, p. 226.

26. *Selected Essays*, pp. 28, 118–19.

27. *Collected Later Poems*, p. 7.

28. *Paterson*, pp. [11], 65; *Paterson*, 5 (New York, 1958), [6], 65; *Journey to Love* (New York, 1955), pp. 37–40.

29. *Collected Later Poems*, p. 5.

30. *In the American Grain*, pp. 227, 231–33.

31. *Ibid.*, p. 216.

32. *Selected Letters*, p. 130.

33. *Ibid.*, p. 185; *The Great American Novel*, p. 61.

34. *The Great American Novel*, pp. 47, 61, 62.

35. *Cf. Selected Essays*, pp. 86–87.

36. *In the American Grain*, pp. 60–62.

37. *Ibid.*, pp. 194–97.

38. *Cf.* Williams's Preface to his libretto for an Opera "The First President," *Many Loves and Other Plays*, ed. J. C. Thirlwall (Norfolk, Conn., 1961), pp. 303 ff.

39. *In the American Grain*, p. 174.

40. *Ibid.*, pp. 63–68, 80 ff., 111, 114, 116, 120–21, 174, 177–78.

41. *Ibid.*, p. 213.

42. *Ibid.*, pp. 39, 41, 128; *A Novelette and Other Prose*, pp. 97–98.

43. *Ibid.*, p. 175.

44. *The Great American Novel*, p. 25.

45. *A Novelette and Other Prose*, pp. 97–98, 100–101.

46. *Selected Letters*, p. 33.

47. *Ibid.*, p 214.

48. *Ibid.*, p. 61; *The Build-up* (New York, 1952), p. 301.

49. *In the American Grain*, pp. 213–15; *Selected Essays*, p. 18. *Cf.* Stevens's "Notes Toward a Supreme Fiction" and Whitman's 1855 preface.

50. *The Great American Novel*, p. 61.

51. *Yes, Mrs. Williams* (New York, 1959), pp. 30, 136–37.

52. *The Great American Novel*, pp. 45–46, 49–52.

53. *Selected Letters*, pp. 269, 288.

54. *I Wanted to Write a Poem*, pp. 65, 74–75; *Selected Essays*, pp. 256, 286.

55. *The Great American Novel*, pp. 11, 17–19, 22, 26. *Cf.* also *Selected Letters*, p. 126.

56. *I Wanted to Write a Poem*, pp. 14, 15, 23.

57. *Paterson*, p. 65; *Many Loves and Other Plays* (Norfolk, Conn., 1961), pp. 32–33.

58. *Selected Letters*, pp. 269, 285.

59. *Selected Essays*, pp. 13–14.

60. W. C. Williams, "Measure," *Spectrum* 3 (Fall 1959): 157; *Selected Letters*, p. 228; Vivienne Koch, *Williams Carlos Williams* (Norfolk, Conn., 1950), p. 47.

61. *Spectrum*, pp. 136, 149, 153, 155, 156, 157. *Cf.* also *Selected Essays*, pp. 289–91.

62. *I Wanted to Write a Poem*, pp. 65, 80, 81–83; *In the American Grain*, p. 221; *Selected Letters*, pp. 257–58.

63. *Selected Letters*, p. 127.

64. *Ibid.*, pp. 315–16.

65. *Paterson*, p. 53; *Paterson* 5 (no pagination); *Selected Letters*, p. 299.

66. *In Defense of Ignorance*, p. 154.

67. *Selected Essays*, p. 16; *I Wanted to Write a Poem*, p. 8.

68. *Selected Essays*, p. 218; *In the American Grain*, 213; *Spectrum* 3 (Fall 1959): 136; *Selected Letters*, pp. 270, 286, 287. *Cf.* also Williams's essay in *Leaves of Grass: One Hundred Years After*, ed. Milton Hindus (Stanford University, California, 1955).

69. *Selected Letters*, p. 269; *Collected Later Poems*, p. 4; *Selected Essays*, pp. 13, 217. *Cf.* also Laurence Lerner, *The Truest Poetry* (London, 1960), pp. 86 ff.

70. *I Wanted to Write a Poem*, p. 52; *Selected Letters*, pp. 263–65.

71. *Selected Letters*, p. 137, 146; Vivienne Koch, *op cit.*, p. 91.

72. *Many Loves and Other Plays*, pp. 9, 14–15, 33.

73. *Selected Essays*, pp. 285, 286; *The Great American Novel*, p. 60.

74. *Selected Letters*, pp. 25, 257; *Selected Essays*, p. 21.

75. *Selected Essays*, pp. 208, 217.

76. *Selected Letters*, p. 286; *Selected Essays*, pp. 14–15; *Paterson* 5 (no pagination).

77. *Selected Essays*, p. 143; *Selected Letters*, p. 142.

SHERWOOD ANDERSON: AN AMERICAN MYTHOPOEIST

I

IT IS NOT SURPRISING that during the past generation Sherwood Anderson's literary reputation should have suffered an eclipse, for the renascent American literature he envisioned and in part exemplified half a century ago was rooted in the soil and in a sense of wonder and mystery alien both to the realism that preceded it and to the sophisticated naturalism that followed it. To be sure, his work has rarely evoked the degree of condescension found in the dictum of Susan Sontag, who, somewhat ironically upbraiding Anderson for taking himself too seriously, dismissed *Winesburg, Ohio* as "bad to the point of being laughable." In view of her affinity with the New Wave of French fiction, with its commitment to sensory surfaces and psychic fragmentation as contrasted with Anderson's concern for inwardness and identity, her verdict is inevitable.[1]

That such a reversal in his literary fortunes would occur Anderson himself predicted more than forty years ago. Acknowledging himself to be not a great writer but rather a "crude woodsman" who had been "received into the affection of princes," he prophesied that "the intellectuals are in for their inning" and that he would be "pushed aside." And indeed, though more judiciously than Sontag, estimable critics have concurred in assigning Anderson a lesser rank than did his early contemporaries. Soon after the author's death Lionel Trilling, while confessing a "residue of admiration" for his integrity and his authenticity as the voice of a groping generation, nevertheless adjudged him too innocent of both the European literary

126

heritage and the role of ideas in psychic maturity. More recently Tony Tanner, in an analysis of the naiveté of American writers, found in Anderson a distressing example of such writers' penchant for "uncritical empathy" and for dealing in discrete moments of feeling without the "exegetical intelligence" that has shaped all durable literature.[2]

Between these two extremes of detraction grounded on the one hand in an aversion to "meaning" and on the other in an intellectualization of art through formal control and complexity, Anderson has consistently had, as a 1966 volume assessing his achievement shows, his body of apologists. William Faulkner, Van Wyck Brooks, Irving Howe, and Malcolm Cowley have been among those who have found a distinctiveness and a distinction in the best of his work, especially when it is seen in relation to the literary atmosphere of the first quarter of the century. Indeed, Anderson himself throughout his career could never separate his writing from its national context, and this cisatlantic cultural context impelled him toward the mythic, toward the archetypal and elemental, rather than toward the urban and sociological. Repeatedly he spoke of his love for America, sometimes as "this damn mixed-up country of ours," sometimes as a land "so violent and huge and gorgeous and rich and willing to be loved." Moreover, he thought of himself as representatively and comprehensively the "American Man," as he wrote Brooks, explaining that by virtue of his varied occupational background he could take into himself "salesmen, businessmen, foxy fellows, laborers, all among whom I have lived." But not only did he feel himself to be a "composite essence of it all"; he also could experience, he declared with Whitman-like assurance, an "actual physical feeling of being completely *en rapport* with every man, woman, and child along a street" and, in turn, on some days "people by thousands drift[ed] in and out" of him. Like Whitman, too, he contained not just multitudes but also contradictions; he was, as he said, a compound of the "cold, moral man of the North" and "the warm pagan blood of the South . . . striving to become an artist" and "to put down roots into the American soil and not quite doing it."[3]

In reiterating through the second and third decades of the century his view that the crucial deficiency among American writers was that "Our imaginations are not yet fired by love of our native soil," Anderson had in mind of course more than the affirmation of a simple American pastoralism. The "soil," indeed, included the darker lives of the people who lived on it or near it; or, as he wrote to Dreiser in the mid-1930s, the redemption of such lives must lie so far as the writer is concerned not in any philosophical or ideological projection from his pen but in telling "the simple story of lives" and by the telling, counteracting the loneliness and "terrible dullness" that afflicted the American people. He had in mind, no doubt, such a story as the first that he had drafted for *Winesburg*, as he later related its genesis in "A Part of Earth"—a story called "Hands," in which he conveys the pathetic misunderstanding of the character he described as the "town mystery" of Winesburg, Wing Biddlebaum, whose hands reached out to others like "the wings of an imprisoned bird." Later the same motif is repeated in the hero of *Poor White*, whose loneliness and vague ambition impel him to a restless wandering and finally to an awkward and alienated marriage, and in the heroine of *Kit Brandon*, whose intense loneliness Anderson asserts to be characteristic of American life. Indeed Anderson's return to his native "soil" led him to the discovery of what he called "the loneliest people on earth," and his sensitive treatment of these people has led the novelist Herbert Gold to call him one of the purest poets of isolation and loneliness. To Irving Howe he seemed to have expressed the "myth" of American loneliness. Even with this theme, therefore, the mythopoeic Anderson apparently had initially found his imaginative stance. He was not, of course, in the strict etymological sense of the word a "mythopoeist," a maker of myths; but his imagination achieved its finest expression in narratives such as "Death in the Woods" or in parts of *Dark Laughter* where the preternatural or archetypal not only gave it unity and direction but also evoked a connotative style approaching the idiom of poetry. The term is therefore broadly used here as the most adequately comprehensive one to indicate the orientation and mode of Anderson's fiction as contrasted with those of such contemporary naturalists or realists as Dreiser and Lewis.[4]

II

This persistent concern with loneliness both in Anderson's own life and in that of his characters, Lionel Trilling asserted, is in part traceable to his excessive reliance on intuition and observation and to his unfortunate assumption that his community lay in the "stable and the craftsman's shop" rather than in the "members of the European tradition of thought." That Anderson was only superficially and erratically involved with the literary and philosophical past of Europe is undoubtedly true. As late as 1939 he could declare that he did not know what a "usable past" is and that his concern was rather to live intensely in the present. In effect Anderson was emphasizing the inductive and the autochthonous as primary in the literary imagination, as Emerson, Thoreau, and Whitman had done before him; or, in anticipation of William Carlos Williams, he was committing himself to the principle that only the local thing is universal. By concentrating on the elemental tensions of provincial life he was assuming, as Mark Twain had done with the Mississippi, that the archetypes of human character and situation would most surely emerge, and that by returning to "nature" or the "soil" American literature would find at once its uniqueness and its authenticity. Hence his dismissal also of recent European art as a model for American artists. How irrelevant is Whistler's pictorial mode, he wrote in the 1920s, to a valid expression of the "rolling sensuous hills . . . voluptuously beautiful" in California; and how silly are those painters who follow Gauguin when the varied life and color of New Orleans is available to them. The "half-sick neurotics, calling themselves artists" as they stumbled about the California hills, apparently resembled the "terrible . . . shuffling lot" of Americans he later observed in Paris.

Yet from writers whom he venerated as the great fictional craftsmen of Europe—Turgenev, Balzac, Cervantes—he induced what seemed to him to be the fundamental principle for a durable American literature: indigenous integrity. These au-

thors were "deeply buried . . . in the soil out of which they had
come," he asserted in *A Story Teller's Story*; they had known
their own people intimately and had spoken "out of them" with
"infinite delicacy and understanding." With this indigenous
comment, Anderson believed, he and other American writers
could belong to "an America alive . . . no longer a despised
cultural foster child of Europe."[5]

Although Anderson found only a limited relevance for the
cisatlantic writer in the literary modes and cultural traditions of
Europe, he was by no means indifferent to the American past.
His involvement lay deeper than the love that he professed to
Gertrude Stein for "this damn mixed-up country of ours"; it
approached, indeed, a mythic assent to what he viewed as a
liberating cultural destiny often reiterated from the early days
of the Republic—a belief in what his younger contemporaries
Pound and Fitzgerald praised as the old largeness and generosity
that they felt had marked the antebellum national character.
The substance and inclination of Anderson's nationality may be
inferred from the names of the five Americans whom he concluded, in an evening's discussion with his wife, to be the greatest his country produced: Jefferson, Lincoln, Emerson, Whitman,
and Henry Adams. For Lincoln and Whitman, as well as for
Twain and Dreiser, he confessed a special affinity because they,
with origins like his own, had had to take time to put roots down
in a thin cultural soil and, ingenuous and confused, to confront
a "complex and intricate world." The somewhat unexpected inclusion of Henry Adams may be accounted for by the common
anxiety that both authors felt not only about the shattering effects
of the machine on the older American values but also about the
redemptive agency of some new mythic force that would bring
unity out of multiplicity in American life. A more sustained
influence, however, Anderson felt in Whitman, whose attempt
to supplant a narrow and repressive Puritanism with large democratic vistas of brotherhood and loving perceptions he believed
had been betrayed by later generations of American authors.
Like Whitman he tried to project the democratic beyond concept
into myth—into man's link with primordial forces of earth and
into an eventual return to what the older poet in "Passage to
India" had called "reason's early paradise."[6]

Although early in his literary career Anderson was puzzled that Twain had not generally been placed with Whitman "among the two or three really great American artists," he was especially drawn to the Missouri author as a salient example of the American writer's plight and failure. In Twain he perceived a literary pioneer whom the "cultural fellows," as he termed them, had tried in vain to get hold of. Yet ironically, despite Twain's brave achievement and his bold disregard of literary precedent, Anderson sadly observed, he had never been able to attain full literary stature because the America that nurtured him was a "land of children, broken off from the culture of the world." As a part of this, Twain seemed to Anderson to have been caught up in the country's dominant shrillness and cheapness, with his literary talent thereby perverted and dwarfed. But an additional factor in Twain's failure seemed to Anderson to be his voluntary removal during the latter half of his literary life to the East, where he became subservient to what the latter termed the "feminine force" of the "tired, thin New England atmosphere." It is not surprising, therefore, that in *Dark Laughter* Anderson, through his hero Bruce Dudley, should charge Twain with deserting the imaginatively rich Mississippi River milieu and reverting to childhood or trivial themes that could be summed up as "T'witchetty, T'weedlety, T'wadelty, T'wum!" By ignoring the "big continental poetry" of rivers before it was choked off by the invasions of commerce, Twain in Anderson's eyes was in part responsible for the fact that the great River had become a "lost river," now "lonely and empty," and perhaps symbolic of the "lost youth of Middle America." Indeed *Dark Laughter* may be viewed as Anderson's mythopoeic projection of the repressed Dionysiac forces that the early Twain at times adumbrated and then gradually abandoned for genteel values and concerns. At the heart of the book is Anderson's elegy for a literary ancestor who should have expressed the mythic force of the heartland but who lost his touch with elemental things.[7]

For Anderson, therefore, America evoked both intense devotion and recurrent despair—perhaps an inevitable dualism in one whose deepest cultural convictions were grounded in an antebellum version of the American dream as articulated by his five greatest Americans. Jeffersonian as he essentially was, he inclined to trace the confusion and vulgarity of his age to the displacement of the agrarian base of American society. This older America he could envision in *Windy McPherson's Son* as a kind of pastoral paradise, a land of milk and honey wherein the shocks of abundant corn were "orderly armies" that the American pioneer had conscripted from the barren frontier, as it were, "to defend his home against the grim attacking armies of want." It was this agrarian faith, he wrote in *Mid-American Chants*, that had lured the immigrant races westward and had developed a deep affinity with the earth spirit, with the fields as "sacred places" in whose fertility the impulses to human aggression had vanished. And as small organic centers in this agrarian richness, he felt, there had developed the Midwestern villages, which, in turn, had nurtured a vital individualism whereby both men and women lived with courage and hope and with a pride in craftsmanship and independence such as that joyously possessed by Sponge Martin in *Dark Laughter*. Hence Anderson's characterization of Bidwell, Ohio, the setting of much of *Poor White*: It was a pleasant and prosperous town whose people were like a "great family" and, like those in other Midwestern towns in the 1880s, were undergoing a "time of waiting" as they tried to understand themselves and turned inward to ponder the utopianism of Bellamy and the atheism of Ingersoll.[8]

The snake that had crept into this agrarian Eden and its village culture was, in Anderson's reiterated view, a new reliance on the external benefits supposedly conferred by technological progress rather than on the inner resources conferred by Nature and the Soul on the Emersonian and Thoreauvian and Whitmanian self. On this contest of the humane self and the non-human machine most of Anderson's major works revolve—especially *Windy McPherson's Son*, *Winesburg*, *Poor White*, *Dark Laughter*, and *Beyond Desire*.

During his youth, Anderson told a college audience in 1939, the increasing obsession with getting ahead had resulted in a pervasive confusion through the identification of happiness with possessions. Inevitably the towns had become tainted with a competitiveness and greed that left them, as he phrased it in *Windy McPherson's Son*, "great, crawling slimy thing[s] lying in wait amid the cornfields." Young Sam McPherson's success in Chicago, like Anderson's, brought its disenchantment with such "blind grappling for gain"; having "realised the American dream" in its perverted form at the end of the century, Sam felt impelled toward the larger quest of seeking truth—toward the risks of that "sweet Christian philosophy of failure [which] has been unknown among us." Because of a ruthless greed whetted by the new industrialism, Anderson suggests in the novel, "Deep in our American souls the wolves still howl." The consequent dehumanization of the old communities could be seen in both city and village. Reflecting on the brutal crowds in New York, Sam is no doubt expressing Anderson's attitude when he concludes that "American men and women have not learned to be clean and noble and natural, like their forests and their wide, clean plains." And in villages like Winesburg, as Anderson declared in his *Memoirs*, the blind faith in machines had not brought beauty but had left a residue of fragmented grotesques—villagers who, as he explains in introducing the stories of *Winesburg*, in the disintegration of the agrarian community had been driven to seize upon some narrow or partial truth and, in a desperate attempt to sustain their lives, to make it an obsessive and destructive absolute. In a disconsolate mood of acceptance Anderson conceded in his *Memoirs* that "it may just be that America had promised men too much, that it had always promised men too much." In effect he was conceding the subversion of a major myth—one fused by his own experience from the old dream of the garden, Jeffersonian agrarianism, Transcendentalism, the repudiation of Puritanism, and the pastoral abundance of the West. His vision of a land where the earth and brotherhood would allow the satisfaction of the basic human desires had yielded to the reality of masses of "perverse children," lost and lonely.[9]

III

Anderson's mythic focus, however, lay below the national or politico-economic level. America and the West were at last but symbolic media or indices for him, as they had been for the Transcendentalists—transient entities to be valued only to the degree that they proved instrumental in releasing the deific forces or primal satisfactions of man's being. This assumption Anderson made clear in his early days as a writer by insisting in the *Little Review* that the so-called new note in American literature was in reality "as old as the world," involving as it did the "reinjection of truth and honesty into the craft" of writing and also the "right to speak out of the body and the soul of youth, rather than through the bodies and souls of master crafts-men who are gone. In all the world there is no such thing as an old sunrise, an old wind upon the cheeks." Similarly, as he later recalled in his *Memoirs*, he and other members of the Chicago group during World War I were, above all, trying "to free life . . . from certain bonds" and "to bring something back," including the "flesh" that the genteel realism of the preceding generation had excluded. In short, they wished to divert Amer-ican literature from what they conceived to be its secondary focus on the sociopolitical and redirect it to the primary and recurring experiences—to what Anderson in his later years was willing to call "the great tradition," which, he said, goes on and on and is kept straight only with difficulty. "All the morality of the artist," he concluded, "is involved in it."[10]

Convinced as he was that the greatest obstacle to the return to the "oldness" and the "great tradition" lay in the fidelity to fact espoused by the realistic school, Anderson insisted that American writers look primarily within themselves, for "there is this common thing we all have . . . so essentially alike, deep down the same dreams, aspirations, hungers." In effect Ander-son was urging a mythopoetic approach to the same native scenes that William Dean Howells and Twain had often depicted. Like Joseph Conrad, he believed that "the artist descends within himself " and "appeals to that part of our being which is not dependent on wisdom" by speaking to "our capacity for delight and wonder, to the sense of mystery surrounding our lives; to our sense of pity, and beauty, and pain." In the Midwestern lives about him Anderson found the "dreams, aspirations, hun-gers" that could evoke the "sense of mystery . . . of pity, and beauty, and pain," and the transatlantic understanding and ap-proval his stories had elicited confirmed his belief that the American writer could best strike the universal note through such an emphasis. That the "subjective impulse" and the imagined world should take precedence for the author over fact he continued to affirm throughout his life, proclaiming consistently the satisfactions that he had found as a "slave to the people of [his] imaginary world."[11]

Anderson, like Hawthorne and Twain before him, used, as the clearest repository of archetypal emotions and situations, the small town or village for his settings. In the commonplace Midwestern world, he wrote in 1918 in "A New Testament," there is a "sense of infinite things." As an illustration of this "sense" he proffered his story "In a Strange Town," in which the persona observes an ordinary couple—a woman and a man accompanying her to place her husband's coffined body on the train. The people are of no importance, he explained in a comment on the story, but they are involved with Death, which *is* "important, majestic." The very strangeness of the town, he also explained, served to afford a kind of aesthetic distance in which the irrelevant and superficial disappeared and the elemental constants of mortality emerged. To be sure, Anderson at times and for the most part in nonfictional works, did view the town, both Midwestern and Southern, in a sociological perspective. But even here he frequently sounded mythic overtones, as he did in his perceptive remark in *Home Town* (1940) that the small community had always been the "backbone of the living thing we call America" because it lies halfway between the cities (which breed ideas) and the soil (which breeds strength).[12]

On this soil as an autochthonous matrix Anderson consistently relied for the vital norms of his stories as well as of the villages themselves, enclosed as they generally were with their cornfields. It was the soil that in his belief gave the "power" to life and literature (to use Emerson's dual terminology from "Experience") as the towns and cities gave the "form." The towns and villages, therefore, of *Winesburg* or *Dark Laughter* and *Poor White*, rich as they may be in human archetypes, are never autonomous, but always have their traffic with the surrounding fields and woods. Acknowledging the "bucolic" in his nature, Anderson spoke of himself as a "Western novelist" and of his region as the "corn-growing, industrial Middle West." It is "my land," he wrote in 1918 to Van Wyck Brooks. "Good or bad, it's

all I'll ever have." But only incidentally was he concerned with
its industrial aspects; for what he wished to do, he said, was to
"write beautifully, create beautifully . . . in this thing in which
I am born"—indeed, to "pour a dream over it." His perspective
was thus visionary; his imagination was committed to distant
vistas, not merely democratic but essentially mythic. Stirred
during the years of the Chicago renaissance by something new
and fresh in the air, as he said in the *Little Review*, he was
convinced that "the great basin of the Mississippi . . . is one day
to be the seat of the culture of the universe." The current industrialism of the region he interpreted in a quasi-mythic figure
as a cold and damp winter beneath whose lifeless surface something was "trying to break through." Envisioning that vernal
rebirth in the West when "newer, braver gods" would reign and
a new and joyous race would develop, he composed his *Mid-
American Chants*—essentially a volume of free-verse hymns
extolling an American paradise where nature and man were one.
In the very term "chants" Anderson suggested both the style
and purpose of his poems. Eschewing both the elegiac disenchantment with the region to be found in Edgar Lee Masters's
Spoon River Anthology and the virile bravado of Carl Sandburg's
contemporaneous *Cornhuskers*, these visionary poems in their
diction and movement and tone are Anderson's most explicit
venture into the mythopoeic strain. [13]

In the *Chants* Anderson essentially invoked the earth spirit,
as he wrote in "Mid-American Prayer," with its Indian memories
and rites to supplant the Puritanism dominant in the region and
to remind the Midwestern people of the "lurking sounds, sights,
smells of old things." The theme of the repressive sterility of
New England was, indeed, an oft-reiterated one in Anderson's
most prolific years, for he had come to feel that the major mission
of the Midwestern writer, as he explained in his *Memoirs*, was
on behalf of a new race to put "the flesh back in our literature"
and thereby to counteract the "feminine force" of the older
section. The New England notion of America was not blood
deep, he asserted in a Lawrentian vein in *A Story Teller's Story*;
and since blood will tell, the increasingly thinner blood of the
Northeastern man must yield to that type more richly blended
from the "dreaming nations" that had settled the Midwest. In

place of an "old-maid civilization" derived from a cold, stony New England, Anderson saw emerging from the "rich warm land" and polyglot racial strains a kind of Dionysiac brotherhood in which the humane spirit of Lincoln would be the heroic and brooding presence. Thus, as he wrote in *Dark Laughter*, the "whole middle America empire" would be restored as a land of rivers and prairies and forests "to live in, make love in, dance in."[14]

Despite Anderson's invocation of rivers and forests and the "old savages" therein "striving toward gods," the dominant symbol in *Mid-American Chants* was the pastoral cornfield—a symbol indigenous to the country as a whole, though especially so to the Upper Mississippi Valley. Confessing himself to be a "kind of cornfed mystic," Anderson was always moved by the sight of a cornfield, and later in his life at Marion, Virginia, he remarked that such fields were distinctively American. Not surprisingly, the cabin where he chose to do his first writing in Virginia was, as he wrote Alfred Stieglitz, a "deserted one in a big cornfield on top of a mountain. Cowbells in the distance, the soft whisper of the corn." Nearly a decade earlier, in *Windy McPherson's Son* he had protested the popular conception of corn as being merely the feed for horses and steers; instead the shocks of corn stood for him as majestic symbols of a land in which man had been freed from hunger. Yet two years later, in *Mid-American Chants* the cornfields moved from a mere symbol of well-being into the sacramental: They became a "sacred vessel" filled with a sweet oil that had reawakened man to a sense of the beautiful, old things. Moreover, the long aisles of corn in their orderly planting not only signified man's conquest of the forest; they seemed even to run to the throne of the gods. He wrote in "War," "Deep in the cornfields the gods come to life, / Gods that have waited, gods that we knew not." In the cornfields, indeed, Anderson found a new impulse to prayer through what he felt to be their mythic reincarnation of the earth spirit; in them he found an elemental vitality to counteract the sterile religious tradition of New England. Back of the "grim city," Chicago, he saw "new beauties in the standing corn" and, in "Song to New Song," dreamed of "singers yet to come" when the city had fallen dead upon its coal heap. Or again, in "Song

for Lonely Roads," he reasserted his faith that "The gods wait
in the corn, / The soul of song is in the land." During these
years, indeed, as he wrote in one of his letters, he felt that "a
man cannot be a pessimist who lives near a brook or a cornfield";
and in another he confessed to the "notion" that none of his
writing "should be published that could not be read aloud in
the presence of a cornfield."[15]

IV

By the 1930s, and especially with the stringencies of the
economic depression, Anderson's corn gods had proved illusory.
In his earlier romantic commitment to the divinely organic he
had construed the machine as a seductive threat to a Mid-
American reunion with the earth. In those days he could still
believe in the triumph of the egg—to use the title of one of his
volumes, which contains the story "The Egg," a humorous treatment of the effort of the persona's father to subdue a simple egg
by standing it on end or forcing it into a bottle. His humiliating
defeat, one may suppose, may be taken to reflect Anderson's
earlier view of the futility of human attempts to contain or subdue the primal, organic forces of nature. From a similarly organic
perspective the inventor-hero of *Poor White* (1920), appearing
at evening and pantomiming with his flailing arms and mechanical strides the motions of his cabbage-planting machine, becomes for the farmers a frightening specter whose grotesque
movements are a graphic index to consequences that Anderson
felt must follow the replacement of the organic by the mechanical. As imposed behavior and technological demands had succeeded freedom and personal pride in craftsmanship, he
commented in *Poor White*, men and women had become like
mice; and in *Dark Laughter* he spoke of the "tired and nervous"
cities, with their "murmur of voices coming out of a pit."

Over a decade later in his Southern novel *Kit Brandon* only
a few of the mountain girls seemed to him to have retained a
self-respect and proud individualism akin to that of "the day of
America's greater richness." Of this older richness another symbol was the horse, which as a boy in the livery stable he had

found to be the most beautiful thing about him and superior to many of the men with whom he had to deal. In the industrial era, he wrote in *A Story Teller's Story*, since machines had supplanted horses, his own nightmare as a writer was that of being caught as a prisoner under the "great iron bell"—that is, we may interpret, under the great humanly wrought inanimate doom. Perhaps his vivid story "The Man Who Became a Woman," in which a young boy, whose devotion to the horse Pick-it-boy has cleansed his lustful thoughts and dreams, is mistaken for a girl at night in the stable loft by drunken horse-swipes and flees naked to the neighboring slaughterhouse yard, where he undergoes a kind of traumatic burial in the skeleton of a horse—perhaps this story reflects something of the psychic effect on Anderson of the destruction of his mythopoeic America. At any rate, even by the time of the publication of *Horses and Men* (1923), in which he celebrated both the vibrant fascination of the horse and the innocence of youth, he confessed to Stieglitz that he had learned at last that horses and men are different and that in the confrontation of human dilemmas the equine would no longer "suffice."[16]

Although by the mid-1920s Anderson felt obliged to abandon many of the mythic assumptions of his Midwestern years, he could not renounce entirely the demands of his mythopoeic imagination. During the last fifteen years of his life, therefore, he sought new centers and media for a viable myth that would bring unity and beauty to his life. This he found in the mill towns of the new industrial South and in the girls who worked therein. Formerly the South had been for Anderson New Orleans and the southern Mississippi, where the dark, ironic laughter of the Negroes had seemed to express for him an elemental spontaneity and a vital sense of life—a "touch with things" such as stones, trees, houses, fields, and tools, as Bruce Dudley enviously concedes in *Dark Laughter*—which made the members of a subject race humanly superior to the sterile life about them. In the later Southern novels the Negroes have all but disappeared, and though the mill girls, who as a vital center supplant them, are too much at the mercy of their factory world to embody any mythic assurance, they do point to a redemptive feminine principle, which Anderson, like Henry Adams, found in his later years the surest counteragent to the disintegrating power of the machine. It was the American woman, he concluded in the 1930s, who alone could reintroduce the "mystery" that a technological age had dispelled and without which "we are lost men." Since American women at their best had not yet been "enervated spiritually" by the machine or accepted from it a "vicarious feeling of power," perhaps women, he argued in his book entitled by that phrase, might rescue the American man "crushed and puzzled" as he was in a mechanical maze.[17]

Yet, just as Anderson's phrase "perhaps women" suggests an acknowledged tentativeness in his later mythic formulations, so his treatment of the machine in his late works often discloses a new ambiguity. As his recourse to woman for salvation reflects Henry Adams's adoration of the Virgin, so his discovery of the poetry as well as the power of the machine follows the example of another of his five "greatest Americans," Whitman, who abandoned the pastoral milieu of "the splendid silent sun" to discover the poetry of ferries and locomotives and crowded streets. Yet Anderson, with his earlier sustained distrust of the machine, could not free himself from an ambivalence in his later years; he felt both awe and impotence, he confessed, in the presence of the vast order and power and beauty of machinery, and his tribute to Lindbergh as an emergent culture hero, the new type of machine man, as well as his sympathetic portrayal of the speed-obsessed Kit Brandon, the heroine of a late novel, betrays an uneasiness not present, say, in his characterizations of Sponge Martin and the Negroes in *Dark Laughter*. Yet watching the superb technology of the whirling machines, his hero Red Oliver, in *Beyond Desire*, no doubt reflected much of Anderson's later attitude by confessing that he felt "exultant" and that here was "American genius" at work—America at "its finest."

Two years earlier, in 1930, Anderson had declared that he would no longer be "one of the . . . protestors against the machine age" but henceforth would "go to machinery" as if it were mountains or forest or rivers. Hence his poem to the beneficence of the automobile and his attempts to catch the excitement of the cotton mills in his "Machine Song" or "Loom Dance." Yet he also felt impelled to express the more sinister admixture of fear and awe experienced in the presence of the textile machines,

whose hypnotic speed and incessant shuttle rhythms could induce in Molly Seabright, a mill girl in *Beyond Desire*, an indifference and confusion that led to a loss of identification with
the human world about her. Modern American industry, he
concluded ambivalently in *Perhaps Women* (1932), was indeed
a "dance," a "flow of refined power," to which men lifted up
their eyes in worshipful adoration. Surely in such statements
the failure of Anderson to approach the machine as if it were
mountains and rivers is manifest. The earlier mythopoeic imagination has become bifurcated into myth and poetry; the validity
of the myth is not felt, and the poetry is an act of will rather
than of imagination. In this bifurcation and desiccation one may
no doubt find much of the explanation for Anderson's decline
in his later years.[18]

V

To his inclination and commitment to a mythopoeic approach
to American experience both Anderson's literary achievements
and his shortcomings may ultimately be traced. From the time
of World War I until his death at the beginning of World War
II, he consistently aligned his writing with a focal purpose summarily stated in *A Story Teller's Story*: "It is my aim to be true
to the essence of things." In probing for the "essence" he ran
the romantic risk of neglecting the existential substance of
American experience, and hence one may feel, as Lionel Trilling
has asserted, a deficiency of the sensory and concrete in his
work. If one adds to this mythic concern for patterns and forces
behind the phenomenal world Anderson's addiction to the
psychic and intuitive as the arbiters of reality, one approaches
what to Anderson seemed the "poetic" factor in the mythopoeic
imagination. Hence neither the region nor the nation was a
substantial entity for him; neither ideologies nor sociological
formulas were significant norms for his fictional perspective. The
"new note" in American literature, as he said, was really a return
to the old sensations and desires; and hence his women have
few social concerns or ambitions, nor are they regional types:
Aline Grey and Clara Butterworth and Kit Brandon play their

roles rather as versions of the White Goddess reasserting primal humanity, as did Adams's Virgin.[19]

Anderson's style, like his larger fictional perspective, is an organic product of his mythopoeic approach. Rooted in the naive, in wonder, in the mystic and intuitive, his expression shapes itself subjectively from emotions or associations, as Tanner has shown, at the expense of tight syntax, controlled structure, and purified or precise diction. And yet Anderson's vagaries are, for the most part, those that he inherited (and somewhat intensified) through a major native tradition initiated by the Transcendentalists and involving in its course Whitman, Twain, Stein, and J. D. Salinger. If from Anderson's pen this style becomes one in which each sentence affords only a fragmentary glimpse, as Tanner contends, perhaps the limitation is in part explained by Anderson's conclusion that in an immense land where all men are strangers to one another, the writer can "only snatch at fragments" and be true to his "own inner impulses." That a cisatlantic orientation may be necessary for a full comprehension of Anderson's style, with its indigenous tone and idiom, is suggested by Gertrude Stein's contention that "Anderson had a genius for using the sentence to convey a direct emotion, this was in the great american [sic] tradition, and that really except Sherwood there was no one in America who could write a clear and passionate sentence."

Early in his career Anderson in "An Apology for Crudity" asserted that if American writing were to have force and authenticity, it would have to forgo objectivity for the "subjective impulse," and that an honest crudity would have to precede the "gift of beauty and subtlety in prose." However consciously stylized and contrived his own apparent artlessness may have been, his "subjective impulse" extended outward like Whitman's in an effort to catch "the essence of things," and his reputation will be most secure among those who can accept the mythopoeic assumptions that nurtured and shaped his imagination.[20]

Notes

1. S. Sontag, "Notes on 'Camp,' " in *Against Interpretation* (New York, 1966), p. 284.

2. S. Anderson, in *Saturday Review of Literature* 4 (December 3, 1927): 364–65; *Letters*, ed. H. M. Jones and W. B. Rideout (Boston, 1953), pp. 36, 38, 108; L. Trilling, in *Kenyon Review* 3 (Summer 1941): 293 ff.; 4 (Spring 1942): 171; T. Tanner, *The Reign of Wonder* (Cambridge, U.K., 1965), pp. 206, 209 ff.

3. See *The Achievement of Sherwood Anderson*, ed. Ray Lewis White (Chapel Hill, N.C., 1966), *passim*; S. Anderson, *Letters*, pp. 95, 104, 275; *A Story Teller's Story* (New York, 1924), pp. 307, 308.

4. S. Anderson, *A Story Teller's Story*, p. 79; *Letters*, pp. 344–45, 455; "A Part of Earth," in *The Sherwood Anderson Reader*, ed. Paul Rosenfeld (Boston, 1947), pp. 321–28; *Memoirs* (New York, 1942), pp. 6, 184–85; *Kit Brandon* (New York, 1936), p. 255; H. Gold, in *Hudson Review* 10 (Winter 1957–58): 548 ff.; I. Howe, *Sherwood Anderson* (New York, 1951), p. 129.

5. L. Trilling, in *Kenyon Review* 4 (Spring, 1942): 171; I. Howe, *Sherwood Anderson*, pp. 245–46; W. C. Williams, *Selected Essays* (New York, 1954), pp. 118–19, 132; S. Anderson, *Letters*, pp. 126, 165; *Dark Laughter* (New York, 1952), pp. 45, 47; *A Story Teller's Story*, pp. 390, 395.

6. S. Anderson, *Letters*, pp. [3], 37, 40–41; cf. B. T. Spencer, "Pound: The American Strain," *PMLA* 81 (December 1966): 460, 465–66; "Fitzgerald and the American Ambivalence," *South Atlantic Quarterly* 66 (Summer 1967): 374, 377–80; R. L. White, ed., *The Achievement of Sherwood Anderson*, p. 149; S. Anderson, *Windy McPherson's Son* (Chicago, 1965), pp. 33–40; *Memoirs*, p. 440.

7. S. Anderson, *Letters*, pp. [3], 31, 33, 34, 41, 43; *Dark Laughter*, chaps. 2, 11, *passim*.

8. S. Anderson, *Memoirs*, pp. 87, 289, 396; *Windy McPherson's Son*, pp. 57–58; *Mid-American Chants* (New York, 1923), pp. 69–71; *Poor White*, in *The Portable Sherwood Anderson*, ed. Horace Gregory (New York, 1949), pp. 153–55, 156, 162, 271–72.

9. *The Sherwood Anderson Reader*, ed. P. Rosenfeld, pp. 337 ff., 342; S. Anderson, *Windy McPherson's Son*, pp. 66, 98–106, 131, 242, 244, 294, 324, 325; *Memoirs*, pp. 80, 396, 401, 495, 501; *The Achievement of . . . Anderson*, ed. R. L. White, p. 34. For the larger context of the garden myth, see Leo Marx, *The Machine in the Garden* (New York, 1964).

10. *Little Review* 1 (March, 1914): 23; *Memoirs*, pp. 240–45; *Letters*, p. 442.

11. S. Anderson, in *Little Review* 1 (April 1914): 16–17; *Memoirs*, pp. 445, 495; *Notebook* (New York 1926), pp. 139–46; *Letters*, p. 457; "Man and His Imagination," in *The Intent of the Artist*, ed. A. Centeno (Princeton, 1941), *passim*; for Conrad, see preface to *The Nigger of the "Narcissus."*

12. S. Anderson, in *Little Review* 6 (October 1918): 4; *Short Stories*, ed. M.

Geismar (New York, 1962), pp. 155–57; "Home Town," in *The Sherwood Anderson Reader*, pp. 743–47.

13. S. Anderson, *Letters*, pp. 7, 10, 13, 21, 43, 79, 80; *Memoirs*, pp. 241–42; *Mid-American Chants* (New York, 1923), pp. 18, 51, 71; in *Little Review* 6 (October 1918): 6; I. Howe, *Sherwood Anderson*, pp. 57–58, 73–74.

14. S. Anderson, *Mid-American Chants*, pp. 69–71; *Memoirs*, pp. 246, 247; *A Story Teller's Story*, pp. 80, 101; *Dark Laughter*, pp. 68–69; *Letters*, pp. 40–41, 43.

15. S. Anderson, *Memoirs*, p. 360; *Windy McPherson's Son*, pp. 57–58, 246; *Mid-American Chants*, pp. 11–12, 13, 22, 29, 30, 35, 38–40, 47, 60, 62–63, 67, 68, 69–71; *Letters*, pp. 21, 33, 145.

16. S. Anderson, *Poor White*, in *The Portable Sherwood Anderson*, pp. 188, 215; *Dark Laughter*, p. 75; *Kit Brandon*, pp. 84, 85; *Memoirs*, p. 79; *Letters*, p. 106; *A Story Teller's Story*, pp. 187–90.

17. S. Anderson, *Letters*, pp. 58, 68; *Dark Laughter*, chaps. 7, 11; *Perhaps Women* (New York, 1931), pp. 41–43, 112, 113, 142.

18. S. Anderson, *Perhaps Women*, pp. 9 ff., 14–17, 21–29, 30 ff., 36, 107–8, 125–26; *Beyond Desire* (New York, 1961), pp. 49–51, 288–89; *Letters*, pp. 202–3, 206, 207, 208.

19. S. Anderson, *A Story Teller's Story*, p. 100; in *Little Review* 1 (March 1914): 23; L. Trilling, in *Kenyon Review* 3 (Summer 1941): 298–99.

20. T. Tanner, *The Reign of Wonder*, pp. 206 ff., 220–21; S. Anderson, *The Modern Writer* (San Francisco, 1925), pp. 2–3, 37; "An Apology for Crudity," *Dial* 63 (November 8, 1917): 437–38; G. Stein in *Sherwood Anderson: A Bibliography*, ed. E. P. Sheehy and K. A. Lohf (Los Gatos, Calif., 1960), p. [x].

FITZGERALD
AND THE
AMERICAN
AMBIVALENCE

I

THAT F. SCOTT FITZGERALD'S FICTION bears an American stamp to a unique degree has been frequently asserted and rarely denied. In choice of character and scene, in temper and theme, and even in the recklessness of his own literary career he reflects comprehensively his national origins. It is not surprising, therefore, that he could never remember the times when he wrote anything, as he said in his "Note-Books," for he "Lived in story."[1] From Basil Duke to Pat Hobby, from St. Paul to Hollywood, from early adolescence to his last year as a scriptwriter, his own experience and his fiction fuse like the dancer and the dance and resist clear demarcation. Hence for a time in the early 1920s he wondered if he and Zelda were not fictive rather than real, so closely did their life reflect the situations and tone and impulses of his stories. Accordingly, if he and Zelda were indubitably American, so his work was ingenuously and authentically representative of one aspect of life in the States.

That Fitzgerald, despite the indigenous stamp, gave any sustained consideration to his role as an American writer is less evident—nor is it a liability per se that he did not. His lack of generalizing power has been remarked by Arthur Mizener, who nevertheless is convinced that the substance of his stories is more thoroughly American than that of any of his contemporaries. And yet Fitzgerald's failure to probe disinterestedly and consistently either the relation of the American writer to his material or the nature of American culture may ultimately account for Paul Rosenfeld's conclusion that he was overwhelmed

145

by his subject matter and would have been unable to imply the decadence of the life he depicted had it been measured by the values and texture of high civilization. Indeed, when compared to the stringent assessments of American experience as a national composite made by such novelists as James and Faulkner and by such poets as Pound and Williams, Fitzgerald's perspective seems not only peripheral and casual but also impoverished by its involvement with one stratum of the American people. Hence his candid admission in his fortieth year that except within the "technical problems" of his "craft" he had done "very little thinking," that for twenty years for his intellectual conscience he had depended on Edmund Wilson and for his artistic conscience on Hemingway; as for his political conscience, that "had scarcely existed for ten years save as an element of irony."[2]

Nevertheless, even if Fitzgerald's confessional mood did not incline him to overstate his derelictions in sustained and judicious thought, his sensibility, constantly responsive to the world about him, cumulatively impelled him toward what William Barrett has termed a "brooding" on the image of America. The course of this brooding is manifest in his "Note-Books" in the numerous obiter dicta relating to America and forming a trail of allusions pointing the direction of his concerns as an American author: "When Whitman said 'O Pioneers,' he said all"; or "The ferry boat stood for triumph, the girl for romance . . . but there was a third symbol that I have lost somewhere, and lost forever"; "Books are like brothers, I am an only child. Gatsby my imaginary eldest brother, Amory my younger, Anthony my worry, Dick my comparatively good brother, but all of them far from home. When I have the courage to put the old white light on the home of my heart then . . ."[3]

In his brooding, therefore, Fitzgerald tends to allow his sensibilities free play over American life as he experienced it rather than subjecting it to an established system of values. The clue to his imaginative stance is his early adoration of Keats, whose "Ode on a Grecian Urn" he found "unbearably beautiful" and with whom he might have sighed, "O for a Life of Sensations rather than of Thoughts." In his "Note-Books" (under "Bright Clippings"!) he copied a portion of Keats's doctrine of "negative capability," which equated the greatness of "Men of Genius" with that of "certain ethereal Chemicals operating on the Mass of neutral intellect—but they have not any individuality, and determined Character."[4] Yet perhaps one of Fitzgerald's shortcomings as a writer was that he was not Keatsian enough—that in his fiction he could never lose his own identity sufficiently, that he had always to project himself through Anthony or Gatsby or Dick Diver rather than reflect the world of the rich as a neutral catalyst. His own later version of "negative capability," enlarged beyond merely literary relevance and evidently enforced by his own experience, appears in his observation that "the test of the first-rate intelligence is the ability to hold two opposed ideas in the mind at the same time and still retain the ability to function." Even early in his literary career he had concluded that "There is no such thing as 'getting your values straightened out' except for third-class minds" willing to accept the views of some Illinois or South Carolina messiah.[5] In effect he was thus concurring in Keats's doctrine that the great writer is crippled by too rigid a grasp on certainties. In his "ever-new, ever-changing country," with its consequent "moral confusion," as he described it in "The Swimmers," Fitzgerald neither succeeded in becoming a "first-rate intelligence" nor pretended to messianic conclusions. If he did not achieve that full measure of "negative capability" that would have allowed him wide and dispassionate reflection on his country, his very lack of commitment at least kept his imagination flexibly responsive to much of the contradiction and ambivalence of American experience.

The literary consequence of this uncommitted openness was that even Fitzgerald's avowed romanticism was constantly qualified by fortuitous circumstance. Like his young Basil Duke, in "The Scandal Detectives," he cherished the moments wherein he would be sent "plunging along through the air of ineffable loveliness"; or such moments, as in "Forging Ahead," when at the sight of a child's face "there was beauty suddenly all around him in the afternoon; he could hear its unmistakable whisper, its never-inadequate, never-failing promise of happiness." A "great dream," he wrote his daughter in her seventeenth year, lay at the center of his own life at her age. In a vast continental sense the greatest of human dreams captivated the minds of the Dutch sailors at their first sight of the New World, and in lesser

and vulgarized shapes it was the radical impulse of his rich boys
and tycoons, though rarely of his women. In 1937, when he
conceded that he had no more dreams, he nostalgically looked
back to that earlier time "when the fulfilled future and the wistful
past were mingled in a single gorgeous moment—when life was
literally a dream." Yet this "conviction that life is a romantic
matter," whether the dreams were of money or the girl or the
"eternal Carnival of the Sea," he characteristically held (or professed to hold) in conjunction with an opposed belief that "life
is too strong and remorseless for the sons of men."[6] But this
latter deterministic view, which he said that he shared with
Joseph Conrad and Theodore Dreiser, was neither deeply
enough felt nor sufficiently rewarding in the literary marketplace
for him to make convincing use of it in his fiction. For all his
early admiration for Dreiser, Frank Norris, and Harold Frederic,
he was not a naturalist either by temper or by conviction, and
he feared the popular magazines would have no interest in such
depressing narratives as theirs from his pen. Yet that in 1936
he could write to his daughter of his "particular view of
life . . . (which as you know is a tragic one)" suggests that the
undercurrent of tragic awareness had persistently flowed with
increasing strength beneath the surface of his reiterated dreams
of the future.[7]

II

Though in designing his fiction, Fitzgerald admittedly gave
most of his thought to technical problems of narrative art rather
than to a substantive national context, in his "Note-Books" he
recognized the significance of the context: "Art invariably grows
out of a period when, in general, the artist admires his own
nation and wants to win its approval." Though his admiration
for his country was often severely qualified, his desire for its
acclaim was constant. This acclaim, however, he wished to be
spontaneous and based on aesthetic grounds; he had no desire
for the "huzzas of those who want to further a worthy American
Literature," which a comment on the jacket of *Gatsby* had urged
for him, though no doubt while at college he had, like his Amory

Blaine in *This Side of Paradise*, "sought among the lights of Princeton for some one who might found the Great American Poetic Tradition."[8]

Hence his revolt against current aspirations for what he termed "national" or what some of his contemporaries called a "significant" literature: the earthy fiction that dealt with rural American life or insisted on cisatlantic themes or settings. Irving, Whitman, and even Henry James, he thought, had "stupid-got with worry" over the obligation of native writers to use American materials. The result had been an "insincere compulsion to write significantly about America" conjoined with the assumption that the "significance" of literary art lies in the substance rather than in the imaginative treatment of it. Most of the novels of the 1920s, with their "drab . . . subject matter" of inarticulate farmers or racial and political strife, he argued, could at best be considered "muddy lakes" out of which the "clear stream" of a mature literature might flow. No real tragedy could be wrought from the American countryside, he declared in 1925, "because all the people capable of it move to the big towns at twenty. All the rest is pathos." Contemptuous of the "fourth rate imaginations" which fixed on such themes and characters—of the "Barnyard Boys" composing their "epics of the American soil"—Fitzgerald elected to stake his literary fortunes on a donnée of the well-to-do and on the responses of urban and sophisticated readers. "An author ought to write for the youth of his own generation," he asserted as a part of his literary creed in 1920, and in another letter the next year he professed that his "one hope is to be endorsed by the intellectual elite and thus be *forced* onto people as Conrad has."[9]

Though Fitzgerald's literary orientation was thus genuinely American, it was narrowly so. Nor was his familiarity with previous American literature, except possibly the fiction of the recent naturalists, any more inclusive or perceptive than were his concern for and grasp of American life as a whole. Almost a half century earlier, James could both devote a discriminating book to Hawthorne's art and also build his own fiction in part on his predecessor's achievement; but except for an occasional and often superficial allusion Fitzgerald shows no familiarity with the major figures in his own native literary tradition. To be sure, in the mid-1920s he could discover no vital tradition in Europe either: Italy was a "dead land" where a few were deceived by "the spasmodic last jerk of a corpse," and the crowd around Pound in Paris were "mostly junk-dealers." Therefore, finding little in Europe worthy of his literary allegiance, yet convinced that the example of the American naturalists turned toward drabness and that Wolfe's "stuff about the GREAT VITAL HEART OF AMERICA is just simply corny," he apparently concluded that his purpose must continue to be that of his hero in *The Romantic Egotist*—to set down the story of his own American generation, with himself "in the middle as a sort of observer and conscious factor."[10]

Given his avowed concern to portray his own generation in America, the character of the society that both formed and confronted his contemporaries assumes a major significance as both agent and ethos in his fiction. In his own brooding way Fitzgerald throughout the 1920s apparently sought some quintessential national impulse or trait underlying American experience. America was not a "land" like France or a "people" like England, he wrote at the end of the decade; its distinction lay rather in its "having about it still that quality of the idea," and hence it "was harder to utter." To "utter" it Fitzgerald of course resorted to the fusion of the characters, plots, and symbols of his narratives, but no doubt the passage in his "Note-Books" (later expressed as the "discovery" of his expatriate hero in "The Swimmers") expresses his own view in 1929 that the surest index to the national character is to be found in "the graves at Shiloh and the tired, drawn, nervous faces of its great men, and the country boys dying in the Argonne for a phrase. . . . It was a willingness of the heart."[11] While this sensitive apostrophe, one realizes, might well serve as a description of the America that emerges, say, from Whitman's poems, it is scarcely that evoked by most of Fitzgerald's fiction. Perhaps one may assume that Fitzgerald's portrayal of the brittle and moneyed world implicitly constitutes a long lament over the loss of "that quality of the idea" in American life and thereby by indirection reinforces it; but where, except for Gatsby and Carraway, is the "willingness of the heart" as contagiously conveyed as the glamor and power of the rich?

In depicting the America of the 1920s and 1930s Fitzgerald indeed displayed his characteristic ambivalence. As America plunged into what he called "the greatest, gaudiest spree in history," he readily became a willing accomplice and participant. In the decade in which he saw the "whole race going hedonistic" in a great surge of emancipation, he confessed, it was "pleasant to be in one's twenties" and to observe the upper 10 percent living with the "insouciance of grand ducs [*sic*] and the casualness of chorus girls." Accordingly, he watched what he called "the death struggle of the old America" with mingled regret and acceptance. The old patriotism of a homogeneous race, as Amory Blaine reflected, was no longer easy amid the "stinking aliens"; the "old generosities and devotions" had to struggle in "the heart of the leaderless people"; indulging in the splendid privileges of wealth, vulgar and neurotic Americans wandered everywhere like "fantastic neanderthals." Yet if Fitzgerald's Americans were damned, they were also often beautiful, and in the "most opulent, most gorgeous land on earth," he fancied, Beauty may well have had her cyclical rebirth disguised as a "susciety gurl" or even been known during her fifteen-year sojourn as a "ragtime kid, a flapper, a jazz-baby, and a baby vamp." In the America of the 1920s "all those impersonal and beautiful things that only youth ever grasps" were abundantly present.[12]

Yet beyond the "quality of the idea" that Fitzgerald supposed American experience to have distinctively embodied, beyond that "willingness of the heart" that he revered but so rarely represented, lay the strong impress of two not always compatible regional cultures, those of the Old South and the old Midwest. Even in his boyhood stories he wrote of the Confederacy that his ancestors in Maryland had known, and later in a brief piece on his father's death he spoke of his "good heart that came from another America"—that of the old Southern aristocratic order before the corrosive materialism of the Gilded Age. No doubt there was much of Fitzgerald in Henry Marston, in "The Swimmers," a seventh-generation Virginian to whom the "mighty word [American] printed across the continent" meant less than the memory of his Confederate grandfather; and similarly in *Tender Is the Night* Fitzgerald reveals again his veneration for his Virginian heritage when Dick Diver in Paris, perceiving something of "the maturity of an older America" in the dignity of the Gold Star mothers, remembers sitting on his father's knee and listening to tales of the campaigns with Mosby. Later, returning to his father's funeral and hearing again "the lovely fatuous voices, the sound of sluggish primeval rivers flowing softly under soft Indian names," Dick said goodbye to all his ancestral fathers, whose souls he felt had been "made of new earth" in the seventeenth-century forests around Chesapeake Bay. Yet despite his nostalgia for the Old South, Fitzgerald in writing to his daughter in 1936 proclaimed himself a "northerner," and accordingly in such stories as "The Ice Palace," with its counterpoint of temperaments and attitudes of North and South, there is a sympathetic understanding rather than a glorification of the Southern mind and sensibility.[13]

By his term "northerner" Fitzgerald no doubt intended to include the complex of attitudes derived not only from his boyhood in St. Paul but also from his education in New Jersey and from his life in or near New York. Yet even within this northern stratum there was a marked dichotomy of values, which, as has been frequently noted, issued in the polar symbols of East and West. In responding to this dichotomy Fitzgerald was typically ambivalent. As a young undergraduate visiting New York, he thought of the "metropolitan spirit" as "essentially cynical and heartless," with the "warm center of the world out there" in the Middle West, where his "girl" lived; and indeed a decade later, though largely converted to urban life, he concluded that New York was not a self-contained universe but "faded out into the country on all sides into an expanse of green and blue that alone was limitless." Probably it is this expanse projected westward to which Fitzgerald alludes in his "Note-Books" as the "home of my heart" and from which all his imaginary brothers (Gatsby, Amory, Anthony, and Dick) are said to be far away. He has not yet had the courage, he confesses, to "put the old white light" on his home.[14]

To be sure, Nick Carraway, realizing that all of the major characters of *Gatsby* are Westerners, concludes that this "has been a story of the West, after all." But in returning to the West as an antidote to the brutality of the Eastern metropolis, he is conscious that his personal Midwest (a replica of Fitzgerald's) is no simple pastoral homeland of "prairies or . . . lost Swede towns" but a composite of the gaiety of Christmas and returning trains and the lighted windows of the Carraway house, "where dwellings are still called through decades by a family's name." If Carraway's West is comparatively a world of innocence, it is nevertheless a tainted Eden—the "snobbish West" to which Fitzgerald refers in "The Rich Boy" as the place where "money separates families to form 'sets.' " Actually, of course, the West of *Gatsby* had bred its own corrupt Codys and Buchanans and Jordans, and Nick felt no assurance that innocence might be reclaimed there. As for Fitzgerald, in the early 1920s he found St. Paul as "dull as hell" and longed for New York, the glittering white city, which, he "knew" by 1927, however often he "might leave it, was home."[15] Had there been a garden of lost innocence in the West, he would have been among the last to wish to live there.

III

However firmly or tenuously attached to real life in America as Fitzgerald knew it and liked it, the West and the East of his fiction increasingly assumed overtones respectively of the perennial human quest for the promises of life and of the reactionary disillusion that has consistently followed. Because his own experience was largely American, it was natural that he should trace the course of this disenchantment in an American donnée. Moreover, since the "fresh, green breast" of the New World had provided the last great spectacle commensurate with man's "capacity for wonder," as Nick said at the end of *Gatsby*, this world inevitably became the symbolic West to the European East, the theater for the acting out of the "last and greatest of all human dreams." Thus *Gatsby* is not so much a specific indictment of the American dream as a threnody to an archetypal human quest placed in an American setting. The Dutch sailors after all were not Americans or Jeffersonian democrats corrupted by an ingenuous faith in reason; their hopes for an "orgiastic future" were born in Europe.

Yet the frustration of their illusory hope for the realization of the "greatest of all human dreams" presages a similar fate not only for Gatsby but also for the last of Fitzgerald's dreamers, Monroe Stahr, who as a poor boy in the Bronx felt the pull of California and thus became a part of the ageless human story, which, the author observes in his notes for *The Last Tycoon*, is the "most beautiful history in the world. . . . It is the history of all aspiration—not just the American dream but the human dream and if I came at the end of it that too is a place in the line of pioneers." If the culmination of the "beautiful history" was likely to be a disillusioned return to the East, or, as he wrote in his "Note-Books," if the "end of the adventure which had started westward three hundred years ago" resembled the "pilgrimage eastward" of the "rare poisonous flower of his race" or "the long serpent of the curiosity" turning too sharply on itself and "bursting its shining skin, at least there had been a journey. . . . The frontiers were gone—there were no more barbarians. The short gallop of the last great race . . . had gone—at least it was not a meaningless extinction up an alley."[16]

Fitzgerald thus envisaged all human experience, at least in the American-European world, as an endless counterpoint of westward thrust and eastward recoil. Such, it may be said, was his ultimate cultural perspective, his archetypal plot. Though he once supposed that "When Whitman said 'O Pioneers', he said all," his own concern was rather with the "pilgrimage eastward." Hence his letter to his daughter in 1937, wherein he not only warned her specifically against "accepting the standards of the cosmopolitan rich" but also, by way of larger cultural context, added that "if there is any more disastrous road than that from Park Avenue to the Rue de la Paix and back again, I don't know it." Accordingly his dreamers go eastward and perish (Gatsby), or capitulate (Diver), or return to the West (Carraway, Diver). Cities and nations seemed to him also to undergo the cyclical transmutations of westward inception and eastward recoil. In twenty-five years, he predicted in 1921, New York will be as London is now. "We will be the Romans in the next generations."[17]

For the embodiment of this age-old pattern of the sober fate of human aspiration, Fitzgerald utilized his own experience in America and Western Europe. "America's greatest promise is that something is going to happen," he wrote just after the appearance of *Gatsby*, "and after a while you get tired of waiting because nothing happens to people except that they grow old, and nothing happens to American art because America is the story of the moon that never rose." That the moon had not risen for his contemporaries, he thought in 1924, was due to the dullness and obtuseness of the previous generation. It was they, as it were, who had permitted a devastating war or had obsessively acquired diamonds as big as the Ritz and thereby set the atmosphere of corruption whereby the young Jim Gatzes, aspiring for the stars, were transformed into Jay Gatsbys deluded by a "vast, vulgar, and meretricious beauty." His younger contemporaries, Fitzgerald observed at the time of *Gatsby*, were therefore "brave, shallow, cynical, impatient, turbulent, and empty"—the issue of an "America . . . so decadent that its brilliant children are damned almost before they are born." The extent of his concern over this decadence is suggested by his turning toward Marx in the early thirties and by his early plan, according to his notes for the plot of *Tender Is the Night*, to have Dick Diver save his son by sending him to Russia for his education. Indeed, for the past two years, he confessed in 1934, he had "gone half haywire trying to reconcile my double allegiance to the class I am part of, and the Great Change I believe in."[18] That he scarcely effected the reconciliation is clear from *The Crack-up* and *The Last Tycoon*.

If the young men of his generation seemed to Fitzgerald to bear the stamp of a corrupting milieu, even in a greater measure did his fictional women. At least his men could maintain an allegiance to large aspirations, as did Gatsby, Carraway, Diver, and Stahr; but their feminine counterparts compromised and destroyed. The nature of their failure in Fitzgerald's mind is suggested by a line from Shakespeare's sonnets that he quoted on several occasions and that he commended to his young daughter in 1933: "Lilies that fester smell far worse than weeds." The American girl in Fitzgerald's fiction, indeed, has ceased to play the redemptive or heroic role that she played in James's narratives; there are no Isabel Archers or Milly Theales, no Maggie Ververs or even Daisy Millers; Fitzgerald's women are no longer James's "heiresses of all the ages," no longer the vehicles of civilized sensibility in American life as the earlier novelist often conceived them to be. Unlike James's women, Fitzgerald's rarely have either disinterested awareness or acute intelligence; for the most part their aspirations do not transcend the pattern of Gloria Gilbert's in *The Beautiful and Damned*: to be young and beautiful, gay and happy a long time. As the description of Nicole makes clear, though the American girl could still be portrayed as an heiress, she had become a pampered one whose inheritance was not of the culture "of all the ages" but of wealth, parental irresponsibility, and technological progress. Like Nicole, she was the culminating "product of much ingenuity and toil," served by workers in "chickle factories" and on plantations, on trains and in five-and-tens. For all her beauty and grace, as the inevitable consequence of a "whole system" she contained "in herself her own doom."[19]

Until *The Last Tycoon* Fitzgerald's disenchantment with the American girl as a self-centered and destructive agent was frequent if not continuous. Much of his portrayal of the feminine role no doubt derived from his life with Zelda, however abiding his loyalty to and consideration for her may have been. His own youthful "great dream," he wrote his daughter, had grown until he had "learned how to speak of it and make people listen"; but Zelda had wanted him to work "too much for *her*" and not enough for the dream. Hence, though for a time he took pride in his early stories wherein, he supposed, he had "created a new type of American girl," he soon was so repelled by the "preposterous, pushing women and girls" whom he saw in Paris that he confessed that if he had had "anything to do with creating the manners of the contemporary American girl," he had "made a botch of the job." But the flaw, he later felt, lay deeper than manners. Park Avenue girls, he admonished his daughter, were the offspring of a type of "Yankee push," with a hardness that was only a feminine "sublimation" of the "peddler's morals" of Jay Gould. As early as *The Beautiful and Damned* he had surmised that this "most gorgeous land on earth" was a matriarchy "where ugly women control strong men." The culmination of the type, perhaps, was Baby Warren—"the American Woman . . . the clean-sweeping irrational temper that had broken the moral back of a race and made a nursery out of a continent."[20]

Within this substantial and cumulative indictment, however, something of the usual ambivalence remained, for in his mid-career Fitzgerald used a young American girl as the redemptive character in his most memorable apostrophe to what he called the "quality of the [American] idea." When the tired expatriate Virginian of "The Swimmers" first sees the young American girl on the French seashore, he is entranced by her grace and beauty and independence; and yet he wonders if "the male is not being sacrificed" to this "perfect type" from his homeland as in former times the English lower strata were sacrificed for a governing class. Although she is not an intellectual and cannot formulate the reasons for her own delight and skill in swimming, Henry (already betrayed by his French wife) relates it to a sub-conscious love of cleanness, which in turn he analogizes with the essential heart of his country. Repossessing his masculine self through her presence, he returns to America, where he continues to swim almost as a symbolic act, moving in "a child's dream of space" and fancying himself "setting off along the bright pathway to the moon." Americans need "fins and wings," he mused, in their dream of escaping the past. After a second betrayal by his wife he sails for Europe with a new "gratitude . . . that America was there" and a conviction that, though now leaderless and mercenary, his country is not a "bizarre accident."

Perhaps the central image of America as the "clean" venture toward the future and the explicit comment at the end of the story on the "willingness of the heart" as the supreme quality of the American idea are not wholly reconciled and fused; but plot, character, and symbol are sufficiently consistent to form a compelling affirmation, to be echoed a decade later in *The Last Tycoon*, that the authentic American dream is historically and essentially not an obsession with a diamond as big as the Ritz but a compassionate society founded on the "old generosities and devotions." The tragedies of Gatsby and Diver therefore bespeak neither the collapse nor the punitive culmination of the American dream, but rather its betrayal by the non-dreamers. "The best of America was the best of the world."[21]

For two decades Fitzgerald's imagination responded to the color and energy of American life and especially to the omnipresent wonder and aspiration that he both felt and observed.

As a consequence in part of his own mixed heritage—Southern, Midwestern, urban, Catholic, Irish—the impulse of the affective moment rather than the demands of the ideological or cultural pattern shaped his narratives. All authors, he remarked, retell under different guises the two or three great and moving experiences of their lives; moreover, in his own writing he was obliged to "start out with an emotion—one that's close to me and that I can understand." Even in revision, he admonished himself while working on *The Last Tycoon*, he must "rewrite from mood."[22] Sensitized by his own central and romantic involvement in the "promise of happiness," he therefore wrote with affective authority on the inception and decay of these promises in the individual and collective life of America and, by implication, in the world at large.

From year to year as his own experiences and moods varied, he shifted accordingly his record and assessment of human aspirations and defeats. Hence the ambivalence of his attitudes: Was the Midwest dull or redemptive? Was the South the norm of civilization or decadence? Was the basis of humane values urban or agrarian? Did money liberate or corrupt? Was the American dream disastrous illusion or unexpendable center in the national life? Was the American girl incarnate Platonic beauty or Eve in the New Eden? To those and similar questions raised by his fiction Fitzgerald offers chiefly ambivalent and at times paradoxical clues. As for the American dream, he seems to cherish it as the indispensable root of a living culture whose flower will always be blighted. The disillusion, the vulgarization, the exploitation are inevitable; but better these than the sterile and corrupt despair of its absence.

Notes

1. *The Crack-up*, ed. Edmund Wilson (New York, 1945), p. 176.
2. A. Mizener, in *F. Scott Fitzgerald*, ed. A. Kazin (New York, 1951), pp. 23, 43; P. Rosenfeld in *ibid.*, pp. 75–76; *The Crack-up*, p. 79.
3. W. Barrett, in *Partisan Review* 18 (May–June 1951): 347; *The Crack-up*, pp. 23, 176, 178.
4. *The Crack-up*, p. 95; an almost exact quotation from John Keats, *Letters*, ed. H. E. Rollins (Cambridge, Mass., 1958), I, 184, 185.

5. Fitzgerald, *Letters*, ed. A. Turnbull (New York, 1963), p. 470.

6. Fitzgerald, *Letters*, pp. 32, 462; *The Crack-up*, pp. 89–90.

7. H. D. Piper, *F. Scott Fitzgerald: A Critical Portrait* (New York, 1965), p. 84; Fitzgerald, *Letters*, p. 12.

8. *The Crack-up*, p. 179; *Letters*, p. 191; *This Side of Paradise* (London, 1960), p. 111.

9. "How to Waste Material," *Afternoon of an Author*, ed. A. Mizener (Princeton, 1957), pp. 118–19; Piper, *Fitzgerald: A Critical Portrait*, p. 135; Fitzgerald, *Letters*, pp. 151, 179, 185–87, 190, 191, 459; *The Crack-up*, p. 190.

10. Fitzgerald, *Letters*, pp. 97–98, 479, 486; see Sergio Perosa, *The Art of F. Scott Fitzgerald*, trans. Charles Matz and Perosa (Ann Arbor, Mich., 1965), p. 18.

11. *The Crack-up*, p. 197.

12. *The Crack-up*, p. 87; *The Fitzgerald Reader*, ed. A. Mizener (New York, 1963), pp. 326, 330, 331; *This Side of Paradise*, p. 149; "The Swimmers," *Saturday Evening Post* 202 (October 19, 1929): 154; *The Beautiful and Damned* (London, 1961), pp. 33–34, 154.

13. See *The Apprentice Fiction of F. Scott Fitzgerald*, ed. John Kuehl (New Brunswick, N. J., 1965), pp. 34–35, 67, 68; "The Swimmers," p. 13; *Tender Is the Night* (London, 1960), pp. 177, 290; Fitzgerald, *Letters*, p. 12.

14. *The Crack-up*, pp. 24, 32, 176; *cf*. Robert Ornstein, "Scott Fitzgerald's Fable of East and West," *College English* 7 (December 1956): 139 ff.

15. *The Great Gatsby* (London, 1958), p. 265; "The Rich Boy," *Bodley Head Fitzgerald* (London, 1963), V, 288; *The Crack-up*, pp. 30–31, 256.

16. See Piper, p. 269; *The Crack-up*, p. 199.

17. *The Crack-up*, pp. 178, 288; Fitzgerald, *Letters*, p. 326.

18. Fitzgerald, *Letters*, pp. 417, 488, 489; *The Great Gatsby*, p. 202; Piper, p. 176; A. Mizener, *The Far Side of Paradise* (New York, 1951), p. 309.

19. *The Beautiful and Damned*, p. 244; *Tender Is the Night*, pp. 127–28; see Edwin Fussell, "Fitzgerald's Brave New World," *Journal of English Literary History* 19 (December 1952): 295–301.

20. Fitzgerald, *Letters*, pp. 12, 32; *The Crack-up*, p. 271; *The Beautiful and Damned*, p. 33; *Tender Is the Night*, p. 320.

21. "The Swimmers," pp. 13, 150, 154; *The Crack-up*, pp. 108, 109.

22. Fitzgerald, *Afternoon of an Author*, pp. 132, 133; see also John Kuehl, in *Modern Fiction Studies* 7 (Spring 1961): 6.

HART CRANE:
AMERICA AS CATHAY

IN ANY EXPLORATION of major twentieth-century American authors who have expressed their views of nationality not only through explicit comment but also in fictional or poetic works, Hart Crane must be accorded a distinctive place. The cumulative scholarship on Crane that began with Phillip Horton and Brom Weber has issued in many discerning studies, and in recent years two learned and meticulous apologies by R. W. B. Lewis and Sherman Paul have persuasively asserted the integrity of his vision and the rich coherence of his poetry. Their general conclusion on Crane's position as a major American poet of this century is assumed in this essay, which will attempt rather to assess him as a "national poet," that is, to describe his extrapoetic as well as his poetic version of his native land, to examine the formation of his sensibility and poetic principles, to trace the vicissitudes of his national attitudes in the last ten years of his life, and, with especial attention to his visionary literary ancestor, Whitman, to consider the distinctive national configuration of his poetry.

If readers of Crane have expected national emphases in his work, it is surely in part due to the poet's reiterated statements of his lofty expectations and epical intentions between 1923 and 1930. When he first conceived *The Bridge*, he enthusiastically wrote his friend Gorham Munson in February 1923 that it would be a "mystical synthesis of 'America'," and that the bridge itself would be a symbol of "our constructive future" and our "unique identity" including "also our scientific hopes."[1] Although in July his "head [was] simply bursting with the 'Bridge' poem," by

160

August, as he wrote both Alfred Stieglitz and his mother, his mind had become "like dough, and *The Bridge* is far away."[2]

In December 1925, having made little progress on his poem for nearly three impoverished years and having heard of the philanthropist Otto Kahn's interest in "the creation of an indigenous American poetry," Crane informed him of his stalled attempt to "enunciate a new cultural synthesis of values in terms of our America."[3] Kahn responded, as Crane wrote his mother, by giving him $2,000 for a year's living expenses to write the "most creative message I have to give."[4] After two further years, in a long letter to Kahn the poet reviewed the completed sections and explained that in the five poems of Part II ("Powhatan's Daughter") he was "really handling . . . the Myth of America" from aboriginal days to the present. Yet in outlining the range and scheme of *The Bridge* as a whole at the end of the letter, he explains that he is "really writing an epic of the modern consciousness." And as if to counter any charges of procrastination and to stress the epic implications of his poem, he compared its "historical and cultural scope" to that of *The Aeneid*—a work, he reminded Kahn, that had required more than five years to write![5]

Although Crane in his early years was occasionally impelled toward expatriation by what he regarded as the philistine vulgarity of American society, he later viewed foreign residence as being chiefly valuable for affording in brief intervals sharpened perspectives on the character of his country. In his 1927 letter to Kahn (p. 309) he declared that the "foreign-ness" of the Isle of Pines (near Cuba) had "stimulated" him "to the realization of natively American materials and viewpoints" that he had not previously "suspected." Three years later he based his application for a Guggenheim Fellowship in part on his desire to study "European culture . . . with especial reference to contrasting elements implicit in the emergent features of a distinctive American poetic consciousness."[6] Though he actually utilized his Guggenheim award for a final year in Mexico, his concern for indigenous expression persisted. He was, he said, "too attached to the consciousness of his own land to write 'tourist sketches' elsewhere," and, though Mexico was "well enough," he would rather be in his "favorite corner of Connecticut."

Moreover, contemporary Mexican poets held little interest for him, he wrote Waldo Frank, because they were not "really interested one iota in expressing anything indigenous" but preferred to ape Valéry and Eliot.[7]

What, then, in the light of Crane's large aspirations and apparent devotion to the indigenous, were the formative forces and resultant attitudes that culminated in his epical venture in *The Bridge*? The purpose of this essay is to provide one view of this complex issue by exploring first his explicit view of America as expressed primarily in his letters but also reflected in his short poems; second, the literary influences that shaped his sensibility; third, his literary principles; fourth, the imagistic thrust of his poetry; fifth, the visionary example of Whitman; and finally, *The Bridge* as a national poem.

I

The America of which Crane writes in his letters and criticism is viewed as in decline from its nineteenth-century glory and from the idealism and integrity of its founders, colonial and Revolutionary. For the young poet much of its contemporary vulgarity was focused in cities like Akron and Cleveland, in which or near which he spent most of his first twenty years. With a cultural bias nurtured by fin-de-siècle, romantic, and symbolist poets, he pronounced Pound to be "right" in deploring the plight of "the helpless few in my country, O remnant enslaved"—of those who could not wear themselves out "by persisting to successes."[8] Yet Crane recognized that as an aspiring poet he would have to make some compromise with those who, like his father, had "succeeded." Working temporarily in his father's candy store in Akron in 1919, when he was 20, he stated in a newspaper interview that a compatible relationship with the business world could exist if a writer or artist would for a time recognize the dominance of that world and work within it without becoming subservient to it. The writer, he conceded, would thus become a split person, ostensibly serving Mammon, so to speak, but really worshiping the Muses.[9]

The vulgarity and essential rapaciousness of that world, how-

ever, Crane continued to deplore. Repelled by the character of
Cleveland's celebration of its 125th anniversary in July 1921, he
wrote to Munson of his "disgust at America and everything in
it. . . . No place but America could relish and applaud anything
so stupid and drab as that parade. . . . Our people have no *atom*
of a conception of beauty—and don't want it."[10] For a while in
1921–22 he found in Cleveland enough congenial artistic and
literary friends, such as William Sommer and Ernest Bloch, to
feel relatively happy there; but the city's "smug atmosphere"
and its indifference to its gifted artists like Sommer and the
lithographer Ernest Nelson continued to depress him. The latter's death in 1922 moved him to compose a sardonic commem-
orative tribute, "Praise for an Urn," and also led him to
characterize his friend as "one of many broken against the stupidity of American life in such places as here. . . ." In a similar
vein a few weeks earlier he had written Allen Tate that the work
of E. A. Robinson was both permanent and tragic—"one of the
tragedies of Puritanism, materialism, America, and the last century."[11]

By Easter of 1923 Crane had fled Cleveland's philistinism
and returned to New York, where, stimulated by his association
with such friends as Eugene O'Neill, Waldo Frank, Stieglitz,
and Charlie Chaplin, and confident that he, too, was "making
a real contribution to American literature," he resisted his
father's appeal that he return to Ohio because, as he said, his
art would be stifled and he had "a terrible fear" of his reaction
to the city after "a month or so."[12] His persistent contempt for
Cleveland's cultural provincialism is reflected in his description
of his own family's library as mostly "atrocities" of interest to
the "rural minded."[13] It is therefore not surprising that after the
publication of his *White Buildings* (1926) he prophesied that
among his Cleveland friends and relatives it would be "farther
from their grasp than the farthest planets." Soon thereafter he
"rocked with laughter" when he learned that a Cleveland lady
proposed to read poems from the volume to a women's club,
convinced as he was that the "poor dears" wouldn't know what
to make of it.[14]

Although Crane at twenty conceded Akron and Cleveland
to be less vulgar than Greenwich Village, the vitality of the New

York literary milieu as well as family problems in Ohio dictated his return to that city for much of the rest of his life.[15] It is "really a stupendous place," he wrote in 1923, and "the center of the world today," as Alexandria had been in ancient Egypt. In his letters to his family he spoke of its spirit of "cordiality and abandon," of its "sparkling simplicity," of its stylish people in their "bright clothes," of its lively social life, and of his exciting association with major literary figures.[16] Yet over the beauty of the upper sections of the city he preferred "as a steady thing," he said, "the wonderful streets of this lower section crowded with life, packed with movement and drama . . . ," and his room at the end of the Brooklyn bridge seemed to him to provide the "finest view in all America."[17]

Despite its bright sophistication and color, however, New York scarcely afforded Crane stable or durable satisfactions. With minimal financial resources and prosaic assignments in advertising companies, he complained that he had little inspiration for writing poetry. The New York summer, with its noise and frenetic pace and the "insidious impurity in the air," he wrote his family, drove people to the limit of endurance.[18] Though he sought even in 1923 to escape to the isolation of the family house on the Isle of Pines he was obliged to limit his respites in the mid-1920s to veering back and forth between the city and the homes of friends in Patterson or Woodstock, New York. If the city was a virtually uninhabitable milieu for him in summer, the rural retreats soon became a "kind of shell" that the Slater Browns and the Allen Tates seemed to "have retired into lately"—a shell in which he felt it impossible to effect the "actual fleshing of a concept." To be sure, he experienced a reinvigoration from the wholesome food and outdoor activities, and his pastoral inclinations found satisfaction in the Patterson countryside and especially in the "profusion of wildflowers"; but by 1927 such beauty and solitude could no longer compensate the lack of urban diversion and stimulus. He was, he admitted in 1926, a "rum-scallion" who "never planned to stay put anywhere very long in the woods."[19]

Crane's shift to New York and events of the later 1920s, therefore, wrought no substantial change in his view that as a poet he was a victim of a vulgar and insensitive society. Radio, crossword puzzles, and "other such body-rattles for the American public" seemed to him to have "cut so badly into book sales" that the publishing of "good poetry" had become a great risk. Two more years of monotonous work at Sweet's Catalogue Service, he prophesied, "will kill my imagination." Noting the widespread European influence of O'Neill and Frank, he lamented that in contrast the "American public is still strangely unprepared for its men of higher talents." Moreover, his own experience in New York convinced him that the situation for such "higher talents" was "getting harder and harder," since the earning of a decent living left them too little time for their "real work."[20] Hence by the mid-1920s Crane could not so confidently reiterate his earlier belief that in "fifty years or so" in an increasingly standardized world "the American scene will be the most intricate and absorbing one" and that he and such New York associates as Munson and Matthew Josephson were forming a "kind of aristocracy of taste."[21] New York, after all, had evidently proved to be scarcely different from Cleveland.

The generally disparaging assessment of American culture and institutions that appears in Crane's letters frequently has explicit or implicit reflection in his early poems. Smoke-ridden "Akron, 'high place,' " is a far cry from the Acropolis, he implied in "Porphyro in Akron"; but its Greek workers have fortunately retained their Old World memories and native pride as well as a cultural cohesiveness that he feared they might lose if they became "Americans / Using the latest ice-box and buying Fords." Although scarcely a reverential medieval lover, he considers himself a Porphyro in a city whose "stars are drowned in a slow rain" and whose "axles need not the oil of song." Here a Keatsian poet like himself, he sighed, could only "whisper words" to himself, "pitch quoits," and "try to sleep." In another expression of resignation to the indifference of a materialistic society, "Black Tambourine," Crane as a white poet identified himself with a black man—actually a porter in the cellar storeroom of one of his father's Cleveland restaurants where he also worked.[22] Both poet and porter were, so to speak, "underground men," unable to get beyond "the world's closed door," and hence they wandered in "some mid-kingdom dark" between man and beast where their "tambourines" were "stuck on the wall."

Although Crane occasionally made a frontal attack on American behavior, as he did in his Cummings parody "America's Plutonic Ecstasies," wherein he scoffed at the national penchant for preferring laxatives to wine and righteousness to Dionysian celebration, his social criticism inclined toward the oblique and ironic strictures of "Chaplinesque." His tribute to Chaplin after seeing *The Kid* is one of his deftest prescriptions for evading "the doom of that inevitable thumb" of power and oppressive authority, economic or otherwise. Chaplin's distinctive comic art as the unnoticed little man allowed Crane to give an American focus to Laforgue's figure of Pierrot who, as clown or fool, could provide the poet a role whereby he, too, might "dally" his "doom." In the poem the "famished kitten" rescued from "the fury of the street" is aligned implicitly with the American poet, who is also all but overwhelmed by an indifferent and busy world of trade. For kitten and poet salvation lies in an obscure humane community in which the moon in "lonely alleys" can "make / A grail of laughter of an empty ash can."

A more substantial and affirmative projection of the two worlds, however, came in Crane's first major poem, "For the Marriage of Faustus and Helen," in which the latter stands for "an abstract sense of beauty," as he wrote to Frank, and the former is a "symbol of myself, the poetic or imaginative man of all times."[23] In "General Aims and Theories" Crane said that he was trying to build a bridge between classic experience or the Grecian attitude toward beauty and the divergent realities of our "confused cosmos of today."[24] Presenting in the first section the philistine money-centered world of the stock market with its "smutty . . . equivocations," Crane also suggests the humane impulse to escape from it toward somewhere "Virginal, perhaps, less fragmentary, cool." The Faustian persona of the poem, observing in a street car the beauty of an office girl whose hands are "Stippled with pink and green advertisements," envisions her as an American Helen whose love he may share in a "white" (or transformed) city beyond the "million brittle, bloodshot eyes" that pervade contemporary skyscrapers. The second section, however, does not further the realization of the persona's vision but rather, as Crane explained in "General Aims and Theories," reflects Helen of Troy's seduction and the Dionysian revels of her court. Crane's parallel is set in a Metropolitan roof garden where indigenous jazz rhythms express a primitive eroticism that Crane apparently assumes, as R. W. B. Lewis believes, will exorcise the guilt of a fallen world and prepare for a higher spiritual music.[25]

The third complex section, in which Helen is abandoned, identifies the suffering and destruction of World War I with the "*katharsis* of the fall of Troy," though in fact a victorious America emerging from that war as a world power would seem to have little in common with the permanent destruction of Troy. Through the "religious gunman," whose varied aerial maneuvers are impressively projected, Crane accepts, as he wrote Frank, a Dionysian view of experience—the inevitable bond of destruction and creation. Or, as he described the third section in a letter to Munson, it comprised "Tragedy, War (the eternal soldier), Résumé, Ecstasy, Final Declaration."[26] Thus the section ends with praise for the "lavish heart," which will "atone / The abating shadows of our conscript dust," and for those founders of new cultures such as Anchises and Erasmus. The final Dionysian exhortation is to "Delve upward for the new and scattered wine" because the "imagination spans beyond despair." Perhaps Crane implies that the vision of Helen's "gold hair" persists despite war's destruction. In this secular and esthetic faith in the redemptive power of Beauty married to the poetic imagination Crane avowedly gave his New World answer to what he considered the retrospective despair of *The Waste Land*.[27]

The poem that envisioned an American marriage of Faustus and Helen may be regarded as a kind of halfway mark in Crane's productive poetic life. It both synthesized poetic modes and cultural attitudes that he had cumulatively refined in recent years and pointed to an enlarged national context that was for seven years to occupy his attention as he erratically struggled to complete *The Bridge*. Whereas his earlier poetry at times dealt with the threats of corporate America to "Beauty," as did the first part of "Faustus and Helen," he declared that the affirmation of "certain things" was the "persisting theme of the last part of 'F and H.' "[28] That theme, with its linking of creation and destruction, implied that the technological and commercial dominance that he had so often deplored might, like war, be sublimated into a richer cultural life for the nation. Though ultimately visionary the affirmation also recognized the interdependence of the quotidian and the transcendent. "I am concerned with the future of America," Crane declared in 1925, "because I feel persuaded that here are destined to be discovered certain as yet undefined spiritual quantities. . . . And in this process I like to feel myself as a potential factor."[29] The prolonged effort with the structure and substance of *The Bridge* is in part a reflection of the vicissitudes of his affirmative expectations. What, then, were the literary and personal influences that molded and modulated the changes in his poetic utterance so far as its national implications are involved?

II

Crane's "education" was apparently almost wholly "literary," and in achieving it he was his own persistently involved mentor. He read little history per se, and, if one may judge by his letters and poems, he had no interest in politics in either the narrow or the wider Aristotelian sense. The dreary weeks he spent in Washington in late 1920 as a representative of his father's candy business reflect no curiosity about Washington or Jefferson, no pilgrimages to Mount Vernon or Monticello. As for his command of foreign languages, the level of his competence has not been definitively established, although at times he uses them impressively in translations or epigraphs. Declining parental advice to pursue linguistic studies at Columbia, he had some tutoring in French and he rather freely translated some of Laforgue. But he read literature and criticism avidly in his late teens and before twenty discerningly wrote confident evaluations of recent works for the little magazines. In his earlier poems the changes in style and focus reflect the literary "masters" by whom he was successively influenced.

In his youthful years it is natural that he should have been attracted to modish contemporaries, to such fin de siècle favorites as Algernon Charles Swinburne and Oscar Wilde with, respectively, their world-weariness and sophisticated aspersions on bourgeois values and behavior. But even at nineteen he had already concluded that Swinburne had never "possessed much beyond his 'art ears,' although these were long . . . adequate to all his beautiful, though often meaningless mouthings." As for Wilde: "After his bundle of paradoxes has been sorted and conned,—very little evidence of intellect remains."[30] Recent French authors (Rimbaud, Laforgue, Valéry, and Baudelaire) took a firmer hold. As a participant in the postwar vogue of Laforgue, Crane became "mad about him," made free translations of three of his Pierrot poems, and also reflected his influence in his own "Chaplinesque." The influence of Rimbaud is not so readily definable, but Crane procured his poems from Paris along with Laforgue's in 1920 and earned from Carl Sandburg the designation of the "Cleveland Rimbaud." Simultaneously he was reading Baudelaire's *Fleurs du Mal*, and he later praised him with Joyce for evincing a "penetration into life common only to the greatest."[31] Clearly so long as Crane was dominated by such Symbolist influences, he would have no interest in writing an indigenous American poetry or an American epic related to our "constructive future."

From the British Isles the two strongest influences were Joyce and Eliot. Defending Joyce against charges of "immorality and obscenity" in 1918, Crane proclaimed Stephen Dedalus "too good for this world" and *A Portrait of the Artist as a Young Man* to be "Bunyan raised to Art" and "aside from Dante . . . spiritually the most inspiring book I have ever read." Although Crane smuggled early copies of *Ulysses* into America, he linked that work with *The Waste Land* as an expression of "renunciation" lacking the vision that America and the whole world needed.[32] Although he deplored Eliot's pessimism and, in a letter to Munson early in 1923, admitted differences in outlook and temper, he declared that his own recent work had been influenced more by the expatriate poet than by "any other modern." Crane's hope was that he could apply as much as possible of Eliot's erudition and technique "toward a more . . . ecstatic goal."[33]

Among other foreign contemporaries the influences were less sustained. The Padraic Colums, as he wrote his family, during his first stay in New York introduced him to Irish literature and the French Symbolists; and his French tutor enriched his knowledge of the "aristocratic and literary side of Parisian life."[34] By

1920 he had consciously turned to Pound, Eliot, and the minor Elizabethans "for values," and though he does not seem to have been markedly impressed by Shakespeare's major plays, he did find *The Tempest* to be the "crown of all the Western World."[35] Keats and Blake, of course, had a major impact, which is often reflected in his poetry and his allusions. Thus most of the authors for whom he felt a special affinity through his early twenties (before Pound's *Cantos*) impelled him toward a romantic or visionary poetry as yet unrelated to an American myth or epic and, indeed, intensified his hostility to a national milieu that would not easily tolerate a Keatsian Porphyro. Furthermore, his transcendental predilections were so much enhanced by his "reading of the philosophers of the East" that, as he wrote to Malcolm Cowley in March of 1926, "I actually dream in terms of the Vedantic scriptures." As a result, as L. S. Dembo has shown in *Hart Crane's Sanskrit Charge*, not only did Crane infuse his Vedantic reading into *The Bridge* but he also concluded that even his "Falcon-Ace" in the "Cape Hatteras" section must be given a "Sanskrit charge / To conjugate infinity's dim marge— / Anew!"[36]

Countering these generally antinational influences, however, were Crane's admiration for, and affinities with, indigenous American writers and artists. But early enthusiasms sometimes faded, for example, that for Maxwell Bodenheim's imagist poems, which their author composed on the assumption that "true poetry is . . . unconnected with human beliefs or fundamental human feelings"—a "definition" that in 1919 Crane judged "inordinately precious."[37]

This suspicion of the "precious" is reflected later in the same year in his newspaper interview in Akron when he declared that the American poet or artist who would not lose "the essential, imminent vitality of his vision" must know the commercial world about him. Among the writers who had absorbed their environment and were providing for the growth of a "national culture" he included Sandburg, Theodore Dreiser, Edgar Lee Masters, and Sherwood Anderson. Such indigenous inclinations on Crane's part were further strengthened by his close association with the Ohio painter and mystic, William Sommer, whose view of art as a celebration of life Crane reflects in the poem "Sunday

Morning Apples." He was also drawn to Sommer's view that form arises out of objects, and in later discussion with Josephson he declared that he believed with Sommer that the " 'Ding an Sich' method is ultimately the only satisfactory principle to follow."[38] In such a view lies the implication that native objects or situations expressed through organic form can effect mature aesthetic responses, but Crane's later "logic of metaphor" suggests he lost interest in Sommer's principle. In later years and especially in 1923 Crane drew similar sustenance from his association with Alfred Stieglitz, whose ability to suggest in his photography "an inherent order behind the superficial disorder of represented objects" he found congenial. They shared, as Crane wrote to Stieglitz, "common devotions, in a kind of timeless vision."[39] This visionary quality Crane perceived in the work of the photographer, who in turn read the poems with admiration.

More directly relevant on the literary plane, however, was the influence and example of Sherwood Anderson. Reviewing *Winesburg, Ohio* in 1919, Crane described its achievement as an expression of the author's self, of humanity, of a period in the "Middle West," and of "art." "America should read this book on her knees," he said, for "It constitutes an important chapter in the Bible of her consciousness." Two years later in a further assessment of Anderson's art, including *Poor White*, he emphasized the novelist's distinctive treatment of the "inscrutable soil"—"a contact with animal and earthy life," which forms "a very foundation" of his stories. Anderson's love and sensuous comprehension of Ohio hills and barns, he declared, has lent a lyricism to his style and has afforded a vivid contrast to the "mechanical distortions of humanity" in urban life.[40] Yet Crane was not a ready convert to Anderson as a complete artist despite the latter's "sincerity." As he wrote Munson in late 1919, he was torn between the hard, classic quality of Josephson and the "crowd-bound" Anderson, "with a smell of the sod about him, uncouth. Somewhere between them is Hart Crane with a kind of wistful indetermination, still much puzzled."[41]

In listing for his friend William Wright in 1921 those poets of the past most worthy of attention Crane said that he ran "joyfully toward Messrs. Poe, Whitman, Shakespeare, Keats,

Shelley, Coleridge, John Donne!!!, John Webster!!!, Marlowe, Baudelaire, Laforgue, Dante, Cavalcanti, Li Po, and a host of others."[42] One may suspect that the last two names were gestures toward Pound, as were Dante, Laforgue, Webster, and Donne toward Eliot. Indeed Crane seems not to have read much of Dante until the late 1920s, and Cavalcanti and Li Po seem to have left no impact on his style or imagery. *As poets* Melville and Emerson—whom he mentions only once (p. 73) in his *Letters* as "Poor dear Emerson"—seem to have been less influential than Emily Dickinson, whom he refers to in the *Letters* (p. 324) as, like Blake, being in an age of Relativity "more incontrovertible than ever." She appears as the singer of Eternity in a sonnet honoring her and in the epigraph to "Quaker Hill" because of her "mapled vistas" through which the old American dream may be glimpsed. Yet how pervasive the Emersonian transcendental temper and how inescapable Melville's treatment of the sea were has been convincingly shown in R. W. B. Lewis's *The Poetry of Hart Crane.* Certainly *Moby Dick,* which Crane read at least four times, was an integral part of his imagination when he wrote "At Melville's Tomb" and *The Bridge.* (Whitman's inclusive impact, especially through "Passage to India," will be given especial attention in a later section.)

Had the direction of Crane's poetry after 1923 been fixed wholly by foreign or even many cisatlantic authors and literary modes surveyed in the preceding paragraphs, it is doubtful if the composition of *The Bridge* would have ever been undertaken. The crucial tilting toward an exaltation of the American heritage and the nation's potential future was essentially furnished by a few journalists and aspiring authors clustered in postwar New York. When Crane left Cleveland in early 1919, his immediate interests were focused on writing for advertising and other remunerative assignments. He acknowledged to his friend George Bryan that it is "a long way from poetry to scenario writing," and that if he should not be successful with scenarios, he would enter the "advertising game" where there is "a lot of money . . . for the man who can write good adds [*sic*]."[43] Yet his poetic aspirations soon drew him to such writers as Bodenheim, Munson, and Josephson, and *The Little Review* group.[44] He also gradually became acquainted with Waldo Frank, Van

Wyck Brooks, and Paul Rosenfeld, who were voicing through *The Seven Arts* their concern for a "usable past" as a basis for an American cultural and literary renaissance.

By 1922 he thought of himself as a part of a new establishment, an incipient "aristocracy of taste." His conclusion that Josephson was doing better work before he "got in touch with the Paris crowd" suggests that his occasional temptations to become an expatriate were being dispelled by a new faith in his country's cultural rejuvenation. Yet the homogeneous and unified literary community that he had envisioned scarcely emerged during the years ahead. Rifts appeared on such issues as the compatibility of a pervasive technology and a mature, humane culture and on the degree of aesthetic purity appropriate to a national poetry. By 1926 Crane and his friend Munson had serious "theoretical differences . . . on the function of poetry" and, also stung by Munson's picture of him as "waiting for another ecstasy," Crane in turn wrote scoffingly to Yvor Winters of Munson and other friends going through "all sorts of Hindu antics."[45]

Among the varying impacts of Crane's New York associates on the direction and character of his poetry, that of Waldo Frank was the greatest, as Philip Horton long ago observed.[46] Frank's *Our America* in 1919 was the catalyst that initiated sustained discussions among Van Wyck Brooks, Munson, and others concerned with the linking of the imagination to a national heritage and vision. Crane, finding Frank's analysis "pessimistic," and fearful of the restriction that he supposed an "extreme national consciousness" would impose on the imagination, argued that Frost, Dreiser, and Anderson had attained their stature through "natural unconsciousness combined with great sensitiveness" rather than by the "logical or propagandistic" approach advocated in *Our America*.[47] Yet three years later, after he had begun *The Bridge*, Crane proudly wrote his family that Waldo Frank, whom he called "present day America's greatest novelist," had seen fragments of the poem and, like Munson and Jean Toomer, had given it high praise; and when in 1926 Crane went to the Isle of Pines to try to complete his fragmentary poem, the novelist accompanied him and for three weeks provided crucial encouragement. "I can't forget how steadfastly you have per-

severed in helping me," he wrote Frank a month after the latter's
return to New York.[48]

By 1926 Crane had surely discovered that he had no grounds
for distrusting Frank's "extreme national consciousness," and
that his solicitous friend was also a mystic and a visionary who
construed America as a land whose culture was still caught between a Europe that dominates our ideas and arts and a machine
world that has made us worshippers of power. Hence our literature, Frank declared, is a "success machine." To rectify this
bifurcated culture, he said in 1929, an apocalyptic method is
needed to transfigure and unify American experience—a "direct
recreation of a formal world from the stuffs within us." Already
he had seen that Crane and William Carlos Williams "are of this
class."[49] It is not surprising, therefore, that in a 1957 foreword
to his edition of Crane's poems, he should have paid tribute to
Crane as the "poet of our recent time who . . . most superbly"
sustained the tradition of taking "the term *New World* with
literal seriousness." But the American "jungle of machines and
disintegrating values . . . soon destroyed him."

III

From the interplay of various literary mentors, from his own
concern with his poetic craft and from the often destructive
forces in his personal or family life Crane had gradually for-
mulated by the time he had written most of *The Bridge* cogent
statements of his own literary principles. Frequently they were,
as is often the case with authors turned critics, rationalizations
or defenses of his own practices and predilections. Although
"romantic" authors had been dominant influences—Blake,
Keats, Coleridge, and the French Symbolists—he could at
twenty be crisply authoritarian. "A piece of work is art, or it
isn't; there is no neutral judgment," he proclaimed in praising
the Joyce of *A Portrait of the Artist*.[50] Even earlier he had
concurred in the artist Carl Schmitt's view that art is a tension
created by the conflict of good and evil or of beauty and ugliness.[51] Yet he was markedly hostile to any art that slanted toward

what he thought of as didacticism or propaganda, though his own persistent strictures on commercialism and corporate power were surely tendentious. Hence his indignation toward Edmund Wilson for the latter's "half-baked" article that admonished poets not to be narrowly professional and toward Yvor Winters for his "easy talk" about poets' ethical function and their obligation to express the "complete man." He conceded that his own "type of vision" did not include "those richer syntheses of consciousness" found in Chaucer and Shakespeare. He was convinced that the "essential to all real poetry" lies in its creator's "sincerity,"[52] and while writing *The Bridge* on the Isle of Pines he mentioned another resource in a letter to his family: "Suffering does, if borne without rancour . . . build something that only grows lovelier with time." As Sherman Paul has suggested, when Crane in "The Tunnel" was writing of Poe's tortured existence, he implied the inextricability of poetic creation and anguish.[53]

With his "romantic" resistance to any prescriptions on his creative modes, Crane could write his mother in 1924 that the "freedom of my imagination is the most precious thing that life holds for me."[54] This "freedom" evidently implied for him virtually a religion of art in which, as he said in "Faustus and Helen," "The imagination spans beyond despair, / Outpacing bargain, vocable and prayer." As a kind of surrogate religion, poetic creation ideally for him involved mystical vision and ecstasy—a sense of transcendence, as he wrote Munson, much as he had experienced on a visit to a dentist's office, where, under the influence of ether, his "mind spiraled to a kind of seventh heaven" of consciousness and "something like an objective voice kept saying . . . 'You have the higher consciousness. . . . This is what is called genius.' "[55] The ecstatic joy that Crane experienced on this occasion led him to suppose that he had "known moments of eternity" and also to start writing "Faustus and Helen." Apparently he felt a similar need for such elevation in writing other poems. In starting anew on *The Bridge* in 1926, he wrote his mother that "one has to keep one's self in such a keyed-up mood for the thing" that he did not know how "steadily" he could work on it. Two days later he reported that he had been working in an "almost ecstatic mood" and had never felt "such range and symphonic power before." Through Otto Kahn's benefaction he supposed that he had been "set free to build the structure of my dreams."[56]

If the "higher consciousness" that Crane experienced seemed to him to resemble the "fourth-dimensional order of consciousness" prophesied in Ouspensky's recent *Tertium Organum*, as Philip Horton believes,[57] his prosodic assumptions were often aligned with those of Poe, with whom, as "The Tunnel" shows, he felt a strong affinity. As Poe insisted in "The Poetic Principle," "a long poem is simply a flat contradiction in terms," and such protracted works as epics were for him, as Northrop Frye has phrased it, "intense poetic experience stuck together with connective tissues of narrative or argument" that are really "versified prose."[58] This view influenced the French Symbolists, Pound, and Eliot and, in effect, was observed by Crane, who composed the fifteen short poems of *The Bridge* over a period of seven years and declined to alloy his art with prosaic connective tissues. Crane's use of wine, phonograph music, and other means to induce a "keyed-up mood" has, of course, scores of precedents among previous romantic poets, and it is given most appropriate comment by R. W. B. Lewis, who, quoting William James and Emerson, notes that the latter "reminds us of Milton's saying that the lyric poet may drink wine and live generously; but the epic poet who shall sing of the gods and their descent into men, must drink water out of a wooden bowl."[59] That anti-Miltonic Crane could suppose that he could write an American epic on a Homeric or Virgilian pattern seems incredible; but that an indigenous national poem as a series of lyrics was possible Whitman had already proved. With a greater thematic coherence Crane followed his example.

Consistent with Crane's need for "keyed-up moods" for writing was his conception of himself as a visionary poet. In a letter in early 1923 dealing with the reassuring sense of community that he felt with Frank and Munson, Crane declared that it rested on "something more vital than stylistic questions"; it is, he said, "vision, and a vision alone that not only America needs, but the whole world." Against the background of his "Faustus and Helen" he related this vision to their shared feeling of a "new vitality" lacking in *The Waste Land* and *Ulysses*; and he added, "There is only one way of saying what comes to one in ecstasy"—a pronouncement of which Munson was to remind him to his discomfort four years later.[60] Linked vision and ecstasy were no doubt for him integral aspects of his belief, expressed a few weeks earlier, that "The true idea of God is the only thing that can give happiness,—and that is the identification of yourself with *all of life*."[61]

That Crane himself identified with *all* of America, let alone *all of life*, is doubtful; but that his focal concern was on the transcendent rather than the national is evident in his "General Aims and Theories," where he states that his interest in America is not due to an assumption that it had "any so-called par value as a state or as a group of people" but only because he feels "persuaded that here are destined to be discovered certain as yet undefined spiritual quantities." Supposing himself to be "a potential factor" in this "new hierarchy of faith," he "must speak in its terms and what discoveries I may make are situated in its experience." The poet as seer or visionary, he explained in "Modern Poetry," "has nothing to do with factual prediction or with futurity" but, rather, possesses a "peculiar type of perception, capable of apprehending some absolute and timeless concept of the imagination."[62] To Crane, therefore, America was primarily a vantage ground for apprehending the absolute through the "higher consciousness."

The nature and manifestations of the Absolute so frequently alluded to by Crane are not always consistent or clear. Undoubtedly one should not expect an avowed mystic and visionary to reduce the "higher consciousness" to the discursive processes of a Socratic dialogue—a process that Crane frequently disparaged. Yet at times he uses the vocabulary of the rational intellect, as he does in speaking of "concepts of the imagination." Had Crane said, as Emerson tended to do, "the intuitions or revelations of the imagination," his statement would be logically consistent and impregnable. At times his Absolute seems to be the Brahman—Emerson's Over-soul—to be approached or intuited by some of the methods with which he presumably became acquainted in reading the Vedantic scriptures. At any rate, he concluded that poets and artists must be guided by "spirit" rather than by mind or intellect because in the latter lie "no mystical possibilities," and "spirit" included the "ecstasy" of homosexual affairs, which, he was convinced, were a channel to absolute Beauty.[63]

In his aspiration for absolute experience, he was persistently attracted by the "mystical possibilities" of things or situations. Thus, writing in 1923 of his projected poem *The Bridge*, within a few lines he speaks of the poem as a "mystical synthesis of 'America,' " and the "mystic portent of all this" floats through his mind—or, he adds, rather the "mystic possibilities."[64] To this "mystical" sense of the Absolute the poetic imagination seems to Crane to be an infallible vehicle. Admitting that "strictly speaking" an "absolute experience" may not exist, he nevertheless contends that "certain aesthetic experience . . . can be called absolute inasmuch as it approximates a formally convincing statement of a conception or apprehension of life that gains our unquestioning assent, and . . . our imagination is unable to suggest a further detail consistent with the design of the aesthetic whole." In contrast, the "impressionist" is concerned only with projecting "selected factual details" and is indifferent to the "*causes* (metaphysical)" or the "utmost spiritual consequences" of his materials.[65]

In this contrast Crane would seem to be using somewhat differing criteria: The "absolute poet" is judged primarily (as Poe would also have it) by a poem's self-contained aesthetic effect; the "impressionist" by a concern for "metaphysical causes" and "spiritual consequences," though of course he may feel that holding a mirror up to life is, as Hamlet and also Chekhov supposed, the best means of revealing values. Furthermore, quoting Blake on the limitations of seeing "*with* and not *through* the eye," Crane construes "our 'real' world somewhat as a springboard . . . to give the poem *as a whole* an orbit . . . of its own." As at least "a stab at truth," he added, this kind of autotelic poetry "may be differentiated from other kinds . . . and called 'absolute.' " "Its evocation" will be "toward a state of consciousness, an 'innocence' (Blake) or absolute beauty." From this consciousness he supposed that "certain spiritual illuminations, shining with a morality essentialized [that is, abstracted and reshaped] from experience directly" might be discovered.[66] From such a view of "the absolute" poem one may infer the sense in which *The Bridge* would become a national poem. The body and texture of American life would be primarily a springboard for projecting the "higher consciousness." The poem would presuppose a metaphysical context but would provide little insight into the character of the Absolute such as that provided by Homer's gods or Dante's Hell and Paradise or Milton's God, Satan, and Christ, or Blake's Biblical engravings. But it would be concerned with the "spiritual consequences" of American culture and its possible evolution into that spiritually harmonious Cathay that Crane's Columbus envisioned.

Whether, with its "stab" at the truth or Absolute, Crane's poetry may be best described as essentially Platonic, Neoplatonic, or religious is an issue too complex for discussion here.[67] He thought of the poem as ideally a "new *word*" in that it was "essentialized from experience directly" and not from tradition, and hence involved "new forms of spiritual articulation." In effect, this "new *word*" did not imply an Absolute that defined or directed experience but an Absolute of feeling that was derived from it. He was interested, he wrote Yvor Winters in 1927, "in recording certain sensations, very rigidly chosen," which seemed "suitable to—or intense enough—for verse."[68] When these sensations coalesced into euphoria they could be accorded, it would seem, honorific if not absolute status as Beauty or Love. For Crane the certification of mystical fusion with the Absolute seems to have been simply and ultimately the experience of ecstasy.

To project the "new *word*" and to convey the "higher consciousness" Crane felt that he must transmute the normal poetic modes that rely either on a substratum of logical progression or on "impressionists' " representations. His innovative "logic of metaphor," he explained to Harriet Monroe, editor of *Poetry* magazine, makes use of the "illogical impingements of the connotations of words" and is "organically entrenched in pure sensibility."[69] That his adherence to this principle issues in some of his most resonant and memorable poetry is unquestionable; that in its very compressed richness and subjectivity it was more appropriate to the short lyric than to the longer narrative-historical poem of epic or narrative tradition (whether the *Divine Comedy* or E. A. Robinson's *Tristram*) would seem clear. Furthermore, Crane's assumption that the "truth" of a poem rests primarily in consistently harmonious relationships among its metaphors gives such poetry an autotelic existence immune to extrapoetic national or ethical concerns such as those he accused Munson of imposing in 1926.[70] Surely neither Dante nor Milton nor the later Eliot would have concurred in such a view. Inevitably the "logic of metaphor" impelled Crane toward the kind of poetry that, as he said, has "an orbit of its own." In modern terminology Crane embraced the ideal of "satellite" poetry in which the poem, launched from the "real" world away from the earth's maximum gravitational pull, could stay aloft indefinitely in its own rarified metaphorical altitude. Such was Crane's essential method for relating the quotidian American life to the Absolute.

IV

Crane's devotion to the Absolute and his aversion to much of American life and culture resulted in persistent imagery of transcendence throughout his poetry. His very "logic of metaphor" played a part in diverting him from a celebration of much of both rural and urban America and also from "contact" with most of the quotidian phenomena with which Williams and Whitman so insistently gave an indigenous body to their poetry. It is therefore not surprising that in an obituary in *Contempo* in 1932 Williams should have spoken of Crane's lack of reliance on what "he knew . . . his life to be . . . rather he continually reached 'up,' out of what he *knew*, to that which he didn't know. . . . He grew vague instead of setting himself to describe in detail. . . . His eyes seem to me often to have been blurred by 'vision' when they should have been held hard . . . on the object."[71] Hence, despite his fervid praise of Pocahontas in "The Dance" as the fertile body of America, Crane's explicit attention to her beauty in *The Bridge* is virtually confined to the praise by the hoboes. In fact he employs a poetic cosmography as Ptolemaic as Milton's, in which the godhead is above and hell is below in a New York subway. The compulsive flight toward the "higher consciousness" whose voice he had heard in the dentist's office, he embodied in images of birds, towers, heights, and stars. As H. A. Leibowitz has noted, the verbs "lift" and "leave" are among the seven he used most often. Even at eighteen he wrote his father that he was "preparing for a fine life" and that his powers if "correctly balanced" would enable him to "mount to extraordinary latitudes."[72]

With the affirmative mood of "Faustus and Helen" images of ascent became persistent: "The mind is brushed by sparrow wings," Helen is "Among slim skaters of the gardened skies," the "religious gunman" flies in "nimble blue plateaus, / The mounted yielding cities of the air!", and we are exhorted to "Delve upward for the new and scattered wine." With the opening lines of *The Bridge* the sea gulls set the tone of transcendent aspiration as their wings shed "white rings of tumult, building high / Over the chained bay waters Liberty—." In "Atlantis," however, the bridge itself is ascendant motion with its "arching path / Upward . . . the flight of strings,— . . . / As though a god were issue of the strings, . . . / White tempest nets file upward, upward ring / With silver terraces the humming spars, / The loft of vision, palladium helm of stars." The bridge is, indeed, a "steeled Cognizance whose leap commits / The agile precincts of the lark's return; . . . / Of stars . . . the stitch and stallion glow." It is a "white seizure . . . / Kinetic of white choiring wings." Walking in "ecstasy" across the bridge with his beloved, Crane wrote in 1924, with the "cables enclosing us and pulling us upward," was "such a dance" as he had never walked before. In an earlier poem, "The Bridge of Estador," he had also linked the bridge with exalted vision and a dance and had exhorted presumably himself to "Walk high on the bridge of Estador . . . / Where no one has ever been before—" and he had supposed that as "Beauty's fool" he would not forget "the Gods that danced before you / When your fingers spread among stars."

With Crane's symbolic addiction to height, it was inevitable that he should realize that the invention of the airplane had given man access to space never reached by lark or sea gull. Even though he may not have flown, his imagination could project in "Faustus and Helen" the vicarious intoxication of ascent and of aerial maneuvers in the "tensile boughs" and "nimble blue plateaus" and the "mounted, yielding cities of the air" that the "flesh remembers." And in "Cape Hatteras" the fact that the "star-glistered salver of infinity, / The . . . blind crucible of endless space, / Is sluiced by motion,—subjugated never" evoked rhapsodic passages akin to those in "Atlantis." Aware in 1927 that "the eagle [Lindbergh?] dominates our days" and that "Time and Space is the myth of the modern world," Crane confessed to his father that he was "a bit jealous of 'Lyndberg' [*sic*]."[73] His uneasiness over the destructive use of the plane in war did not impair for him its mythic and transcendental implications. While in France, as L. S. Dembo has noted, he became interested in "Verticalism," a movement inaugurated by Eugene Jolas and concerned with, among other things, "flight and particularly ascent" and its mystic manifestations. "The poetry of mystic flight," Jolas said, sought a transcendental reality; and it is significant that Crane not only contributed to a 1929 manifesto entitled "The Revolution of the Word" but also, still at work on "Cape Hatteras," reported that as a result of "Verticalism" he had improved and augmented passages in the poem.[74]

The "twin monoliths" of the bridge in "Atlantis" that support the "cable strands" of "the arching path / Upward" reflect the transcendental implications of towers elsewhere in Crane's poems. Indeed, when he first wrote to Munson about the many "mystic possibilities" in the projected "Bridge poem," as he often called it, he had his doubts about being able to complete such an ambitious work; but if he did succeed, he added, "such a waving of banners, such ascent of towers, such dancing, etc. will never before have been put down on paper!"[75] Several years later in "Virginia," the last of the "Three Songs" in *The Bridge*, virginal blue-eyed Mary, who with her golden hair leans from the "high wheat tower . . . / High in the noon of May," apparently so transmutes the "nickel-dime" tower [Woolworth's] where she works that she becomes "Cathedral Mary," possibly a twentieth-century surrogate for the Virgin Mary of "Ave Maria." Similarly the skyscrapers of New York, which were the matrix of so much in American corporate life that Crane deplored, could become in his vision the "white buildings" of the spiritually harmonious Cathay of which Columbus had dreamed.

Unfortunately Crane's fractured life in his last months in

Mexico involved experiences and assessments that issued in a final image of "The Broken Tower," his final poem based on a traumatic pre-dawn ringing of the Taxco cathedral bells in which he participated with the bell ringer in a celebration of an Indian fiesta. "The bells . . . break down their tower," he discovered, and "Their tongues engrave" his own "long-scattered score of broken intervals." The old high "Banked voices" of pagodas or campaniles now seem "slain . . . —terraced echoes prostrate on the plain!" Seeking in a "broken world / To trace the visionary company of love," he felt the "crystal Word" now "cleft to despair" and doubted if the "steep encroachments" of his own blood "could. . . hold such a lofty tower." Instead, he found his "latent power" regenerated by "the sweet mortality" of a woman [Peggy Baird] who "builds, within, a tower that is not stone / (Not stone can jacket heaven)." The "wings of silence" now "dip / The matrix of the heart, lift down the eye."

Although Crane in "Quaker Hill," the last section he wrote for *The Bridge* in 1929, had implied a descent from the hotel's cupola and from "the hawk's far stemming view" to the plaintive song of the whip-poor-will, he still apparently resisted the need to "lift down the eye." This descent in "The Broken Tower" to "sweet mortality" is of a much more sweeping and profound character. As Marius Bewley persuasively concludes, this poem "expresses what he had learned of his own limitations by writing *The Bridge* . . . and the anguish of that discovery." In *The Bridge*, as Bewley observes, he had tried "to transcend his transcript dust" by vague "cosmic consciousness," only to learn at last that the "tower of absolute vision was much too lofty for him to climb in his poetry" and that "the poet, dedicated to an absolute, a Platonic vision, must necessarily fail to achieve it in his art." The rich symbolism of the poem is, of course, susceptible of various readings. The bells, for instance, in their fiesta context may well suggest Crane's early dedication to the Dionysian celebration of life rather than the word or voice of the poet, as in Bewley's interpretation; but he is thoroughly convincing in his view that the key to the last stanzas is the Angelus, with a tone of "humility and quiet acceptance," and that Crane had realized that Apollo and the lady of "sweet mortality" must play their interacting parts. Or, as Sherman Paul has summarily said, in "The Broken Tower" Crane abandoned the transcendental stance of "The Bridge of Estador."[76]

In this final descent from the tower to "sweet mortality" Crane probably moved closer to Whitman than ever before, and had he made his descent in 1923, *The Bridge* would have been a much more autochthonous poem than it is. In view of Crane's veneration for Whitman and as a transition to a final consideration of his "epic," a general consideration of their views of the American "literatus" would seem to be useful.

V

It was not until early 1923 that Crane, influenced by Frank and Munson, could write that he was "beginning to feel . . . directly connected with Whitman." He could feel himself "fit to become a suitable Pindar for the dawn of the machine age," he added—an age that he assumed Whitman had accepted for imaginative assimilation. He was then envisaging *The Bridge* as a continuation of the affirmative American tenor of "Faustus and Helen" and as a poem of approximately the same length. It would be, as previously noted, "a mystical synthesis of America," and the bridge itself would be a "symbol of our constructive future."[77] The prime literary exemplar of such a vision was inevitably Whitman. As Crane wrote in 1930 in a short piece called "Modern Poetry": "The most typical and valid expression of the American *psychosis* seems to me still to be found in Whitman. . . . He, better than any other, was able to coordinate those forces in America which seem most intractable, fusing them into a universal vision which takes on additional significance as time goes on . . . ; his bequest is still to be realized in all its implications." Crane's persistent espousal of Whitman drew strictures from his antiromantic friend Allen Tate, who regarded his attitude toward Whitman as "sentimentality." Conceding in turn that his "rhapsodic address" to Whitman in "Cape Hatteras" was not an "exact evaluation of the man," Crane nevertheless charged Tate and other critics with ignoring *Democratic*

Vistas and hence making irresponsible assertions about Whitman's encouraging materialism and industrialism.[78]

Crane's attachment to Whitman lay primarily in his view of him as a visionary poet whose poetry and prose had most consistently been directed toward a realization of Columbus's dream of Cathay—a new land that Crane avowedly used as "a symbol of consciousness, knowledge, spiritual unity."[79] It is not surprising, therefore, that "Passage to India" was his favorite Whitman poem and that he should have written Otto Kahn in March 1926 of his intention of portraying Whitman as the "Spiritual body" of America as a complement to the section devoted to Pocahontas as the "natural body." A year and a half later he informed Kahn that this still unfinished section, "Cape Hatteras," would be "a kind of ode to Whitman."[80]

Finally in the completed, multifaceted, and at times eloquent "ode," Crane, often echoing or adapting Whitman's own lines, paid him tribute as the poet both of the sea in his early Paumanok days and of the open road as the "Saunterer on free ways still ahead." Yet he recognized that Whitman was also the first comprehensive poet of the modern city—a "labyrinth" with its Exchange and "canyoned traffic." Furthermore, he was the poet whose eyes, "bright with myth," could range over the "abandoned pastures" of Connecticut. After considering the "new verities" of power in the dynamo and the airplane, Crane returned to Walt as the visionary who in "ascensions" higher than those of the plane brought "upward from the dead . . . a pact, a new bound / Of living brotherhood!" He was the "Mourner" who kept the "sum" of wounds "That then from Appomattox stretched to Somme!" In concluding his apostrophe, Crane endowed Whitman with a number of spiritual or mythic personae: He is a sacramental figure, *Panis Angelicus*, with eyes "tranquil with the blaze / Of love's own diametric gaze"; he is "Our Meistersinger," who "flung the span on even wing / Of that great Bridge, our Myth, whereof I sing!"—the bridging of the gulf, in Whitman's view in "Passage to India," between Man and Nature through a return to "reason's early paradise"; he is a Vedic Caesar who "to the greensward knelt," a Sanskrit conqueror in a redeemed green world; he is a "joyous seer" who, like Columbus, perceived the "rainbow's arch" of a New World above the "Cape's ghoul-mound."

Despite the visionary affinities that drew Crane to Whitman and led R. W. B. Lewis to call them "the grandfather and father" of a new American poetry,[81] there were also diversities in emphasis, vision, temperament, and prosodic concepts. Some of them were the inevitable reflection of mutations in the national milieu—cultural, social, and political—during the two generations that separated the major works of the two poets. Though the limited scope of this essay does not permit a full and definitive examination of the issue, a general juxtaposition of the views in Whitman's 1855 preface and *Democratic Vistas* and of Crane's literary principles as treated in an earlier section should reveal some of the salient concurrences and dissimilarities.

The two concurred in a confidence that America was the richest nurturing ground for a restitution of Eden or Atlantis, and in an assumption of a teleological impulse working toward a new spiritual harmony among men. Apparently *Democratic Vistas* was especially reassuring to the young poet. Whitman emphasized the need for an American poetry that was "transcendent and new"; to express a New World "higher consciousness" was also Crane's persistent concern. Both cultivated a new poetic idiom that only slowly received popular acceptance. Whitman's insistence near the end of *Democratic Vistas* that a new theory of literary composition was imperative and that proper reading involved a "gymnast's struggle," with the text furnishing only hints and clues, was consonant with Crane's theory of the "logic of metaphor." Equally congenial in the 1855 preface was the dictum that poetic expression should incline toward the indirect rather than the direct or epic; and Whitman's prophecy that poets would replace priests as the spiritual arbiters of the land was essentially reiterated in Crane's conviction that the poetic imagination was more powerful than "vocable and prayer." Both were mystics. In addition, both made large symbolic use of the sea.

Beyond these fundamental affinities, however, lay marked divergences of attitude regarding the character of the poet, his resources, and his relationship to the nation and its people. Although both were, broadly speaking, transcendentalists, their metaphysical contexts differed and issued in contrasting poetic approaches and substance. As a Platonist (or Neoplatonist) Crane tended to accept the absolute Idea, which the poet might grasp through sensation and imagination and thereby nurture a renascent society in a relatively short time; as a Hegelian, Whitman perceived the seed of perfection struggling through the centuries toward its ultimate flowering ages and ages hence. Crane aspired toward the heights to bring down transcendent truth to his less sensitive compatriots; Whitman saw truth emerging from the grass upward. Hence when Whitman in "Song of Myself" was "afoot" with his "vision," he first scanned the continent—its onion patches, its pimpled alligators, its burial coaches, and its coffin'd corpses; Crane was in effect primarily "a-wing" with vision and, envious of larks and seagulls, sought transcendent insight rather than the revelations of the flora and fauna of the land. Though both professed a commitment to organic form, Crane used traditional verse patterns in his "logic of metaphor" and gave full autonomy to the coherence of the poet's own subjective pattern; Whitman, on the other hand, rejected formal metrical patterns and rhyme and, attuned to the idioms and inflections of American speech, allowed his cadences and lines to "bud" from them like "lilacs or roses on a bush." The imagistic movement of Crane's poems tends upward toward the heavens; in Whitman it is downward toward the grass or the haloed faces reflected in the water through which the Brooklyn ferry moves, laterally to the crowds, or forward to the open road. Crane's gulls and larks seek the heights; Whitman's mockingbird and thrush are humanized mourners who sing of the death of a mate or a president. The modern poet above all, thought Whitman, must write great poems of death; Crane virtually ignored the process and idea of "sweet mortality." Convinced in 1855 that America itself is a great poem and that Americans are the most poetic of all peoples, Whitman opposed the formation of a distinct literary class or elite and urged the poet to walk among "powerful, uneducated people"; Crane felt the need of a dedicated and coherent authorial nucleus to transform America and prided himself on being one of a small group representing an "aristocracy of taste." Whitman supposed that the American poet must "flood himself with the immediate age" and must "absorb" his country if it in turn was to absorb him; Crane's "absorption" was highly selective, and hence the South and Southwest and Far West as well as many classes or levels of his compatriots are virtually absent from his poems.

Such contrasts, incomplete as they are, may serve as a general index to the two Americas evoked in their poems. Yet not only Crane's poems but also his veneration of Whitman and his interest in "the emergent features of a distinctive American poetic consciousness"[82] clearly justify a concluding estimate of him as an exemplar of his own conceptions of this distinctive literature. How convincingly did he project Pocahontas and Whitman as, respectively, the natural and spiritual aspects of America?

VI

Had Crane not written *The Bridge*, his special position among those modern authors who have both cogently examined and memorably exemplified such "American poetic consciousness" would be much less secure. In "Faustus and Helen" he had sought to suggest that Helen's beauty and Faustus's confident imagination could conjoin in the New World if not in Eliot's European *Waste Land*. When, as a further projection of his earlier poem, he embarked on *The Bridge* by writing "Atlantis," the concluding section, he evidently had no epic design in mind. Indeed, since "History, fact, location, etc." were to be "transfigured into abstract form that would almost function independently of its subject matter," he in effect intended to denationalize the poem in favor of transcendence and "pure" poetry.[83] Moreover, he apparently composed the rhapsodic and visionary "Atlantis" with little consideration for what was to precede and validate it. Three years later on the Isle of Pines he laid his failure to supplement the section to his conviction that America's best days were in her past—a past that Whitman experienced and of which "the little last section" of his poem is a "hangover echo"; or, in another figure, it hung "suspended somewhere in ether like an Absalom by his hair."[84]

"Atlantis" is, indeed a "Psalm of Cathay"—a Cathay implicitly augured by the bridge itself as its "cable strands" arch upward, a "telepathy of wires. . . . / As if a god were issue of their strings." In this "psalm" Crane pushed his "logic of metaphor" to a frequently untranslatable verbal music—an enriched twentieth-century echo of Marlowe's mighty line and of the eighteenth-century "sublime" in the vein of less inspired earlier American epics like Joel Barlow's *Columbiad*. To be sure, in early 1926 Crane himself admitted that "Atlantis" seemed "a little transcendental in tendency at present," but he expressed confidence that the other sections would serve as "pediments" and would "show it not to have been."[85] Although the first three sections tend to move toward the transcendental "Atlantis," succeeding sections only erratically do so; and the two sections that immediately precede it (one of which was not written until 1929, just before the publication of *The Bridge*) are both poems of disillusioned descent.

"Quaker Hill," a sardonic picture of current American corporate values contrasted to those of the "Promised Land," ends with the falling leaves and the sadly implicit cultural parallel: "Leaf after autumnal leaf / break off, / descend— / descend—." In "The Tunnel," which immediately precedes "Atlantis," the descent goes to further depths in a hellish night ride on the subway, the "Daemon." Although at the end of the section Crane provides a short but masterful ascent to the harbor and to the bridge "bending astride the sky / Unceasing with some Word that will not die," he does not convincingly arrest and reverse the dark momentum of the two preceding sections. Surely no mythic hero ever returned from the underworld to the transcendence of "Atlantis" so abruptly! The "Hand of Fire" that gathers the "Kiss of our agony" at the end of "The Tunnel" seems far removed indeed from the "Hand of Fire" that evokes a "Te Deum laudamus" at the conclusion of "Ave Maria."

In fact, that the long hiatus in sustained work on *The Bridge* between 1923 and 1926 was only the first of many during the seven years of its composition inevitably raises questions about the depth of conviction with which Crane was dedicated to his work and especially to its New World implications as expressed so ecstatically in "Atlantis." To be sure, during these seven years he was constantly beset by financial problems, by his failure to

find employment that was both congenial and sufficiently remunerative, by his own admittedly distracting love affairs, and
by the difficult relationship with his mother and father; yet he
did find time to write many other poems during that time. When
Otto Kahn through his grant eased some of Crane's anxieties,
the poet "finally got started," as he wrote his mother from Patterson in early 1926, in an "almost ecstatic mood" on additional
sections of his "Bridge poem." His quarrel with the Tates and
his reorientation in the Isle of Pines, however, interrupted his
progress until midsummer, though he was gradually regenerated
by his change of scene to the area where Columbus had sailed
and by the fresh perspectives on America afforded by a partially
alien culture as well as by Waldo Frank's visit and by the cordiality of Mrs. Sally Simpson, his housekeeper. Mindful of his
"responsibility to Mr. Kahn," he assured his mother that he had
come to the Isle for work, not pleasure, and that he hoped to
complete *The Bridge* while there.[86]

In early June he admitted that he had not written a line; but
by July 30 he had completed ten pages in as many days and was
confident that the "poem will be magnificent." By September
6 he estimated that the poem was three-quarters done. Returning to Patterson in December (1926), he felt that in view of the
great expectations aroused in the literary community "via that
poem," failure on it would make him a "laughing stock" and his
career would be "closed." Blaming family troubles for rendering
his mind "as clear as dirty dishwater," he lamented that he might
not be able to "complete the conception" of the poem. At any
rate, early in 1927 he declined his father's well-intentioned in-
vitation to him to return to Ohio to help establish a country inn
with the somewhat disingenuous excuse that his acceptance
would interfere with his completing his "Bridgepoem" by "next
fall." In September, however, he assured Kahn that he was "still
absorbed" with *The Bridge*, explained at length the bearing of
"Powhatan's Daughter" on the "Myth of America," expressed
regrets that "Cape Hatteras" was not yet completed, gave an
inaccurate prospectus of what "Indiana" would contain, and did
not even mention "Quaker Hill"![87] Clearly almost nothing further had been achieved by the fall of 1927.

The question therefore persists: Why Crane's sporadic at-

tention to his major poem over seven years? From the changing
tone and substance of his letters one may reasonably conclude
that cumulatively after the confidence bred by "Atlantis," he
became dubious about his compatriots' ability to accept or embody the apocalyptic vision of the section. On the Isle of Pines,
even after the inspiriting visit of Waldo Frank, he had come to
suspect that his bridge was a symbol to whose structural beauty
and transcendent implications Americans were indifferent. To
them it was of only utilitarian "significance" as "an economical
approach to shorter hours, quicker lunches, behaviorism and
toothpicks." A month later in July he wrote boldly: ". . . I've
lost all faith in my material—'human nature' or what you
will—and any true expression must rest on some faith in something." And after denouncing the malicious gossip of his New
York "friends" and the "elite," he concluded: "let my lusts be
my ruin, then, since all else is a fake and a mockery."[88] Acknowledging on the island that in a "substantial vision much has
been lacking all along," he wished that he were "an efficient
factory of some kind" since an artist "more and more licks his
own vomit, mistaking it for the common dirt." He lived, he said,
"in a culture without faith and convictions."[89] Thus instead of
a confidence in America that would, as he had believed a few
years earlier, allow him to supply the pedimental sections justifying the rapturous "Atlantis" finale of *The Bridge*, he in effect
conceded that in the world about him there was no shared vision
of a national future that would approximate Cathay. The transcendental tower was already breaking.

Crane's recent reading of Spengler, therefore, would seem
to have brought not so much a shocking revelation as a confirmation of recent fears—"a ghostliness" of the past two months,
as he wrote to Frank in June—which impelled him to doubts
about his motivation and his integrity in persisting in any national
affirmation in *The Bridge*. In his inclusive despair he asked,
"Is there any good evidence forthcoming from the world in general that the artist isn't completely out of a job?" Not to realize
that his "forms, materials, dynamics are simply not existent in
the world," he decided, would be playing "Don Quixote." Hence
though "emotionally" he would "like to write *The Bridge*, intellectually judged the whole theme and project seem more and

more absurd." In an America which is not "half as worthy . . . to be spoken of as Whitman spoke of it fifty years ago," he felt that he had nothing "to say."[90] Although a convergence of liberating circumstances (previously noted) issued in a rich resurgence of writing for a few weeks, in the following three years long barren periods persisted. In Paris in February 1929 he confessed that for over a year he had written nothing "longer than scratch notes" for *The Bridge* and that he needed "more strength than ever."[91] Little wonder that in order to complete "Cape Hatteras" that year he should have turned for succor to "Our Meistersinger": "My hand / in yours, / Walt Whitman— / so— . . ."

Crane's doubts and delays, however troublesome to him, may well have effected a less transcendental and more autochthonous strain in the poem. As America receded from Cathay and her future darkened in his mind, he was impelled toward what seemed to him the worthier past of the Whitman era, as he did impressively in "Cutty Sark" where, as he mentions in his *Letters* (p. 269), he recounted the romance and rivalries of the whalers and clipper ships. In this emphasis he was implicitly aligning himself with the traditional glorification of the past typical or earlier national epics. Yet whether *The Bridge* is more epical than lyrical is, when assessed by a national norm, of little significance. Whitman had already shown in "Song of Myself" that a tenuously related series of lyrics involving native personae, experiences, and milieu could be pervasively national in reflecting the texture of American life. It would seem to be unnecessary, therefore, to reopen at this time the issue of whether Crane was justified in comparing *The Bridge* with *The Aeneid*. Given his sensibility and prosodic principles and his concern with America, his own view that "it is at least a symphony with an epic theme" is both honest and sufficient.[92]

Although Crane at times continued to profess obedience to the "Sanskrit charge," his thrust toward the godhead as crucial in the American myth has probably not constituted for most readers the focal and durable appeal and impact of the poem any more than Milton's avowed purpose of justifying the ways of God to man in *Paradise Lost* has accounted for the enduring power of that poem. Joel Barlow's cosmic contexts in *The Columbiad* and *The Vision of Columbus* were as grand though not as mystical as Crane's. Thomas Jefferson, no doubt, would have preferred *The Columbiad* to *The Bridge*. Generally, as has been noted, Crane was averse to evoking "America" through the non-metaphorical directness of Whitman's "loving perceptions" of such lowly objects in "Song of Myself" (Section 5) as "mossy scabs of the worm fence, and heap'd stones, elder, mullein and poke weed." Rather than project continental phenomena, he preferred to filter and transfigure them through his "logic of metaphor." His greatest fear seems to have been, as he wrote to Munson in April 1926 regarding his "rough notes" (apparently for *The Bridge*) just before going to the Isle of Pines, that he had so "systematically objectivized" his "theme and details" that the "necessary 'subjective lymph and sinew' is frozen."[93]

In 1923 when he began *The Bridge*, he had hoped to transfigure history, fact, and location into "abstract form that would almost function independently of its subject matter."[94] Had Crane sustained such a mode throughout *The Bridge*, he would have risked not only failure in achieving a credible national "epic" but also his future stature as a poet; for, as Allen Tate has perceptively argued in an essay entitled "Tension in Poetry": The richest and most durable poetry of England and America has been a blend and fusion of intensional and extensional elements—a proper attention to and respect for both the denotative and connotative.[95] Had all sections of *The Bridge* been written in the style of "Atlantis" the poem might have become a national curiosity rather than a national masterpiece. Although Crane's "vision of poetry" continued to be that of a "pure" poetry—that is, "poetry as poetry," as he quite injudiciously described it, in the tradition of "Kubla Khan," Marlowe, and Keats as opposed to that which would "strain to sum up the universe"[96]—the sections he last composed for *The Bridge* ("Cape Hatteras," "Quaker Hill," "The Tunnel") scarcely sustain a Keatsian "purity." Exemplifying as they do Tate's criterion of "tension," these sections are memorable intensional and extensional fusions that, by inclusion of historical contexts as well as transcendental aspirations, are indispensable additions to Crane's attempt to "sum up" America.

Crane's addiction to the transfiguration of his national materials inevitably and appropriately impelled much of his poem

toward the symbolic. The bridge, he said in 1923, was to be
"a symbol of our constructive future"; and in 1930 he assured
Tate that he would be grateful "if *The Bridge* can fulfill the
metaphorical inferences of its title" in an age of transition and
be a "link connecting certain chains of the past to certain chains
and tendencies of the future."[97] Among his historical figures
Columbus is the most substantial fusion of reality and symbol—the
courageous and devout sailor as derived from the *Journal* of his
voyages and the dreamer of a spiritually harmonious Cathay.
Whitman, on the other hand, in "Cape Hatteras" is largely a
composite of symbolic attributes.

Even more removed from historical reality, of course, is
Pocahontas, the fertility goddess in the skillfully devised myth
of "The Dance." As the "body" of America a "forest shudders"
in the "warm sibilance" of her hair, whereon lies "space, an
eaglet's wing."[98] With her richly symbolic attributes she has little
in common with the Indian princess who became the bride of
John Rolfe or who in her earlier years was either the wanton
child or the compassionate adolescent of John Smith's "histories." And, indeed, she is transmuted to an aboriginal plane
beyond that of the "red girl" bride of the trapper in Whitman's
"Song of Myself" (Section 10) who has "long eyelashes" and
"coarse straight locks" descending upon "her voluptuous limbs."
In "Indiana," however, in portraying the "homeless squaw,"
with the "violet haze" of her "eyes, strange for an Indian," Crane
moves close to the realism of Whitman's "red squaw" in "The
Sleepers" (Section 6), with her "bundle of rushes" on her back
and her "tall-borne face" and her "elastic" step and "pliant
limbs."

In "Three Songs" Crane presumably presents three contemporary women in ascending order of their approximation to the
mythical Pocahontas. Symbolically the most puzzling is Mary,
the subject of the third song entitled "Virginia." The first two
are graphically presented in their sexual allure—the Woman of
the South and the burlesque stripper in the Winter Garden—and
they become readily symbolized respectively as a "Simian Venus" and as "Magdalene." Yet Mary, an office worker in the
Woolworth Building, undergoes a Pre-Raphaelite transformation
into "Mary, leaning from the high wheat tower," who is urged

to "let down" her "golden hair." Why does New York Mary appear in a poem entitled "Virginia"? Is it so called because, as Crane describes it in his *Letters* (p. 272), it was "virgin in the process of being built"? Does this imply that Mary is the virginal basis for a new American culture? Is Mary another Pocahontas who in "The Dance" was described as "virgin to the last of men"?

Richard P. Sugg, who supposes that *The Bridge* "is a poem about the creation of a poem," argues that "Virginia" "progresses from plain Mary to Cathedral Mary" to suggest "an ideal of the constructive imagination"! In *Hart Crane's Sanskrit Charge* L. S. Dembo judges that Mary is a "third fallen image of Pocahontas"—a "modern glacier woman" who is so "untouchable" as to become a "shadow" of a vital earth mother. In this context "Cathedral Mary" would be a pejorative term.[99] But is it not probable that Crane, consistent with his previous characterization of Pocahontas as "virgin to the last of men," projects Mary with her daffodils and violets as a symbol of the sacredness and inviolability of the earth who is, indeed, not unworthy of the same homage as that accorded the Virgin Mary in cathedrals? Although Crane presented few contemporary masculine figures, he could at times sacrifice their credibility to symbolism or narrative devices. Such is the case with his three hoboes who, as he wrote Kahn, are "psychological vehicles" to "carry the reader into the interior" but are also "left-overs of the pioneers" who have known Pocahontas's "body under the wide rain."[100] When as a youth he saw them behind his father's cannery works, as he said in "The River," they seemed like children; but the rigors and dark stresses of their nomadic existence he seems never to have known; and hence he could restrict them to his larger symbolic purpose as devotees of Pocahontas.

In the seven years during which *The Bridge* was written, Crane gradually and perhaps unconsciously tended to depart further and further from his initial ideal of abstracting his American materials into an independent metaphorical existence with an orbit of their own. Many of his New York scenes are given a substantial extensional reality, although always shaped and interfused by his imagination and sensibility. This attention to the observable data of New York existence is notable in many sections of the poem, but especially so in "National Winter

Garden," "The Harbor Dawn," and "The Tunnel," which through their detail respectively suggest the decadence, beauty, and terror that Crane had personally experienced in urban life. The most "ghastly"—to use Crane's epithet—[101] of all the sections is surely "The Tunnel," where metropolitan American life becomes a loveless "underground" of vulgarity and "hades in the brain," and where the haunting spirit of Poe presides as Death looks "gigantically down." In "National Winter Garden" Magdalene, as the Biblical name implies, is presumably redeemable. "The Harbor Dawn," as Crane said in his *Letters* (p. 306), is "legato," with both a fog-shrouded beauty and dream-shattering foghorns and trucks. Unlike "The Tunnel," it is not dominated by Death but by a younger Crane's dreams and love, and by the upward thrust of the bridge presaging a transcendent future.

In view of his largely urban environment Crane could not express authentically the essence of the American soil as Anderson seemed to him so admirably to have done; yet he did recognize even in 1921 that Anderson's fiction had also afforded a contrast to the "mechanical distortions of humanity" in city life.[102] Hence *The Bridge* frequently becomes a paean to the American landscape and the extra-urban past. In "Van Winkle," a reflection of America's childhood, the title character as Rip, now a janitor in a New York tenement, is reminded by a hurdy-gurdy of his eighteenth-century childhood school days and Sleepy Hollow and the stoning of garter snakes; and hence on awaking he *"swore he'd seen Broadway / a Catskill daisy chain in May."* As *The Bridge* moves westward the powerful section "The River" jauntily ridicules modern technology and the commercial life and then allows the wanderings of the three "hobo-trekkers" to reflect earlier national experience in the Mississippi Valley. Like DeSoto and the pioneers, the hoboes "feed the River timelessly" and all are "lost within this tideless spell," as "Tortured with history" its "mustard glow" is absorbed in the "stinging sea." Sensing the "epic sweep" of this section, Crane in June 1927 compared the Mississippi to "a great river of time that takes everything and pours it into a great abyss." And feeling also at this time that "the world is quite mad," he seems scarcely the confident redemptive poet of "Atlantis" who could believe that the "multitudinous Verb" might guide the nation to Cathay.[103]

In less somber lyrical passages, however, Crane balanced the abstract and apocalyptic thrusts of *The Bridge* by recalling his own recurrent delight in the landscape and flora of the countryside. In "The Dance," as he wrote Otto Kahn, he took himself backward into aboriginal America and became "identified with the Indian and his world." Leaving the village "for dogwood," he "took the portage climb" to where his "Feet nozzled wat'ry webs of upper flows" in order to observe the rites and phenomena of an "Appalachian Spring" in which birch, oak, and tamarack participate in a cyclonic dance as Pocahontas's "chieftain lover" yields to her seasonal rebirth.[104] And even more lyrically in "Cape Hatteras" Crane recalls the floral setting of his first reading of Whitman: "Cowslip and shad-blow . . . / . . . bloomed that spring / When first I read thy lines rife as the loam / of prairies. . . . / O, early following thee, I searched the hill / Blue-writ and odor-firm with violets, 'til / With June the mountain laurel broke through green. . . . / Potomac lilies,—then the Pontiac rose, / And Klondike edelweiss of occult snows!"

Although Crane could detail an American heroic past of clipper ships and the floral beauty of the present, he declined to project equivalent images of a future as Cathay, and a mere absence of the hellish subway and of corporate vulgarity is scarcely a persuasive vision of Cathay. Thus Crane's promised land is left as a generalized "symbol of consciousness, knowledge, spiritual unity."[105] Indeed, *The Bridge* is not a visionary poem in the sense that it projects a vision but rather in that it conveys the experience and the imperative of man's being a poetic visionary, of possessing the "higher consciousness." To posit the impact of *The Bridge* on its subscription to Columbus's (and Crane's) worthy aspiration to reach a Cathay of spiritual harmony is to credit authorial concepts with an aesthetic power that they do not possess. Crane's vision was simply a nation of visionaries. Whitman, however, expressed his general vision in two short poems, "Passage to India" and "Song of the Universal," and his more explicit hopes in the long *Democratic Vistas*. Yet his richest specification and affirmation of his New World vision lie in his bestowing of haloes on scores of American men and women whose behavior, as in "Drum-Taps," exemplified courage, modesty, and love. In *The Bridge* Crane is apparently his own hero—another Columbus, a poor and suffering outcast whose metaphorical imagination is the crucial desideratum for transforming America into Cathay. The poet has replaced the priest in shaping a spiritual regeneration; but the substance of that regeneration is only negatively provided through the denigration of those aspects of the national life that Crane judged to be antitheses of Cathay.

This essential evasion of the character of Cathay has been noted by Alan Trachtenberg in his comprehensive study *Brooklyn Bridge: Fact and Symbol*. Crane's bridge becomes increasingly abstract as the poem proceeds from the "Proem" to "Atlantis," he declares, and ultimately issues as a "Psalm of Cathay! / O Love, thy white, pervasive Paradigm." Failing to show what the bridge is a paradigm of, Trachtenberg argues, Crane leaves it a "floating and lonely abstraction." Moreover, unable to face the realities of American life between 1926 and 1929, the poet seems to him to have abandoned the real bridge as a persistently vitalizing symbolic object and to have turned toward the ideal of "leaping into a new consciousness." The quotidian functions of the bridge, as Crane revealed in his oft quoted letter to Frank in 1926, seem too mundane for fusion with the culminating sublimity of "Atlantis," and hence, in Trachtenberg's view, as a detached symbol it was stripped of the common ground between myth and history. Since it never reaches its opposite shore, it is scarcely a bridge but rather a "reconciliation detached from space and time."[106] The final section was conceived, as Crane wrote Otto Kahn before going to the Isle of Pines, as a "mystic consummation toward which all the other sections converge."[107] But on the Isle, doubts replaced mystical assurance, and hence even in the "Proem" (written three years after "Atlantis") the bridge is more firmly fixed in the extensional world—a world whose weight increasingly confers a proper "tension" on the poem.

In a sense as the hero of his own poem Crane apparently considered himself a kind of American pioneer fated for a Nietzschean tragic role, as his identification with the dying Sachem of "The Dance" implies. His work, he wrote his family in

1924, is "in advance of the times." Though the substance and setting of the poem were American, he wrote Kahn, the "larger conception" was to "enunciate a new cultural synthesis of values."[108] For him the matrix of the "higher consciousness" was the imagination, of which the supreme articulation is, as he wrote Harriet Monroe, the "logic of metaphor . . . organically entrenched in pure sensibility." As Roy Harvey Pearce has written, Crane "dared to think" that he could "manipulate his language so as to rend from it the secret of the meaning of meaning." In *The Bridge*, "striving to put America into a poem, he rendered into homogeneity all of its particulars and brought forth a 'multitudinous Verb.' In spite of all he could do, it was his Verb and his only."[109]

During his last half-dozen years, however, as Crane's mystical yearnings gradually became a "broken tower," history and memory increasingly escaped the homogeneity implicit in his "logic of metaphor" and allowed *The Bridge* to move closer to an explicitly national context. Moreover, he was an aesthetic example of that minor but doughty strain in American history who stake all on the "inner light." He counted himself, as he said in "General Aims and Theories," among those poets who were concerned with "the utmost spiritual consequences" of their work, and clearly he included the future of America in those consequences. The nature and degree of any transformation he may have effected are not easily assessed; but in his own way he was a national evangelist, however few or many may have been moved by his "multitudinous Verb."

Notes

1. *The Letters of Hart Crane 1916–1932*, ed. Brom Weber (New York, 1952), pp. 124–25. Hereafter cited as *Letters*.
2. *Letters*, p. 142; *Letters of Hart Crane and His Family*, ed. Thomas S. W. Lewis (New York, 1974), pp. 183, 218. Hereafter cited as *Family Letters*.
3. *Letters*, pp. 222–23.
4. *Family Letters*, p. 448.
5. *Letters*, pp. 305, 308–9.
6. *Letters*, p. 354.

7. *Letters*, pp. 372, 374.
8. *Letters*, p. 44.
9. See John Unterecker, *Voyager: A Life of Hart Crane* (New York, 1969), pp. 156–57. Hereafter cited as Unterecker.
10. *Letters*, p. 62.
11. *Letters*, pp. 41, 89, 93.
12. *Family Letters*, pp. 260, 285.
13. Susan Jenkins Brown, *Robber Rocks: Letters and Memories of Hart Crane* (Middletown, Conn.: 1968), p. 29.
14. *Family Letters*, pp. 530, 534.
15. See Unterecker, p. 158.
16. *Letters*, pp. 130, 134; *Family Letters*, pp. 183, 193, 382.
17. *Letters*, p. 134; *Family Letters*, pp. 305–6.
18. *Family Letters*, p. 200.
19. *Letters*, pp. 152, 231, 244; *Family Letters*, pp. 418, 573.
20. *Family Letters*, pp. 372, 400, 406; *Letters*, p. 148.
21. *Letters*, pp. 86–87.
22. Unterecker, p. 188.
23. *Letters*, p. 120.
24. *The Complete Poems and Selected Letters and Prose of Hart Crane*, ed. Brom Weber (Garden City, N.Y., 1966), p. 217. Hereafter cited as Weber.
25. R. W. B. Lewis, *The Poetry of Hart Crane* (Princeton, 1967), pp. 104, 108. Hereafter cited as Lewis.
26. *Letters*, pp. 116, 121.
27. *Letters*, pp. 114–15.
28. *Ibid.*
29. Weber, p. 219.
30. Weber, p. 199.
31. *Letters*, pp. 45, 86; Lewis, pp. 3, 54; Weber, p. 199.
32. Weber, p. 200; *Letters*, p. 127.
33. *Letters*, pp. 114–15.
34. *Family Letters*, pp. 15, 24, 32, 81.
35. *Letters*, pp. 28, 317.
36. *Letters*, p. 242.
37. Weber, p. 204.
38. Unterecker, pp. 156–57, 204–5, 219.
39. Unterecker, p. 307; *Letters*, p. 138.
40. Weber, pp. 206, 208–11.
41. *Letters*, p. 27.
42. *Letters*, p. 67.
43. *Twenty-One Letters from Hart Crane to George Bryan*, ed. J. Katz, H. C. Atkinson, and R. A. Plock (Columbus, 1968), Letters XVII, XX.
44. *Letters*, pp. 86–87.
45. *Letters*, pp. 237, 239, 298.
46. Philip Horton, *Hart Crane* (New York, 1937), pp. 134–35. Hereinafter cited as Horton.

47. *Letters*, pp. 26–27.

48. *Family Letters*, p. 183; *Letters*, p. 259.

49. Waldo Frank, *The Rediscovery of America* (New York, 1929), pp. 95–96, 140.

50. Weber, pp. 199, 200.

51. *Family Letters*, p. 14.

52. Weber, pp. 202, 241–43.

53. *Family Letters*, p. 476; Sherman Paul, *Hart's Bridge* (Urbana, Ill., 1972), p. 272. Hereinafter cited as Paul.

54. *Family Letters*, p. 345.

55. *Letters*, pp. 91–92.

56. *Family Letters*, pp. 458–59.

57. Horton, pp. 136, 144, 154–55.

58. Northrop Frye, *New Statesman* 94 (December 23 and 30, 1977): 897–900.

59. Lewis, pp. 86–87.

60. *Letters*, pp. 127–28, 239.

61. *Letters*, p. 140.

62. Weber, pp. 219, 263.

63. *Letters*, p. 53; Unterecker, p. 276; "Voyages."

64. *Letters*, p. 124.

65. Weber, pp. 219, 220.

66. Weber, p. 221.

67. See Lewis, pp. 230, 268, 272, 285–86, 336, 371–74.

68. Weber, pp. 246–47.

69. Weber, pp. 221, 234, 235.

70. Weber, pp. 226, 227; *Letters*, p. 238.

71. Paul, pp. 51–52.

72. *Letters*, pp. 91–92; H. A. Leibowitz, *Hart Crane: An Introduction to the Poetry* (New York, 1968), pp. 115 ff.; *Family Letters*, p. 21.

73. *Family Letters*, pp. 588–89.

74. "Hart Crane's 'Verticalist' Poem," *American Literature* 40 (1968): 77–81.

75. *Letters*, p. 125.

76. Maurice Bewley, *Masques and Mimes* (New York, 1970), pp. 328, 334, 336.

77. *Letters*, pp. 124, 128, 129.

78. Weber, p. 263; *Letters*, pp. 353–54. As Susan Jenkins Brown explains in *Robber Rocks* (p. 136), in the 1920s Webster defined *psychosis* as "any total consciousness at a given moment."

79. *Letters*, p. 241.

80. *Letters*, pp. 240–42, 308.

81. *Yale Review* 51 (December 1961): 218.

82. *Letters*, p. 354.

83. *Letters*, pp. 124, 125.

84. *Letters*, p. 261.

85. *Letters*, p. 233.

86. *Family Letters*, pp. 458, 459, 471, 478–84, 487.

87. *Family Letters*, pp. 500, 507, 518, 558–60, 573; *Letters*, pp. 304–9.
88. *Letters*, pp. 261, 264.
89. *Letters*, p. 259, 261.
90. *Letters*, p. 260, 261.
91. *Letters*, p. 336.
92. *Letters*, p. 309.
93. *Letters*, p. 244.
94. *Letters*, p. 124.
95. Allen Tate, *The Man of Letters in the Modern World* (New York, 1955), pp. 70–71.
96. *Letters*, p. 353.
97. *Letters*, p. 353.
98. Weber, pp. 56, 66, 74; *Letters*, p. 305.
99. Richard P. Sugg, *Hart Crane's The Bridge* (University, Ala., 1976), pp. 4, 88; L. S. Dembo, *Hart Crane's Sanskrit Charge* (Ithaca, N.Y., 1960), pp. 113–14.
100. *Letters*, p. 306; Weber, pp. 62, 66.
101. *Letters*, p. 274.
102. *Weber*, p. 210.
103. *Family Letters*, pp. 584, 588–89.
104. *Letters*, p. 104; Weber, pp. 70–73.
105. *Letters*, p. 241.
106. Alan Trachtenberg, *Brooklyn Bridge: Fact and Symbol* (New York, 1965), pp. 158, 159–60, 167, 168, 169; H. Crane, *Letters*, p. 261.
107. *Letters*, p. 240.
108. *Family Letters*, p. 291; *Letters*, p. 223.
109. Weber, p. 235; Roy Harvey Pearce, *The Continuity of American Poetry* (Princeton, 1961), pp. 104, 111.

EDWARD DAHLBERG:
AMERICAN LITERATURE
AS BLACK MASS

> I am the enfant terrible of that humbug
> Black Mass we call American Literature.[1]

ALTHOUGH BY THE END of the nineteenth century the existence
of an American literature distinctive in idiom, temper, and cultural implications was generally recognized, after World War I
a number of major American authors sought further to define
and project what they believed to be the authentic national
strains of American life and letters. Notable among these were
Stein, Pound, William Carlos Williams, Sherwood Anderson,
and, somewhat later, Edward Dahlberg. Some sought to ground
American writing in post-Revolutionary or antebellum codes and
attitudes; some found roots in agrarianism, in regionalism, or
in an aboriginal past; some argued for a subtler authorial integrity
in shaping a style that would reflect the pragmatic and technological emphases so pronounced in the ambient American
scene. Dahlberg, with the stance of an Old Testament prophet,
castigated Puritan asceticism and diabolism as well as nineteenth-century pessimism and moral ambiguity. Wrestling zealously for a generation with the issues of a national style and
values, he seems to have placed his deepest confidence in a
literature that would issue from what he termed the "moral
intellect," the "carnal heart," and a rapport with the American
earth.

If indeed Edward Dahlberg was the "most hated man in
American literature," as he himself maintained in a letter to
Lewis Mumford in the early 1950s, he apparently accepted this
status with pride as well as resentment.[2] Consistently over the
years he conceived of himself as a descendant of the great heroes

or prophets from classical and Biblical times whose lot it was to be spurned or ignored because of their affirmation of unpalatable or transcendent "truths." "It was my duty, and is, to sweep the dung out of the Augean stables of literature," he informed Stanley Burnshaw in another letter in the 1960s;[3] and when the latter characterized the intensity of his critical denunciations as "screams," he abandoned his erstwhile identification with Hercules and defensively aligned himself with such other alleged "screamers" as Jeremiah and Ruskin and the "eagle . . . in a mountain eyrie." His greatest affinity, however, he persistently recognized with another figure, that of the wandering Ishmael, with his own mother as another Hagar. In an America that seemed to him not to care whether he was dead or alive, he wrote when forty-eight, "I have been in exile . . . since I was a boy."[4] Yet within this exile and despite his apologia for the bitter voices of Timon, Hamlet, and Ahab, he could at times think of himself as a "jocose iconoclast"—a role, he said in the late 1960s, he long ago resolved to adopt, and one that, no doubt, involved a disillusioned reaction to his youthful vow to "become the living waters of an American Arcady."[5]

Dahlberg's own version of this alienated critical temper is essentially sustained and occasionally reinforced even by his friends and admirers. Thus, Sir Herbert Read felt impelled to write him that "like a Grand Inquisitor, you would send to the stake any author who in any respect offends your dogma."[6] More simply his friend Sherwood Anderson, conceding the brilliance of Dahlberg's mind, could but judge him to be "down on the world."[7] One may, of course, deferring to Eliot's insistence on the distinction between a writer's private and authorial selves, choose to concur in Arno Karlen's view that the inquisitorial Dahlberg is largely a persona—a magnified and distorted version of his real self, whereby he becomes "the great, gorgeous crank of his age."[8] At any rate, since by his own testimony as well as by the judgment of his friends he appears variously as iconoclast, exorcist of the Black Mass, screaming Jeremiah, and Grand Inquisitor, his assessments of American literature often incline toward a negative mode; and yet in this negative increment, as in satire, an ideal perspective inheres as an impelling force. Hence, from Dahlberg's despair over and indictment of the prevailing national culture, not only his tragic view of man but also his own vision of a redemptive American literature emerges.

In view of Dahlberg's continuous denigration of reason in favor of the "pulse" and his dictum that "taste depends upon your body, which is the only mind we have," it is not surprising that he dismisses scientific and systematic criticism as "idle blab" and applauds Chekhov's division of literary works into two simple classes: "those I like and those I do not like."[9] In Dahlberg's literary inquisitions the latter of Chekhov's categories is clearly dominant; and, to revert to his own figure, in his self-appointed mission to cleanse the Augean stables of literature, Eliot and Pound evidently seemed to him to require his most unrelenting labors. Often he linked them together in joint defilement. Neither of them, he wrote Josephine Herbst in 1960, had any blood circulating in his verse, and the salt marshes near Cadiz he pronounced "sweeter than their technical rot"; as "shrewd basilisks of letters" they had blown their "stony breaths upon a whole generation."[10] Dismayed by what he called "the whole Pound and Eliot perfidy in literature," he continued in letters and essays throughout the early 1960s to denounce them as "savagely mediocre" defectors from their classical heritage—as the "mangy jades of our new Hellas," as "bawds in the beauty parlor on Mount Ida," and as "mock Delphic oracles" lacking in learning and in the imaginative comprehension of the "carnal heart" who with their "American tautologies" had slain their mother tongue.[11]

Beyond these joint attacks on Eliot and "his anthill scribbler, Pound," Dahlberg drew up separate indictments. Not content to disparage Eliot as a "bad St. Louis poet" and a *"mungrell versifier,"* he extended his charges to the moral plane by denouncing his poems as actually "evil"—the product of a "robber of other men's gifts" and of "a simpering, peevish man with abundant vile feelings about Donne, Blake, and Hobbes."[12] Although Pound is also accused of debasing the English language, his literary apostasies are more tolerantly viewed. He is adduced as evidence that immersion in art and literature does not necessarily improve a man's character, and he is censured for his failure to produce "a human literature" of "Flesh, Bone, Spirit"; but Dahlberg concedes that he is a "subtle craftsman," and his verdict of "evil" against Eliot is reduced in Pound's case to one of venial "affections": he is "a Polonius gone mad . . . a pedant of the American vernacular."[13]

Although Dahlberg directed his most intensely adverse criticism of American poets at Eliot and Pound, he gave his most sustained and judicious attention to William Carlos Williams, with whom he had a relationship that was uneven and "bizarre" (as he himself described it) and that accordingly prompted judgments frequently erratic and equivocal. As a professed adherent of the principle that "Truth is more sacred [than friendship]"—to use the title of one of his own volumes—Dahlberg felt obliged to disclose to several friends his impressions that Williams was "very spongy," "incapable of being straight," and "perfidious."[14] On the other hand, he dedicated "The Myth Gatherers" (the second American part of *The Sorrows of Priapus*) to Williams, wept after hearing of his stroke in 1958, and extolled his *In the American Grain*, with its search for the origins and nature of the American psyche, as a "wondrous book" written by the "only poet with the historian's faculty of the American earth."[15]

On Williams's most ambitious poem, *Paterson*, however, Dahlberg's strictures were generally severe, owing in part, no doubt, to what he considered Williams's unauthorized and fraudulent use in the poem of one of his personal letters.[16] It was *Paterson*, indeed, that provided Dahlberg with the basis for one of his most cogently sustained critical essays, "Word-sick and Place-crazy," in which he projected the alleged deficiencies of the "homeless desperado poem" with its "lubricious" lines into the larger implications and failures of the national literature.[17] Utilizing for critical leverage both linguistic patterns and quasi-mythic assumptions, he dubbed Williams the "Paterson rock poet," whose pervasive rock imagery, counterbalanced by that of the river and the sea, issues in a symbolic enhancement of inhumanity and death. Conceding that authorial skill, invention, and originality are abundantly present in Williams's work, Dahlberg nevertheless concluded that an excess of such qualities can "slay the spirit." Indeed, Williams became for him a culminating and salient exemplar of those characteristics that seemed to him to inhere in the "wild, watery men" like Melville who are America's most impressive writers: an addiction to watery coldness, a moral ambiguity or nihilism, an outdoor homelessness, a frontier love of violence, and a lack of vision. In the marriage of water (death) to the stone (fortitude) in *Paterson* Dahlberg found a symbolic absence of moral volition and a typically indigenous reflection of "supine pessimism and dingy misanthropy." Such qualities, he apparently supposed, were the perversions that in part had transformed American literature into a humbug Black Mass.

In his assessment of other contemporary celebrants of that Mass Dahlberg has generally been content to forgo the intensive analysis accorded Williams and to allow a few pungent words or phrases to convey his inquisitorial verdict. In view of his displeasure over the fact that Williams placed technical skill at the service of moral ambiguity or indifference, one is prepared for his easy dismissal of Stevens as a "very niggish poet" and of Cummings as a "tedious urchin" and a "shallow-pate" whose addiction to "fatuous banter" must be resisted if there is to be any hope for a mature American literature.[18] Hemingway and Faulkner in Dahlberg's view had not only deviated from traditional modes and styles but also had created "fetal" heroes (or antiheroes) addicted to scatological and primitivistic behavior and so were guilty of literary offenses sufficiently grave to relegate both authors to the level of "bestial provincial scribblers" who massacred "brain, speech, and reason."[19] Though neither fetal nor bestial, the novels of Fitzgerald were also adversely judged in *Alms for Oblivion* to be a "denatured" and *"peopleless* fiction" of "effete male ingenues" acting out their rootless lives in the violence of "slag cities" (pp. 68–71); yet Thomas Wolfe, for all his sense of place and his concern for roots and landscapes, seemed a failure, too: "the overstuffed cyclops of American dithyrambic fiction" (p. 149).

When Dahlberg deals in *Can These Bones Live* with the established authors of the previous century, the stringent aspersions so consistently heaped on his contemporaries generally yield to a more judicious ambivalence. Viewing them often as victims of, rather than accomplices in, the perversion of the national culture, he has disclosed thereby a more dispassionate and convincing critical perspective. Thus, the Puritans he can both admire for their tough integrity and also censure for their "renunciation of the carnal heart" (p. 56). It was their exorcism of "anatomy" and their "ablutionary ethic" that, he insists, account for the "white and holy literature" of Hawthorne and of Poe (pp. 60, 66), whose "songs," as well as those of Dickinson and Melville, were turned into a "vigil of the Tomb" (p. 96). Of the four he thought only Emily Dickinson had escaped the vassalage of Mather's diabolism and hence had averted the writing of his "Devil's Orison" (p. 122). Only she, presumably, had declined to celebrate the perennial Black Mass of American literature in her time.

Among these alleged victims of the Puritan heritage treated in *Can These Bones Live*, Melville held the greatest fascination for Dahlberg—primarily, no doubt, because he could find much of himself reflected in another Ishmael who, as *isolato* and wanderer, had "died to America" (pp. 44, 45). Yet also in Melville as in Williams he found the elements of both the Black Mass and the authentic vision of American letters. By the late 1930s he felt that Melville had become "a veritable Tamburlaine of our imaginative wisdom" by transcending a provincial emphasis on locale and by touching some "forgotten substratum" of larger human experience.[20]

A few years later, however, apparently owing to a shift in his own psychic needs, Dahlberg began to disparage Melville as a Christian artist who had assassinated his "pulses," and by the 1960s both Tamburlainean and Christian identifications had yielded to a more comprehensively negative image: that of the voice of the "demonic," of America's aboriginal temper and energy, of its unreflective passion for the leviathan as "epical."[21] *Moby Dick* was accordingly construed (somewhat unconvincingly) in *Alms for Oblivion* (pp. 114–15, 118–19, 124, 132, 133) both as a "book of monotonous and unrelenting gloom" and also as an example of America's "wizened, intellectual literature." The absence in the novel of amours, doxies, trollops, and trulls seemed characteristically American to Dahlberg in that "Melville, Whitman, Poe, and Thoreau loathed the female." Moreover, berating Melville as a "hydromaniac" for his emphasis on the sea and ignoring his diverse and richly symbolic use thereof, Dahlberg again used the quasi-myth by which he sought to diminish the poetry of his friend Williams: Imaginative addiction to water issues in "a Babel and a confusion," "destroys filial affection," and "maddens the intellect." And such, in part, are the constituents of the Black Mass.

In view of his predilection for "truth" derived through intuition and the substrata of memory, Dahlberg inevitably construed the rise of realism and naturalism in the decades after the Civil War as a dead end for American literature. Howells he could therefore dismiss in *Truth Is More Sacred* as a "cockatrice" and a "mercenary prig" and James as a "debilitated" and "exquisite mediocrity" (pp. 121, 120, 140). In Twain he saw an enemy of Mnemosyne whose *Huckleberry Finn* had merely embalmed place and, through its addiction to humor, had evaded an authentic depiction of the wretched frontier life along the Mississippi. Thus Twain, like Sinclair Lewis, became for Dahlberg an exemplar of the unsound principle of "mimicry" as opposed to "utterance."[22] As for the naturalists, he could concede a cultural inevitability in their work, for they had anticipated his own reaction against the "ablutionary ethic" of earlier American literature whereby man had been robbed "of the cherished moistened kernel of his tissue and bones." Yet in the extremity of their reaction, he thought, they had unfortunately made the recent naturalistic novel "the allegory of human ordure." Hence, even Norris seemed untrustworthy to him because instead of creating a "purificatory naturalism" that glorified nature, as Whitman did, he and his school had "pour[ed] out their spite" on it and with their relentless attention to miseries and diseases had subverted the élan of life. Especially in such later exemplars of the mode as John Dos Passos, Erskine Caldwell, Hemingway, and James T. Farrell, the "whole human fabric has collapsed, and man has fallen from the grace of good and evil into ordure."[23] In such a fall, apparently, they too had become celebrants of the Black Mass.

In pursuing his critical exorcism of the Black Mass, however, Dahlberg did discover a few authors who scarcely needed his ministrations. The most conspicuous of these was Sherwood Anderson, to whom he accorded more consistent approbation than to any other American author. In *Can These Bones Live* Anderson is linked with Thoreau and Whitman as having helped to save America from a philistine doom through a self-reliant

eccentricity and a devotion to his own intuitions; and with Whitman, Melville, and Thoreau he is honored as a "choric fool"
because amid the "bleached bones of Philistia" he also could say
to the heart, "Son of Man, can these bones live?" Moreover, as
a "rural folk bard" Anderson seemed to have escaped the diabolism of the Black Mass and to bespeak elemental divinities
that American "progress" had cumulatively all but buried: the
sense of touch in artisan and lover, the human aspirations and
bonds of the older village life, and the Edenic vision of a sensuous
accord with nature (pp. 81–84, 87–88). Anderson, indeed, as he
wrote in *The Leafless American* (p. 63), was an "Ohio skald"
whose *Mid-American Chants* seemed "like birds treading the
spirit until it flutters." It was in "Midwestern Fable,"[24] however,
that Dahlberg paid his most comprehensive tribute to Anderson
for a "natural integrity" that issued in a life and utterance that
were a "fable of the old rural, wooden midwest." Noting Anderson's escape from busyness and his anti-Dostoevskian mis-
trust of the value of suffering, Dahlberg proffered gratitude for
his genius as a "compact of goodness and love" that could evoke
the atmosphere of a countryside imbued with the "old style
American habits" and easygoing manners.

A similar interpretation of America's authentic culture and
literature emerges from Dahlberg's consistent praise of Thoreau,
whose resistance to the state and the "occidental cult of industry"
entitled him to a place among the "Christian anarchists" and
helped to shape his life into one of the great "moral allegories."
Moreover, in the texture and strength of his writing he left "a
wild quaggy testament," and he belonged with Melville and
Whitman among America's "Olympian trees, half-cultivated but
doughty."[25] And, in turn, to Thoreau's company Dahlberg as-
signed Randolph Bourne, a "Quixotist" who bespoke Dahlberg's
own distrust of both the state and the pragmatism of William
James.[26] Dahlberg also expressed admiration for the cultural
stance of several of his contemporaries with whom he corre-
sponded, especially Allen Tate, Dreiser, and Josephine Herbst,
though the laudatory comments in his letters to them are brief,
personal commendations rather than sustained critical arguments. "Whatever is good or strong in American literature today," he wrote in 1958, "is virtually underground." Who these

redemptive voices were he does not say, though that same year
he asserted to Josephine Herbst that she, he, and other underground writers and thinkers were the authentic "history of
America."[27] To most of his American contemporaries who lived
and wrote "above ground," however, including those awarded
the Nobel Prize, he generally responded with censure or contempt.

Impelling any inquisition or exorcism, one may assume, is
zeal for an explicit or implicit set of attitudes or principles,
though these may well be in varying degrees rationalizations of
cultural or personal biases. Given Dahlberg's emotive intensity
and his avowed contempt for objective or historical critical methods in favor of what, as he said in *Can These Bones Live* (p. 52),
the "naked eyes, the bone and pulses . . . of themselves discover," one should scarcely expect to find within his appraisals
of American authors any systematic statement of what the national literature should distinctively be. Priding himself on being
one of those whose allegiance was to "truth" rather than to deity
or morals, he once professed to understand badness only as those
"things [which] disgust my entrails," and he defined intelligence
as "nothing but clear feelings . . . lucidly understood." Yet,
however valid this declaration of the visceral and affective genesis of his literary assessments may be, he also viewed himself
as one of the "visionary waifs of the arts," and from his cumulative
pronouncements, as Allen Tate has observed, his vision of an
authentic American literature may be discerned.[28]

Despite his disclaimers of either moral or religious allegiances, Dahlberg increasingly revealed a critical stance that
implies both a moral concern and an assumption of his own
cognitions as being mythically if not divinely derived. Impatient
with "the quackery of drab relativism" and the limitations of
rational and scientific understanding, he argued in *Can These
Bones Live* (pp. 52, 53, 55) that the critic must disclose "a secret
wisdom that is prior to logic—the vibrant god-telling PULSE."
Moreover, he avowedly sought to become what he called an
"acolyte of the seminal *logoi*" and, refusing to "submit to the
despotism of matter," as he wrote to Sir Herbert Read, he chose
rather "to partake of the Tree of Good and Evil, which is the
sublime food of Logos, that awakens the angels in our faculties."[29]

With this acceptance of the Edenic fall and also of the persistent revelation of the Word, Dahlberg supposed that he could distinguish between his reliance on the "pulse" and D. H. Lawrence's apparently similar faith in the "blood"—the former being for Dahlberg the throb of the Logos and the latter being, as he declared in *Truth Is More Sacred* (pp. 88–89), "deceitful and unstable, and it changes its shape as often as lust, avarice, sloth, vanity, and stupidity beckon it to be the goat, the swine, or the ass." In effect the "blood" is thus linked to the Black Mass and the "pulse" becomes the medium of the "seminal *logoi.*" It was probably from a complex of such assumptions that in *Alms for Oblivion* (pp. 22–23) Dahlberg deplored the "underground nihilism in modern man" and affirmed that though the poet need not have an explicit creed or religion, he must express "one character." Intensely concerned with humanity's distinctive and creative struggle in a world where good and evil inhere ambiguously linked, he concluded in 1971 in his *Confessions* that "we cannot perceive unless we partake of original sin."[30] Hence, as Raymond Rosenthal observed, Dahlberg may well be viewed as a "religious writer without a religion, or rather in search of one."[31] At least he sought to disengage American writing from the nihilistic celebration of the Black Mass.

In his efforts to awaken his literary compatriots to the debilitation of the national character, Dahlberg became, as his friend Read wrote, "an excoriating flagellator of every element in their civilization."[32] In Dahlberg's view, however, America had never achieved a genuine civilization—a "human civilization that is sane, civil and moral"—but had leaped from frontier strength to decadence and had become, paradoxically, "a young nation already in its dotage." Amid his "pulseless stone buildings" and his defoliated cities the American, Dahlberg prophesied, must surely go mad and spill blood "if only to have pigment in his life."[33] A fetish of whiteness and a lusting after Hygeia, he charged, had supplanted the old blood ties and the brotherly bonds of touch; "Pale Face is famished for a tree . . . utterly sterile, he begs for the Nature he has warped and killed."[34]

Despite his running jeremiad against the national decadence and sterility, however, Dahlberg accepted his "complex fate" of being an American and declined the palliative of extended residence abroad. Convinced at times though he was that "the American author is Bartleby the Scrivener" and that the poet is the sacrificial bull and pariah of an "immense mortuary cartel, AMERICA," he chose not to risk intensifying his deep sense of homelessness by leaving "the only country I know" where "somehow or other [I] touch the ground."[35] Especially was he averse, as he said, to exiling himself in Paris and to visiting the "salon of that squab Buddha, Gertrude Stein."[36] Moreover, the earlier exiles of the 1920s, the bitter and rootless "children of the New," he characterized in his *Confessions* (pp. 193–94, 198) as "sincere charlatans" in whom the typically American "affliction" of "perennial boyism" never disappeared. In contrast, in the 1950s Dahlberg professed in various letters the desire to "write about America as an American author"—to remain in his homeland and help "teach the American to be quiet."[37] Indeed, writing to Josephine Herbst, in whom he saw another who loved "our wretched, dismembered country . . . without being stupid and refusing to see what we see," he declared that "everything American is in my marrow." For all his national consciousness, however, he was determined to avoid becoming a mere "provincial scribbler" through a neglect of his transatlantic heritage. Hence his sardonic question in denouncing the title *New World Writing* as "barbarous": "What's new save that which is old differently expressed?" In other words, from the indigenous matrix the American imagination must transcend the ephemera of time and place and disclose the archetypal patterns and concerns that constitute the substance and continuity of human experience.

When with this concern for mythic substrata Dahlberg wrote in *Truth Is More Sacred* (p. 16) that "Literature is about what is innocent and first," he was echoing an assumption frequently advanced by American Transcendentalists more than a century earlier. In this native tradition he, too, at times supposed that cisatlantic writers had been afforded a distinctive opportunity to respond to the aboriginal self, to rely on intuition rather than the rational understanding, and to nurture a New Eden. "Be primordial or decay," he warned in *The Sorrows of Priapus*; and in the 1950s, urging Isabella Gardner to "shun modern books" and to "Go back to Beginnings," he assured her that ritual would heal "a line, a stanza, your whole head."[38] As Emerson had admonished poets and scholars to be receptive to the influx of the Over-soul, so Dahlberg relied variously on the pulse and bones and heart—at least in theory—for the ultimate revelations of the "seminal *logoi*," and in this reliance and in his search for the lost Atlantis he insisted that the struggle toward the "mythic hour" must be continuous.[39] Moreover, having concluded in the early 1950s that the rituals of the New World are not inferior to those of the old Mediterranean cultures, he supposed that he might attune himself to mythic revelations through a comprehension of his "indigenous ground" as it had been assimilated and celebrated by the Indians and early explorers. As he wrote James Laughlin in describing his essay on the Southwest, "The Myth-Gatherers," "We will never get back to the gods of energy until we have made peace with the ground and come to some worship of the rivers."[40]

In his resistance to his own technological age and in his resurrection of essentially Transcendental assumptions, however, Dahlberg evidently underestimated the difficulties of reinstating a mythic or primordial sensibility in American culture. Indeed his own mythic perspectives derived from tuition rather than intuition, from learning rather than primary experience, from recorded revelations of the past rather than such transporting personal visions as even Emerson experienced. Though with some justice he could claim to be, as he wrote William Carlos Williams, "the vessel of thousands of years of human experience," he was a vessel refilled continuously not by preternatural visitations but, as he confessed, by "some savant or other."[41] Accordingly, though Dahlberg observed in *Alms for Oblivion* (p. 114) after reading the accounts of the conquistadores that "the enigma of North American literature is to be comprehended by putting one's ear to the savage ground" and that "American writing is aboriginal rather than reflective or homiletical," he could not readily involve himself either in a Thoreauvian commitment to aboriginal modes of experience or in an Emersonian venture into an original relationship with the universe. Hence his letter to Allen Tate in the 1960s announcing his plan to "use" the myths of the American Indian as "local color" and American geography as "scenery" in a work "on adages à la Rochefoucauld."[42] Thus, aboriginal culture with its integral reliance on the American earth would serve Dahlberg not so much as an exemplary mode of the indigenous imagination or cognition as for data for what in *The Carnal Myth* (p. 66) he once honorifically termed the "moral intellect." The same synthetic approach recurs both in his advice to Jonathan Williams to "gather up" Indian myths and translate them into "parables and a fabled landscape" and also in his prospectus for a long poem that, though "seeded" by Inca, Aztec, and Maya legend, would also be "mingled" with the Rig-Veda, Plato, and Theophrastus.[43]

If Dahlberg never convincingly assimilated the old deific and demonic forces of aboriginal myth and legend into his imagination or suggested a viable procedure whereby other American writers might do so, in a more secular-historical context he extolled in his letters the disciplinary benefits to be derived both from the literary masters of antiquity (whom he termed the "old gods of Europe") and from the ancient cultures of "those remote mineraled countries" in which he had "long laved" his heart.[44] Accordingly he argued that no durable national culture could be achieved unless a "humbug parochialism" and the native "fetish of originality" yielded to the tempering awareness and assimilation of the heritage of Attica and Rome.[45] His veneration for the ancients was, in fact, so intense that he felt impelled to censure even Sir Herbert Read for an alleged indifference both to Hellenic ideas and to the spirit of the Hebrew prophets.[46] Inevitably, therefore, as he wrote Dreiser in 1938 he deplored an American literature in what he called "that false American sense of the word."[47] The criteria of his assessments of books and art, he added, derived from the rich body of Europe, and there also his compatriots must acquire that requisite racial memory lacking in the bleak and stunted cisatlantic milieu. American literature must be "seeded in all ground, European and American," he declared in 1961, "if we are to come up as the glorious flowers of our own new earth"; and "we can be indigenous enough however profoundly affected" by such writers as Gogol or Cobbett or Thomas Nash.[48]

To the blossoming of such flowers, however, Dahlberg had

increasingly seen a major threat in the American vernacular, which, in his view, mars the work of authors as varied as Pound, Eliot, Twain, and Faulkner. Convinced by the 1960s that no great literature is possible in such "an abominable tongue," he repented of his own indulgence in such "jargon" in his early novel *Bottom Dogs*.[49] "What is known as the American tongue is stylized sloth," he charged in 1958; and again that same year he asserted that "all the rubbish . . . from trade, cupidity, and advertising is now known as the American Language."[50] For a properly distinguished American style, however, Dahlberg did not demand a replica of his own, with its learned allusions, its Old Testament tones and metaphors, and its idiosyncratic archaisms. What he did require of such alleged delinquents as Pound, Eliot, and Cummings is "real English," and though in isolation the phrase is virtually meaningless, he has in affirmative clarification sanctioned the inclusion of "words . . . derived from agrarian or deeply human origins" because of their "pulsing value," and he has also recorded his approval of "plain humble words" and the "diction of a civilized laborer who does truthful, useful work."[51] In view of such prescriptions (and also of his own aural limitations of response to the overtones of American idiom), one can scarcely be surprised that Dahlberg found most twentieth-century American literature mere rubbish. Yet such linguistic fastidiousness and bias seem all too remotely related to the "holy logos" so often invoked as the deliverer of his countrymen from the diabolism of the Black Mass of American literature.

What kind of literature, then, did Dahlberg in sum envisage to help redeem the national character? If one should project the various lines of his dicta, censure, and literary practice, into what affirmative configuration would they emerge? In the largest context he would insist on an imagination sensitized and shaped by the ancient myths as well as by the Judaic-Hellenic concepts and arts, which, in his view, had cumulatively provided a valid and humane vision for Western culture. In what he often regarded as the virtually subliterary continent of America, he would find the soundest matrix in the rugged Western landscapes and the agrarian Midwest, since through an elemental touch with these the writer might counteract the denatured, inhumane, and rootless life of the cities.[52] For the heroic national image he would return to the temper if not always the behavior of such sturdy antebellum figures as Jefferson, Boone, and Jackson;[53] and for a national ethos of sanity and community he would give priority in setting and metaphor to the solid land with its moral struggles as opposed to the fluid seas with their implications of Narcissism, moral ambiguity, and the death wish.[54] Abjuring rationalism, pragmatism, and Puritan asceticism, the American imagination could then through the revelations of intuition and the pulses most fully embrace and portray in both men and women the "carnal heart," with its admixture of vital force and peril, of tragedy and regeneration.[55] As for style, the plain old words with their rich accretions of experience would form a sufficient base for the disciplined and receptive imagination to create the "communal song of labour, sky, star, field, love."[56] With such a holy song of affirmation, Dahlberg implies, American literature would no longer be a "humbug Black Mass."

Notes

1. Edward Dahlberg, *Reasons of the Heart* (New York, 1965), p. 11.
2. Edward Dahlberg, *Epitaphs of Our Times* (New York, 1967), p. 105. (Hereinafter cited as *Epitaphs*.)
3. *Epitaphs*, pp. 276–79.
4. *Epitaphs*, p. 184; Jonathan Williams, ed., *Edward Dahlberg: A Tribute* (New York, 1970), p. 107. (This volume also appeared as the Fall 1970 issue of *Tri-Quarterly*.)
5. Edward Dahlberg, *Can These Bones Live* (Ann Arbor, Mich., 1960), pp. 3 ff.; *The Leafless American* (Sausalito, Calif., 1967), p. 57; *Confessions* (New York, 1971), p. 38.
6. Edward Dahlberg, *Truth Is More Sacred* (New York, 1961), p. 143.
7. *Epitaphs*, p. 196.
8. Williams, p. 72.
9. *Epitaphs*, p. 168; *Confessions*, p. 222.
10. *Epitaphs*, pp. 156, 157.
11. *Epitaphs*, pp. 275, 279; *Truth Is More Sacred*, pp. 12, 170, 176, 177, 187.
12. *Epitaphs*, pp. 69, 166, 274, 276; *Truth Is More Sacred*, p. 172.
13. *Epitaphs*, pp. 69, 94, 122; Williams, p. 94; *Truth Is More Sacred*, p. 208.
14. *Epitaphs*, pp. 137, 156, 212.
15. Harold Billings, ed., *Edward Dahlberg: American Ishmael of Letters*

(Austin, Tex., 1968), p. 65; *Epitaphs*, pp. 143, 156, 212; Edward Dahlberg, *The Carnal Myth* (New York, 1968), p. 85.

16. *Epitaphs*, p. 137.
17. This later appeared in *Alms for Oblivion* (Minneapolis, 1964), pp. 20 ff.
18. *Epitaphs*, pp. 273, 287; Williams, p. 94.
19. Billings, p. 51; *Can These Bones Live*, pp. 76–78; *Epitaphs*, p. 239.
20. *Epitaphs*, p. 13; *Can These Bones Live*, p. 81.
21. *Can These Bones Live*, p. 97; *Alms for Oblivion*, p. 114.
22. *The Leafless American*, pp. 17–19; *Can These Bones Live*, pp. 70–71; *Epitaphs*, p. 13.
23. *Epitaphs*, p. 12; *Can These Bones Live*, pp. 66–67, 69, 77–78.
24. *Alms for Oblivion*, pp. 16–19.
25. *Can These Bones Live*, pp. 13–18, 25; *Carnal Myth*, pp. 87, 88.
26. *Can These Bones Live*, pp. 38, 39; *Alms for Oblivion*, pp. 78–81.
27. Williams, p. 110; *Epitaphs*, p. 164.
28. *Epitaphs*, pp. 148, 166, 171; Billings, p. 83.
29. *Carnal Myth*, p. 2; *Truth Is More Sacred*, p. 101.
30. *Can These Bones Live*, p. 9; *Confessions*, pp. 163–64.
31. Williams, p. 58.
32. Billings, p. 63.
33. *Epitaphs*, pp. 2, 18, 28.
34. *Can These Bones Live*, p. 58; *Carnal Myth*, p. 5; Billings, p. 63.
35. *Epitaphs*, p. 102; Williams, pp. 107, 110.
36. *Epitaphs*, pp. 139–41; *Confessions*, p. 193.
37. *Epitaphs*, pp. 32, 149, 162, 192.
38. Billings, p. 65; Williams, p. 43; *Epitaphs*, p. 208.
39. *Epitaphs*, p. 7; *Carnal Myth*, pp. 3, 4.
40. *Carnal Myth*, p. 7; *Epitaphs*, p. 124.
41. *Epitaphs*, p. 211.
42. *Epitaphs*, p. 248.
43. Williams, p. 94; *Epitaphs*, p. 123.
44. *Epitaphs*, pp. 32, 123.
45. *Epitaphs*, p. 32; *Can These Bones Live*, p. 49.
46. *Epitaphs*, pp. 63–68.
47. *Epitaphs*, pp. 12–13.
48. Billings, pp. 52–53.
49. *Ibid.*, pp. 51–52.
50. *Epitaphs*, p. 216; Williams, p. 95.
51. Williams, pp. 94–95; Billings, pp. 52, 53.
52. *Alms for Oblivion*, pp. 45, 68–71.
53. *Epitaphs*, pp. 30–31.
54. *Alms for Oblivion*, pp. 21, 22.
55. *Carnal Myth*, pp. 2–4; *Epitaphs*, p. 18; *Can These Bones Live*, pp. 46, 48.
56. Williams, p. 13.

MR. MAILER'S
AMERICAN DREAMS

I

SINCE THE DEATH of Gertrude Stein probably no major author
has so consistently and explicitly reflected concern with "the
making of Americans" as Norman Mailer. From his early novella
A Calculus at Heaven, written while he was an undergraduate
at Harvard, through his recent *Marilyn*, the tensions of his works
have generally derived from attitudes that national myths or
regional diversity have nurtured in his characters. Thus in *The
Naked and the Dead* he subtitles the Time Machine chapter on
General Cummings "A Peculiarly American Statement," and
therein he traces the general's views and conduct to the conflicts
during his youth between his philistine Midwestern father and
his genteel Bostonian mother, whose aesthetic ideals for her son
yield to the image of tough "manhood" imposed by her authoritarian husband.[1] Indeed, a notion of what it might mean to be
an American in any inclusive national sense rarely emerges in
this early novel; America instead seems to be a contentious
aggregate of regional and ethnic cultures. Moreover, Mailer's
authorial stance here is neither that of Dos Passos's detached
naturalism nor that of Whitman's joyous acceptance of continental diversity within a national character but, rather, that of
a sectionally oriented condescension toward those soldiers who
lack the sophistication of his own brand of Northeastern urban
culture.

In fact, by 1952, Mailer had apparently adopted such slanting
as a staple of his literary practice by arguing that a literary work
should be shaped by the author's "prejudices, instincts, and

219

sensitivity."[2] Nevertheless, Mailer's interest in American behavior has persisted over three decades as he has probed the quality of life in Hollywood or Texas or Florida or Chicago, seeking as he said of his participation in the Washington march, "to elucidate the mysterious character" of the "quintessential American event."[3] Observing in the 1960s that Faulkner and Hemingway, "perhaps the two greatest writers America ever had," limited themselves to a "partial vision" by devoting themselves to some microcosm of "the beast," he concluded that American novelists must provide a healing vision of America as a whole.[4]

During the past three decades as Mailer's fascination with America has moved, in general, from analytic assessment to frenetic involvement, so his involvement in turn has ranged from sweeping denunciation to passionate devotion. Reacting with bitterness to his diminished standing as a writer in the 1950s and concluding that his "fine America" was a "cruel" soil for talent and did "ugly things" to real people as well as to fictional characters, he felt something "shift to murder" in himself.[5] Nevertheless, during these years he professed the role of a "noble physician" who would by diagnosis and disclosure help heal a cancerous society.[6] Probing beneath the dismal surfaces of American architecture, plastics, and supermarkets, he traced the psychic causes of the national malaise to the "rootless moral wilderness" in which we live in terror that "we are going mad." The national mind, indeed, seemed to him a vast schizophrenia of unresolved tensions such as those between the vertical thrust of the will of the Faustian East and the horizontal compromises of small-town mediocrity of the Midwestern flatlands, or between Christianity with its transcendental context and the corporation with its "detestation of mystery" and its "worship of technology."[7] "We are a sick country," he declared in the late 1950s, and a decade later America remained for him an accursed, beautiful land "with a leprous skin."[8]

In spite of his frequent jeremiads throughout the 1950s and 1960s, Mailer, like Pound and Fitzgerald, increasingly turned for reassurance to what he believed to be historically the nation's fundamental character and mission. "What a mysterious country it was," he reflected on his march to the Pentagon. "The older he became, the more interesting he found her." But beyond mere interest he also felt a "sharp searing love for her" even though she embodied both puzzling contradictions and an "unquenchable even unendurable individuality."[9] Involved with this love was a renewed concern in the later 1960s for what he called "the real—which is to say the potential—historic nature of America," and a national rededication to this historic nature seemed to him imperative during the intensification of the Vietnam War. Hence at Berkeley in 1965 he denounced the "pistol-whipping" repression that had threatened his and others' "optimistic love affair with the secret potentialities of this nation, some buried faith that the nature of America was finally good"—a faith that had survived all his disgust over the country's "vulgarity, misuse of power, and sheer pompous stupidity." Dismayed though he was a few years later by what he regarded as the insanities and warmongering of the Chicago convention, his greatest anxiety was that America might "disappear now in the nihilistic maw of national disorder." He was "too American by now," he realized, to tolerate the thought of living anywhere else.[10]

With this deep involvement, both affective and meditated, with the cultural patterns and the political destiny of the nation, Mailer thought of himself as an American writer in the most inclusive sense. As a fascinated observer of the triumphant launching of Apollo 11, he judged the nation to be "mighty but headless," still lacking an "agreeable culture" and faltering in its larger mission. Sensing in the 1960s an apocalyptic change at hand, he undertook the role of "Novelist-Historian" in order to study the horizon beyond what he called the forest of the present. On this horizon he could envisage his countrymen realizing "a new world brave and tender, artful and wild"; for America now seemed to him a land where a new kind of person was conceived "from the idea that God was present in every man" as both compassion and power, and where the "dynamic myth of the Renaissance—that every man was potentially extraordinary—knew its most passionate persistence."[11]

As an agent in accelerating the movement of the Republic toward its "heroic destiny," Mailer was confident that his work would have "the deepest influence" of any contemporary American novelist; indeed, he would "settle for nothing less than making a revolution in the consciousness of our time." His aim for the 1960s, he announced, was "to hit the longest ball ever to go up into the accelerated hurricane air of our American letters."[12] For such an achievement he was convinced that the writer must no longer be primarily the quiet craftsman but, rather, a bold venturer into "the jungle of his unconscious to bring back a sense of order or a sense of chaos."[13] In effect, therefore, he proposed to reassess the implications and validity of the so-called American dream by exposing it to what he judged to be the traumatic experiences of contemporary American life.

How, then, is Mailer's persistent concern with the national mission and character translated into appropriate fictional correlatives? In what ways and with what efficacy does he project a healing national vision that will help impel his countrymen to achieve their "heroic destiny" and a "new world brave and tender"?

II

One of Mailer's consistent fictional motifs is that of the "dream" or "vision," and these terms are generally honorific staples of his vocabulary. Not only are many of his characters dreamers or visionaries, but also they often believe that the fulfillment of their dreams is involved with the idea or the actualities of America—with the nation's distinctive heritage, or with its cultural and sociopolitical forces, or with its current impingement on their lives. For the larger national aspirations to make America a brave new world he inclines, like early Revolutionary poets such as Joel Barlow, to use "vision"; for the private and ego-centered yearning to rise in the world, to achieve eminence, wealth, or other personally oriented satisfactions he prefers "dream." Hence he has declared that the nation's life is impoverished when its writers toy with manners instead of projecting a worthy social vision; yet beneath this broad visionary bond he has perceived (under Freud's influence) a subterranean river of "ecstasy and violence which is the dream life of the nation"; and especially when the individual feels thwarted by external social pressures, this dream life becomes "agitated, overexcited, superheated."[14] Yet at times he uses the terms interchangeably, as if they were Anglo-Saxon (dream) and Latin (vision) verbal signs of the same phenomenon. Thus *An American Dream* essentially is restricted to the private world of his protagonist, Rojack; yet Marilyn Monroe is given national significance as "the last of the myths . . . in the long evening of the American dream."[15] In Mailer's fiction, in contrast to scriptural prophecy, both old and young dream dreams, and both see visions; and their dreams, like Mailer's own, are changing and diverse.

In Mailer's earliest fiction (written during World War II primarily under the influence of John Dos Passos, James T. Farrell, John Steinbeck, Hemingway, and André Malraux) the vision of a worthier America involves social and cultural transformation chiefly through ideological change. *A Calculus at Heaven* (1944), as Mailer himself declared, reflects the progressive-liberal slant of the newspaper *PM* and, as a Pacific war novella, it portrays the army pejoratively as the mirror of an authoritarian society—"a cold maniacal thing." Mailer's apparent spokesman, the sensitive aesthete Captain Bowen Hilliard, seeking to find meaning in his life by facing death in battle, disconsolately quotes Malraux's view that Americans lack belief in something worth dying for and, instead, make a "crude calculus" at heaven as a "big team" that wins. Yet this undergraduate narrative scarcely projects the pattern of that worthy national vision that Mailer later enjoined his literary compatriots to supply. America had "taught him all the wrong things," laments Hilliard; but neither he nor Mailer convincingly conveys what the "right things" are or how they might be achieved.[16] Indeed, for the next decade and a half Mailer's fiction provided little positive substance for a credible American dream but, rather, implied its large significance by showing the devastation wrought by its absence on his young protagonists, who are baffled victims of a complacent society rather than agents of a redemptive vision.

After his own military service in the Pacific, Mailer was, of course, able in *The Naked and the Dead* (1948) to project much more extensively and authentically the dreams of numerous soldiers and officers, though most of them are private fantasies or

nostalgic recollections of aspects of American life on which the
deprivations of combat with the Japanese on the island of Anopopei have bestowed a new aura: family ties, the birth of a
child, casual erotic indulgence, a pastoral scene, a hunting trip.
Yet the young Brooklyn native, Goldstein, and the Mexican-
American, Martinez, longing to return to the land where one
can most readily achieve affluence and comfort and power, explicitly subscribe to the popular view of the American dream:
the chance to rise in the material and social world. Yet at least
on one occasion the ultimate satisfaction of this dream of "success" is aesthetically challenged: When the soldiers are confronted by the sublimity of the island as seen from their patrol
boat, they experience a "vision of all the beauty for which they
had ever yearned."[17] (Mailer's phrasing echoes the passage at
the conclusion of *The Great Gatsby* when Fitzgerald imagines
the Dutch sailors' first view of Long Island with the "fresh, green
breast of the new world" holding them "for a transitory enchanted moment" under the spell of "the last and greatest of all
human dreams.")

The limited private dreams of the soldiers, however, are
dwarfed by the scope and complexity of General Cummings's
views of America's future glory. Out of man's evolution from the
brute, he believes, "one great vision" has emerged: "to achieve
God." The attainment of omnipotence, he declares, is now at
hand, and the army, in its structure, its technology, and its
reliance on fear rather than on patriotism, is a "preview of the
future" wherein the "only morality . . . is a power morality."
Asserting that the "dream" of the fascists and Nazis "was sound
enough," he prophesies that "America is going to absorb that
dream" and in the current war is in the process of emerging
from the "backwaters of history" and of bringing to fulfillment
the "consolidation of power." The political organization necessary to assure this future is already being formed, Cummings
asserts; and by implementing the hypotheses that most of humanity is essentially dead, that "the idea of individual personality
is just a hindrance," and that power can "flow only from the top
down," America will exemplify and control the final stage of
man's transition from brute to God. Although Lieutenant Hearn
as the general's aide resists this totalitarian American vision, his

own liberal views are too blurred and quixotic to counter Cummings's coherent prophecy. At his death confessing to his ineffectualness as a "bourgeois liberal," he reflects a state of mind shared by Mailer himself and his young protagonists in the decade ahead.[18]

In *Barbary Shore* (1951) the varied American personae of Anopopei have shrunk to a half-dozen Brooklyn Heights roominghouse tenants, most of whom are too disenchanted or confused to have any but the most vulgar or futile dreams: the landlady, Guinevere, a nymphomaniac and erstwhile burlesque queen; her husband, McLeod, a remorseful revolutionist; and Linda, a shattered proto–"flower child." Hollingsworth, a government agent whose mission is to extract revolutionary secrets from McLeod, is a complacent and aggressive WASP. Only the young narrator, Lovett, an amnesiac battle victim, is concerned with achieving a sociopolitical vision humane and durable for the critical years ahead. Thus through the confrontations of these lodgers in what Mailer called the first American "existentialist" novel, he sought to project, he said, the current struggle between authority and nihilism and the "larger horror of that world which might be preparing to destroy itself."

The title—only twice alluded to in the novel—presumably implies the current displacement of any worthy American dream by the ruthless spirit of the Barbary pirates. Accordingly, the most vulgar and self-centered of the dreamers, Guinevere and Hollingsworth, appropriately choose Barbary as their destination when they elope; and near the end of the novel McLeod predicts endless wars and power struggles stripping mankind to "barbary."[19] As the only hopeful counteragent to "barbary," Lovett receives from McLeod a mysterious object that Hollingsworth has failed to capture. Perhaps symbolically it is the political stance of the penitent and seasoned McLeod—a rejection of Stalinist excesses and a search for some remedial political balance between authority and nihilism, between totalitarian power and ineffectual liberalism. Yet Mailer at this time was apparently incapable of describing the object—of articulating such a sociopolitical vision—and hence for a time he explored an alternative in the refuge of the private consciousness.

If *The Deer Park* (1955) reflects the further course of Mailer's fictional journey inward, it also marks the point where an inclusive national vision has virtually disappeared and the American dream has been lowered to the Hollywood dream. At a southern California resort, film producers, writers, actors, and actresses duplicate the sensual preoccupations of Louis XV's Deer Park; life has been reduced to a quotidian desire for sex and power. The young narrator-protagonist, Sergius O'Shaugnessy, though sharing with Lovett of *Barbary Shore* a psychic disjunction with his military past, has none of the latter's insistent concern for effecting a just social order. Overwhelmed by the Deer Park milieu, he is, as Marvin Mudrick has suggested, "a grand lacuna into which whole chapters topple and vanish" in a novel that illustrates the author's persistent assumption that "Hollywood . . . holds the keys to the ultimate arcanum of sex"—an assumption that recurs nearly twenty years later in *Marilyn*.[20]

In the introduction to the later stage version of *The Deer Park* (1967) Mailer, to be sure, proclaimed the work to be about sex and morality, with characters who in their erotic competitiveness are vain, silly, half-mad with delusions, and "marooned forever from a clear sense of the real."[21] Yet in neither novel nor play does Mailer's current "libertarian socialism"[22] or his declared moral perspective emerge as at least a countervailing national vision. Indeed, the dominating figure and "secret center" (to use Richard Poirier's apt phrase) is a nihilistic and Mephistophelean figure with a Nietzschean and Dostoevskian ancestry, the pimp Marion Faye. With his assumption that the soul can be elevated through evil, Faye has fascinated not only Sergius but also Mailer, who ambivalently described him in the stage commentary of the play as having "an angelic smile of pure evil—or is it the evil grin of an angel?" Moreover, near the end of this version, it is Faye who bespeaks Mailer's often reiterated view of God as a finite Being dependent on man—a Being whose failing power can only be reasserted through man's attempt to "go further in his mind than anyone has gone and yet communicate his vision."[23] The fact that this view became an integral part of what Mailer espoused as an "American existentialism" reflects the increasing incorporation into his national vision of an essentially theological dimension rarely present in his early fiction.

In the decade between *The Deer Park* (the novel) and Mailer's next piece of major fiction, *An American Dream*—a decade in which, he later confessed in *The Siege of Miami and Chicago* (p. 188), he was filled with a militant bitterness and rage—he apparently undertook both to achieve the courageous mentality that Faye posited as the prerequisite to rescuing God and also to "communicate his vision." In effect Mailer, abandoning his earlier secular *Weltanschauung* for the eschatological and apocalyptic, accepted the existential sense of mystery and dread as the all-inclusive context of human behavior. In consonance with this shift, the influence of his earlier naturalistic and socially conscious literary mentors yielded to that of "America's greatest living writer" and "greatest living romantic," Hemingway, who had taught him not only the greater importance of becoming "a man than a very good writer" but also the necessity of first learning how to keep one's nerve. Moreover, Mailer applauded the older writer's "macho," his penchant for self-advertisement, and his courageous confrontation of dread and death in the weeks before his suicide.[24]

The especial attraction of Hemingway in the mid-1950s, however, was that, with his "categorical imperative" that "what made him feel good became therefore The Good," he seemed to express the temper and thrust of Hip, which Mailer was envisaging as the germinal cell in the revolution of the national consciousness to which he had committed himself. Hip, he explained in the *Village Voice* in a simplistic contrast with Square, is an expression of an American existentialism that, unlike that of the rationalistically oriented French schools, is "based on the mysticism of the flesh" and seeks "to describe the states of being" as yet unarticulated. With its roots in the American underworld of the psychopath, black, dopester, jazz musician, and prostitute, it is the voice of the alienated, and its allegiance is both to the self as opposed to society and also to the present tense as opposed to the patterns of the past and rigid designs for the future.[25]

These basic assumptions Mailer extended soon thereafter in

"The White Negro" by arguing that the "only life-giving answer" for modern man is "to accept the terms of death," to "encourage the psychopath in oneself," and, having divested oneself of roots, to embark on "that uncharted journey into the rebellious imperatives of the self." Of this mode of alienated and courageous existence the urban black seemed to Mailer to be the noble avatar. It is he who, as a "wise primitive" with his orgasmic jazz and his constant confrontation of danger in a hostile society, is the exemplary mystic who lives by the "very intensity" of his "private vision." In him and his psychopathic white disciples, therefore, Mailer perceived the regenerative force for the creation of a "new nervous system" wherein there are no truths except the "isolated truths of what each observer feels at each instant of his existence" and wherein "apocalyptic" experiences will replace the "moral wilderness of civilized life" and allow one to approach and rescue the "megalomaniacal God."[26] Since man's fate is "tied up with God's fate" and the "single burning pinpoint of vision" in Hip is that "God is in danger of dying," the "heroic activity" of the White Negro must be to embody and implement "that embattled vision."[27] Thus after a decade of portraying baffled young protagonists, Mailer had finally countered General Cummings's calculated, totalitarian American vision by proffering its diametric opposite rooted in individualistic mysticism.

However adequately Hemingway may have served Mailer for a while as proto-Hipster, the author of *The Old Man and the Sea* neither through the character of his fictional heroes nor through the example of his own casually affluent life-style could be convincingly identified with the psychopathic White Negro. Since public life revealed few credible examples of the "heroic activity" that Mailer had posited for this underground figure, it was virtually necessary that a fictional character be contrived to project exemplarily the "embattled vision" of how God might be kept from dying. Hence the creation of Stephen Rojack, the narrator-protagonist of *An American Dream* (1965), in accordance with Mailer's dictum in *Armies of the Night* (p. 219) that a good novel is a personification of a vision enabling a better comprehension of other visions.

As the publicly esteemed forty-three-year-old professor

plunges through his day and night of murder, sodomy, rape, bloody assaults, and a newly found "love," he constantly sustains his nerve by reminding himself of Mailer's existential creed that such bold acts of self-assertion can earn for him a "manhood" that will transcend sexual guilt and attune him to "unheard thunders of the deep."[28] The decisive act of murder, he has concluded, is akin to the "exhilaration" of a symphony in contrast to the suicidal lure of a string quartet. Accordingly he experiences what he construes to be heavenly visions as he strangles his wife, Deborah; he feels manic joy after a subsequent triumph over inner monitors of civilized sensibility and especially after his sexual orgy with his wife's maid, Ruta, and the disposal of his wife's body by thrusting it through the apartment window for a fall to the street far below. The retching that follows his "zephyr of drunkenness" in the Village later in the evening he interprets as a sign of psychic purgation: After twenty years of pretense he has through his violent, existential acts rid himself of the "rot and gas of compromise, the stink of old fears, mildew of discipline."[29]

In this desperate search for "manhood" Rojack indeed begins to feel himself to be something of a saint, though his saintliness assumes not the traditional commitment to the Other but rather a trust in the ultimate authority of the self and a conviction that since God is not love but courage, his criterion for action must be: "That which you fear most you must do." Hence in a crucial confrontation with his dead wife's incestuous and plutocratic father, Barney Kelly, in the latter's Waldorf penthouse, he nerves himself to make further tests of his defiance of death and dread by risking a dangerous walk on the high parapet, from which Kelly futilely tries to dislodge him. Having heard a voice that declares "The sensible are never free," Rojack must abjure rational choices in his dilemma of whether to continue his contest with Kelly or to go to Harlem to challenge Shago Martin, the possessive black lover of Cherry (a night club singer and small-town, Monroe-like Southern white girl with "one of those perfect American faces"), for whom he has contracted an instant passion on seeing her in the street crowd gathered around his wife's mangled body and with whom, a few hours later, he spends an ecstatic, bacchanalian night. Yet this newly found "love," like

any value, he concludes, can only endure through a readiness
to die for it: " 'I think we have to be good,' " he tells Cherry,
"by which I meant we would have to be brave." In turn, in her
rejection of Shago as "evil," Cherry voices Mailer's notion of a
finite and humanly contingent God who is "doing *His* best to
learn from what happens to some of us." The love dream, however, is to be short-lived, for Rojack learns on returning to the
Village that Shago has been murdered and Cherry is beaten and
dying. Presumably in a further quest for courage and "manhood"
Rojack quickly departs for the West and Central America.[30]

Rojack's narrative, as the title suggests, is of course not a
version of the popular view of *the* American dream but a coun-
tercultural inversion of and an implicit comment upon it; his
recorded actions and reflections are essentially a White Negro
fantasy putatively induced by those whose American dream has
been limited to achieving wealth and power—a dream embodied
here by Barney Kelly and already prefigured by Mailer in such
characters as Martinez, General Cummings, and Hollingsworth.
Rojack's dream is also a projection of a psychic world that, liberated from the norms of civilized sensibility, whirls briefly in
a euphoria of sensations and impulses spawned by a psychopathic
self. The ultimate arbiter is wholly subjective: the satisfying of
a manic obsession with "manhood," courage, and the "purifi-
cation" of the soul. In this novel, therefore, Mailer has de-
scended to what a few years earlier in *The Presidential Papers*
he had called a deeper "subterranean river of untapped, fero-
cious, lonely and romantic desires, that concentration of ecstasy
and violence which is the dream life of the nation" (p. 38).
Moreover, in his "best book," as Mailer proclaimed the *Dream*
to be, he was apparently aspiring to achieve his stated ideal of
the "American writer" as one who, abjuring a quiet mastery of
craft, would venture "into the jungle of his unconscious" to
return with a sense of order or chaos and a determination to
"engage the congealed hostility of the world."[31]

In his decisions, deeds, and reflections during the *Dream*,
Rojack behaves as one who has been thoroughly converted to
the proposals of "The White Negro" as the "only life-giving
answer." He confronts death, accepts the psychopath in and
imperatives of his self, and seeks apocalyptic experiences. Such

bold existential courage, Mailer predicted, would issue in an alliance of urban blacks and White Negroes with the will to attain a paradise of "limitless energy and perception" and with a "passion for future power" that would allow them to become an "elite with the potential ruthlessness of an elite."[32] Yet Rojack at the end of the novel has become an almost complete antithesis of such elitism. He has fled to the West, still persistently obsessed by the moon (death), and he plans a further escape to Central America. In the West he had discovered that the deserts are producing "a new breed of men of which he was a part." But surely this new breed (which Rojack does not describe) in the vast spaces of the Western deserts must be markedly different from the urban blacks and White Negroes in needs, temperament, and types of exigencies. And if he is a part of this new breed, why does Rojack decide so quickly to abandon them? It would seem that, having indulged his psychopathic impulses, he has neither discovered nor liberated his imperial self; nor has he heroically embraced and implemented any "embattled vision."[33] Rojack's disconsolate and indecisive last days scarcely project any contagious confidence in the efficacy of his dreams for the future. It would seem that Mailer by the mid-1960s, having fictively tested the White Negro for the commanding role in implementing the requisite national vision, had found him too unstable in conviction and behavior to enact such a heroic and demanding part.

Such speculations about Rojack's final attitudes and conduct of course imply an interrelationship between Mailer's explicit sociopolitical pronouncements, on the one hand, and his fictional characters and structures, on the other. Especially when his explicitly espoused attitudes and beliefs are so often honorifically echoed by various characters, do they have no bearing on a discerning and valid response to his fictional art? Perturbed by what they consider a vulgar fusion of Mailer's roles as citizen, cultural philosopher, and artist, some of Mailer's most astute apologists—Richard Poirier and Leo Bersani most notably—arguing that the imposition of "outside" (for example, linguistic, humanistic, neoclassical) standards accounts for frequent reservations about the impact and worth of Mailer's literary achievement—have defended the manic ruthlessness of

Rojack as psychological verisimilitude in an autonomous fictional
world that is aesthetically immune to social and moral assessments. Mailer's writings are not a series of opinions on subjects,
Poirier insists, but a release of feelings about them; his language
is not a series of referential signs assessing or indicating extensional reality; rather, it is experience itself or else a mere metaphor (for example, cancer standing for diseased society).[34]
Viewing the *Dream* as an aesthetic object, Bersani also gives the
novel complete sanctuary from the intrusion of sociopolitical
implications by insisting that its "verbal tactics" render even the
psychological focus insignificant. Its " 'ugly' events" are "strictly
literary-novelistic situations"—merely excuses for "inventive
exuberance" and verbal "playfulness."[35]

This sophisticated disengagement of Mailer's novel from ideological or moral genesis, purpose, and effect—certainly appli-
cable to the mode of much modern fiction—would be more
persuasive were it not for Mailer's own persistent disavowal of
such autotelic art. His praise of Dreiser and Tolstoy as great
writers of "vision" and his lament for the absence of such authors
in America in the 1960s, his condemnation of Broadway plays
that sin "against the heart of the Lord," his tribute to the romantic novelist as one with "light-filled passion" to capture "an
heroic destiny," his attack on the quarterlies (and implicitly on
their New Critical tenets in the 1950s) for having stripped ed-
ucated readers of "the power to read with a naked eye," his
assertion that "the primary measure of a writer's size" is a "moral
courage to write a book equal to his hatred and therefore able
to turn the consciousness of our time," his disparagement of
Saul Bellow for his failure to accept "an apocalyptic possibility
for literature," his belief that John Updike could be the best
novelist of our time "if he would forget about style" and probe
more deeply "the literature of sex," his explicit rejection of the
ideal of the novelist as craftsman for one in which he recovers
"a sense of order"—all these and many other similar dicta make
it difficult to concur in the view that Mailer intended his fiction
to be read as a mere release of feelings or a playful display of
verbal tactics.[36]

Mailer's fictional mode, to be sure, transcends both simplistic
moralism and simplistic naturalism. His release of feelings is

indeed contagious, but it is so in part because the feelings are often generated by large issues and involve persistent attitudes; his verbal patterns and diction are indeed often playfully brilliant, but they also frequently express, as he said, compulsive hatreds and apocalyptic visions. Though his style inclines toward metaphor, the figures may carry inclusive social comment: Deborah's cancer in the *Dream* is not only a physiological fact but also a symbol of psychic disorder in her social milieu. Metaphors by definition imply allusion to something beyond themselves (ideas, values, states of being, and so on), and the resonance of Mailer's figurative language is notably contingent on abstracts he so constantly alluded to as ultimate human imperatives: the love of the Lord, the acceptance of mystery and dread, the trust in intuition above reason, the redemptiveness of sexual love, and nobility of spirit. Since so many similar affirmations propounded extensively in his essays appear in the reflections and statements of the characters in the *Dream* (especially in Rojack's), it would seem that Mailer, with his devotion to psychic wholeness, would be most averse to having the components of his "embattled vision" reduced to the expendable scaffolding of a fictional edifice erected to display stylistic virtuosity. He was, he asserted, committed to a revolution in modern consciousness. Surely such a revolution required much more than a Poesque devotion to aesthetic "effect" uncontaminated by ideological or moral implications. The "final purpose of art," Mailer declared in the late 1950s, "is to intensify, even . . . to exacerbate, the moral consciousness of a people," and "the novel is at its best the most moral of art forms."[37]

The assumptions projected in the foregoing paragraphs regarding the intent and range of Mailer's fictional mode are firmly sustained by the author himself in an interview published in 1975.[38] Asserting his belief that God "exists literally" and that He is at war with the Devil, he adds that possibly man is "part of a divine vision which is not, necessarily, all loving" (pp. 198, 201–2). Within this cosmic context, which is frequently alluded to in the *Dream*, Mailer explains that he places the characters along a "spectrum of good and evil" in which Cherry has "more purchase on good than the others" and Barney Kelly is the extreme of evil. Rojack inclines toward the "good"; his wife

Deborah is a "more complex" mingling of the spectrum (p. 198). In responding to leading questions about the "highly metaphorical" character of Cherry, Mailer proffers a generalization about fictional levels in his work: "I don't believe a metaphorical novel has any right to exist until it exists on its ground floor." He insists on the "psychic reality" of all action in the *Dream*, even the more "fantastical" incidents, for "we do have telepathic powers" (pp. 199–200). "To me, it was a realistic book . . . at that place where realistic things are happening" (p. 201). Although acceptance of the intent of the author is not a complete determinant for a valid reading of his work, Mailer's replies in this interview, reasserting as they do much of what he had been saying about the scope and ends of fiction for almost thirty years, must surely be given considerable weight in one's interpretation of his style, substance, structure, and purpose. Indeed Mailer's very titles—*Barbary Shore, The Deer Park, Existential Errands*—give the clue to the imaginative fusion of planes (realistic, moral, sociopolitical, cosmic) that inform his writing. In contrast to Poe, with his appropriate inclination to restricted titles ("The Oblong Box" or "Ligeia" or "The Black Cat"), Mailer does not call his novel *Rojack* or even *Rojack's Dream*. It is, after all, *An American Dream*.

Undeniably, however, for the "innocent" reader—that is, one who reads, in Mailer's hortative phrase, with a "naked eye"—the "moral consciousness" may be confused rather than "intensified" by the *Dream*. Indeed, the narrative sequence may cumulatively appear not as a persuasive projection of the author's commitment to a heroic existentialism but as a sheer melodrama enacted by a manic inebriate. Like another more famous dream on a midsummer night, it proceeds from the frenzy that, as Shakespeare's Theseus says, links lover, lunatic, and poet. Although lunar light pervades both scenes, the moon's role has been shifted by Mailer from that of celestial accomplice in sustaining the madness of the Athenian lovers to that of an omnipresent association with existential dread: On a moonlit night during his first killings in the war, Rojack "looked down the abyss," and now again struggling with his fears, he imagines that some part of himself has "streamed away" to the moon's surface.[39] Hence his "secret frightened romance" with her phases, although she lures him toward death and forces him to examine the inadequacies of his "Being." Looking at her while teetering on the parapet, he calls her "the princess of the dead" from whose "cage" he must "earn" his release; and at the end of his flight to the West, having recently experienced life as if it were in the "safety chambers of the moon," he strolls into the desert to gaze upon her face.[40]

Although Shakespeare provided in Hippolyta and Theseus normative counterpoints to lunar madness, Mailer creates within his novel no characters capable of judiciously and humanely assessing what he later called Rojack's "huge paranoia."[41] His qualifications as an exemplary protagonist in a broadly national vision may be further diminished by the fact that he is, as Helen Weinberg has observed, a kind of pop-art and mass-cult hero whose dream involves such stock elements as Mafia figures, spies and the CIA, Harlem and the blacks.[42] Moreover, because the *Dream* reflects the swift action and persistent violence of much television fare, readers may readily incline to dismiss it with little serious consideration. Perhaps, as Richard Poirier suggests, as an "introspective novel" it was for Mailer a necessary cathartic projection of his own psychic struggles—his war with morbidity, perversity, and the Devil—and as such it can be most profitably and sympathetically read.[43] How many readers have been converted by Rojack's dream to the author's brand of American existentialism or to his envisioned revolution in consciousness, however, it would be difficult to say. Indeed, as has been suggested, the ending of the novel may well imply that by 1965 Mailer himself had concluded that Rojack's paranoia could not adequately encompass a truly national vision.

III

Rojack's dream, whether in its urban or Western phase, scarcely allowed for an involvement in political conventions, mayoralty contests, or protest marches. Having ventured through Rojack into the psychopathic jungle of the unconscious and having emerged with only a vacuous new breed of desert men, Mailer in effect became his own protagonist in a new kind of nonfictional novel wherein he could imaginatively test his American existentialism in the tensions of national politics and exhibit his courage in more socially fruitful action than teetering on parapets or murdering women. He hoped, he said in 1975, that all his work so far could be called a "novel of sorts."[44]

Before fully assuming this new fictional role, however, Mailer in *Why Are We in Vietnam?* (1967) indulged in a further and more relaxed and even picaresque version of the White Negro protagonist: eighteen-year-old "D.J.," "Disc Jockey to the World" and a white Texan "trapped in a Harlem head." In his freewheeling broadcasting style and idiom, D.J. scoffs at the capitalistic-WASP world of power incarnated in his father, Rusty Jethroe, whose very eyes with their gleam of yellow fire reflect a corporate will and "kick off the old concept of dread" in his son.[45] The temper and impact of the novel, however, derive not so much from any pervasive existential anxiety as from the persistent abandon of its scurrilous humor—a colloquial mode of counterfantasy praised elsewhere by Mailer as an integral and sanative part of the American democratic heritage because of its "reductive philosophy," which deflates "overblown values" and the excesses of gentility. Mailer may therefore be justified in regarding this short work as one of the funniest books since *Huckleberry Finn* and the best and "most American" two hundred pages that he had written.[46] At least in Mailer's American dreams the gumption of Western humor had finally asserted itself.

Neither the "dread" of the corporate will nor the humorous deflation of Texas mores, however, clearly reflects any national vision that would account for the title, events, and plot of the novel. Even so sympathetic and perceptive a reader of Mailer as Joyce Carol Oates, who regards *Vietnam* as the author's "most important work," concludes that the novel does not answer the question posed in the title, and she finds its "dynamic core" in D.J.'s implicit plea for a "real language" and "adult sensibility" to save himself from the "hell inside his head." In asserting that Mailer blurs the central issue by allowing metaphors to dominate reality in the novel, she anticipates the author's admission a year later that in *Vietnam* he "trusted metaphor" to a degree never risked before.[47]

Mailer himself, however, evidently construed the "core" of

his novel as national rather than linguistic in focus. In an explicit
and defensive interpretation of the novel Mailer resorted to an
elucidation that surely few readers would have fashioned as an
epitome of its implications but that does assert the American
context of this most metaphorical of his works: *Vietnam* is "saying
that America enters the nightmare of its destiny like a demented
giant in a half-cracked canoe," wounded, bewildered, and diseased by greed, vanity, and a Faustian desire to "enslave nature."[48] Although the greed, bewilderment, and enslavement
of nature are undoubtedly projected, no one in the novel suggests that America either is a giant or has a destiny; nor does
the mystical experience of D.J. and his friend Tex Hyde on an
Alaskan hunting trip purge the "glut and sludge" from their
minds. The revelation of God that they receive is that of a beast
whose command is "Go out and kill." Hence they take blood
vows to become killer brothers and, on their return to Texas,
exultantly proclaim their imminent departure to fulfill their
mutual pledge: "Vietnam, hot damn."[49] Is this equivocal ending
a reflection of a demented America or a foreshadowing of Mailer's
assertion a year later that America's image of herself as a "fighting
nation" is "healthy," for one is "existentially tuned" when he
admits that he wants to kill and does it without patriotic rationalizations?[50] If the latter, then Mailer's vision of American manliness in the late 1960s still involved Rojack's allegiance to ego-
centered and impulsive violence.

The persistence of such views is attested by Mailer's *Existential Errands* (1972), a collection of essays and other pronouncements that expound his doctrine of the "Ego" as the
"great word of the twentieth century." This word had already
found its "noble" incarnation, he asserts, in Muhammad Ali and
other great, and especially black, prizefighters who, proficient
in the language and intelligence of the body as opposed to that
of the mind, could approach "being the big toe of God" (pp.
3–4, 6, 9). Yet also, in *Of a Fire on the Moon*, probing the nature
of the self and assigning an even larger significance than Freud
to dreams, Mailer concedes that the figure of the Navigator (the
"agent of the ego in the unconscious") requires the counterbal-
ancing figure of the Novelist (the conscious designer who continuously envisions and revises social patterns).[51]

Through this apparent gesture at the end of the 1960s toward

a reconsideration of ideologies as they might modify his existential championship of the self against society, Mailer enlarged
his conception of both private dream and national vision. In the
process he seems to have retained an initial morality rooted in
the individual unconscious of the "Navigator" but, proceeding
beyond the Hipster-Rojack stance, to have readmitted the inevitability of a contextual frame of social order. In view of his
reiterated affirmation of the dominance of extrarational forces
in the psyche and the cosmos, he deplored the astronauts' deficiency in existential reponsiveness to the unconscious and to
dread—a deficiency that, he thought, issued in their ironic betrayal of America's ideological mission. Conversely, the dreamer,
he concluded, does not merely achieve Freudian self-consola-
tion, for he is "exploring ultimate modes of existence in sex and
in violence, in catastrophe and in death." Lacking this "submersion in dread," the dreamless, stout-nerved astronauts
seemed to him to have achieved only a technological feat without
sensing the more crucial "buried tendencies of our history"; they
were, indeed, the dehumanized agents of the WASPs—of the
"most Faustian, barbaric, draconian, progress-oriented, and
root-destroying people on earth."[52] Nevertheless, impressed by
their selfless courage on what he regarded as a perverse mission,
Mailer felt obliged to revise Rojack's dictum that God is not love
but courage by conceding that even the astronauts' heroic com-
posure had not effected a displacement of charity by courage as
the major virtue.[53]

Since Americans "were no longer ready to share the dread
of the Lord," Mailer declared, the 1960s had been a "spooky
decade," filled with riots, disasters, and assassinations.[54] Apparently accepting with increasing seriousness his obligation to
help his version of God to realize Himself, he in effect linked
a redemptive national vision to a belief in divine mystery and,
like an Old Testament prophet, turned to identifying and denouncing apostates and unbelievers. Unlike Jonah, who found
God's wrath focused on the wicked city, Mailer supposed it to
be destined to fall on the complacent philistine hinterland. To
be close to "the mood of New York in our time," he said in the
mid-1960s, "is to be close to the air of the Western world."[55] In
Mailer's dream, New York became, as it were, the holy city, the

birthplace of an imminent and imperative transformation of the human consciousness of which America is to be the harbinger.

Thus assuming that God will be rescued in the city, Mailer persistently castigated the small town as the generator of reactionary WASPs, a tribe that included in his view such diverse figures as William Sloane Coffin, Barry Goldwater, George Wallace, and the astronauts! It was the natives of the small towns who, he charged, supposing that great wars would destroy the cities, contrived the American intervention in Vietnam; it is they who populate and maintain the Pentagon as the Bastille of WASP values. In the small-town faces of the South, Mailer perceived a "painful pinch between their stinginess and their greed"; in the astronaut Armstrong's Ohio face he saw both "something as hard, small-town and used . . . as the look of a cashier over pennies" and a "dumb smile . . . small-town dumb."[56] In view of such consistent disparagement and stereotyping of nonurban Americans, it is difficult to account for Richard Poirier's view that Mailer has a "Faulknerian mystique about small-town or rural America."[57]

The very assurance and dedication of the WASPs that Mailer observed both at Miami and at Cape Kennedy, however, did impel some reconsiderations and even tributes. Returning to Provincetown to write of Apollo 11, he confessed some doubts about the validity of his aspersions, especially after he had seen in contrast many of his own band of 'liberators" behaving like "outrageously spoiled children" and disintegrating through vulgarity, fanaticism, and self-centered irresponsibility.[58] Indeed, at the Republican convention in Miami he had wondered if the Left did not still lack "a vision sufficiently complex to give life to the land," if the WASPs were not obliged to "enter the center of our history again," and if he and the leftists did not need to ponder anew the elements of vitality in the "conservative dream."[59] And, indeed, having read Burke and having devoted a long essay to salient passages in his writing, he could in *The Armies of the Night* (1968) profess himself to be a Left Conservative, that is, one trying to think in the style of Marx in order to attain certain values suggested by Edmund Burke" (pp. 124, 185).

One of Burke's conservative values that seemed especially

appealing to Mailer was, no doubt, his view of the sublime as a masculine principle involving power in contrast to beauty as a feminine principle involving passivity and love.[60] Such a hypothesis was supportive of Mailer's own predilections, both literary and sexual: his commitment to an antinaturalistic American literature embodying the heroic rather than the merely beautiful, and his reiterated insistence on the dominant role of the male in heterosexual love. Moreover, attempts like those of Rojack to construe aspects and effects of erotic behavior as spiritual or even theological metaphors seem pertinent to that character's psychopathic struggles rather than to the sustained portrayal that Mailer accorded sexual allure over the years. In his treatment it is generally a psychic ultimate or universal, and its most memorable agents or exemplars in his fiction hark back to archetypes as old as Venus and Adonis or Paris and Helen.

It is not surprising, therefore, that in *Marilyn* (1973) Mailer should pay tribute to Marilyn Monroe not only as a "sweet angel of sex" securely fixed in the dream life of the nation but also as the "last of the myths to thrive in the long evening of the American dream." As her fictional counterpart and derivative, Cherry, was linked to redemptive love in Rojack's brief existential euphoria, so Marilyn becomes in a larger context "every man's love affair with America," possessing as she did "all the cleanliness of all the clean American backyards."[61] Yet somewhat unconvincingly Mailer attempts to underline her national significance by involving her with the Kennedys and the political tragedies of the 1960s and to deepen her existential import by linking her psychic ordeals with his own existential sense of dread.

The fact that he calls Marilyn the "last of the myths" would seem to indicate his recognition that though a figure in the American dream, she also archetypically transcends the New World—that, as Whitman said in *Democratic Vistas*, the American dream is rooted in "the old, yet ever-modern dream of earth." Although Mailer merely asserts and does not account for the "evening" of that dream, his later works especially suggest that the decline of the old "dream of earth" as projected through myth and scriptures is in part due to an increasing popular reliance on a technological version of progress that discounts mystery and the imagination. Marilyn, therefore, could well be viewed as a descendant of Henry Adams's medieval Virgin whose vital and compassionate humanity was destined to yield to the force of the dynamo. In another sense, of course, with her commonplace background, she represented what Mailer had earlier praised as America's persistent and "passionate" devotion to the "dynamic myth of the Renaissance—that every man was potentially extraordinary."[62] She would also seem to be for Mailer one of Whitman's "Children of Adam" living in a New Eden where the divinity instead of the guilt of sexuality would be assumed. Although she may indeed have become, as Mailer said, securely fixed in the dream life of America, she was also as old as Aphrodite.

Throughout his more than thirty years of writing, Mailer's series of various American dreams may be said to be a record of his attempts to chart a Northwest Passage to a "new world brave and tender, artful and wild."[63] Many of these visionary ventures have undoubtedly proved abortive, oriented as they have often been in his own psychic struggles and his failure to achieve an empathy such as Whitman's with the total life of the nation. There is still plenty of time for his concern for America's destiny, his imaginative vitality, and his involvement with the nation's political and cultural life to coalesce in a mature vision of whatever democratic vistas credibly remain for the third century of the Republic.

Notes

1. *The Naked and the Dead* (New York, 1948), pp. 352–64. Unless otherwise specified, all citations are of Norman Mailer's works.
2. *Advertisements for Myself* (New York, 1959), p. 196. (Hereinafter cited as *Advertisements*.)
3. *The Armies of the Night* (New York, 1968), p. 216. (Hereinafter cited as *Armies*.)
4. *Cannibals and Christians* (New York, 1966), pp. 93–103. (Hereinafter cited as *Cannibals*.)
5. *Advertisements*, pp. 228–34, 475–76.
6. *Cannibals*, pp. 1–2, 5.
7. *The Presidential Papers* (New York, 1963), pp. 31–32, 95–96; *Armies*, p. 188.

8. *Advertisements*, p. 433; *Armies*, p. 288.

9. *Armies*, pp. 113, 114, 171.

10. *Presidential Papers*, pp. 25–26; *Cannibals*, pp. 71–72; *Miami and the Siege of Chicago* (New York, 1968), pp. 186–88. (Hereinafter cited as *Miami and Chicago*.)

11. *Of a Fire on the Moon* (Boston, 1970), pp. 67, 70. (Hereinafter cited as *Of a Fire*); *Armies*, pp. 217–19, 288; *Presidential Papers*, p. 39.

12. *Advertisements*, pp. 17, 24, 477.

13. *Cannibals*, p. 108.

14. *Cannibals*, p. 98; *Presidential Papers*, pp. 38–39.

15. *Marilyn* (New York, 1973), p. 16.

16. "A Calculus at Heaven," in *Advertisements*, pp. 28–29, 41–42, 51, 64.

17. *The Naked and the Dead*, pp. 390–91, 394–95.

18. *Ibid.*, pp. 150–53, 157, 280–82, 506–8.

19. *Advertisements*, pp. 94, 106; *Barbary Shore* (New York, 1951), p. 282. See also Barry Leeds, *The Structured Vision of Norman Mailer* (New York, 1969), pp. 54–55, 89.

20. Marvin Mudrick, *Hudson Review* 17 (Autumn 1964): 356, 358.

21. *The Deer Park: A Play* (New York, 1967), p. 35.

22. *Advertisements*, p. 271.

23. Richard Poirier, *Norman Mailer* (New York, 1972), p. 30; *The Deer Park: A Play*, pp. 52, 177.

24. *Of a Fire*, pp. 3, 4; *Advertisements*, pp. 19–21, 265–66.

25. *Advertisements*, pp. 311–12, 314–15, 340.

26. "The White Negro," in *Advertisements*, pp. 338–39, 340–45, 348, 351–54.

27. *Ibid.*, pp. 380–81.

28. *Armies*, pp. 24–25.

29. *An American Dream* (New York, 1965), pp. 8, 31–53, 97, 101.

30. *Ibid.*, pp. 61, 131, 164–65, 197–98, 203, 204, 208, 262–64, 265, 270.

31. *Existential Errands* (New York, 1973), p. 220; *Cannibals*, p. 108.

32. *Advertisements*, pp. 338, 343, 351.

33. *Advertisements*, pp. 380–81.

34. Poirier, pp. 55, 58, 83.

35. Leo Bersani, in R. L. Lucid, ed., *Norman Mailer: The Man and His Work* (Boston, 1971), pp. 175, 176.

36. *Cannibals*, pp. 98, 103, 108, 120; *Deer Park: A Play*, p. 32; *Advertisements*, pp. 23, 465, 467, 475.

37. *Advertisements*, p. 384.

38. In *Partisan Review* 42, No. 2 (1975): 197–214.

39. *An American Dream*, pp. 2–6, 208.

40. *Ibid.*, pp. 7, 13, 259, 268–69.

41. *Partisan Review* 42, No. 2 (1975): 199.

42. Helen Weinberg, *The New Novel in America* (Ithaca, N.Y., 1970), pp. 131–32.

43. Richard Poirier, in Lucid, pp. 163–65.

44. *Partisan Review* 42, No. 2 (1975): 211.

45. *Why Are We in Vietnam?* (New York, 1967), pp. 24, 36, 58.

46. *Armies*, pp. 47–48; *Existential Errands*, p. 219.

47. Joyce C. Oates, *New Heaven, New Earth* (New York, 1974), pp. 181, 185–86, 197; N. Mailer, in *Partisan Review* 42, No. 2 (1975): 207.

48. *Existential Errands*, p. 221.

49. *Vietnam*, pp. 179–80, 186–87, 202–4, 208.

50. Lucid, pp. 274–75.

51. *Of a Fire*, pp. 156–59.

52. *Of a Fire*, pp. 10, 159–62.

53. *An American Dream*, p. 204; *Of a Fire*, pp. 108–9, 130–31, 140, 150–52.

54. *Of a Fire*, p. 5.

55. *Cannibals*, pp. 114–15.

56. *Armies*, pp. 71–72, 113–14, 150–55; *Of a Fire*, p. 30.

57. Poirier, p. 4.

58. *Of a Fire*, pp. 440–41.

59. *Miami and Chicago*, pp. 61, 63.

60. See Lionel Trilling, *Sincerity and Authenticity* (Cambridge, Mass., 1972), pp. 95 ff.

61. *Marilyn*, pp. 15, 16.

62. *Presidential Papers*, p. 39.

63. *Armies*, p. 288.